PROUD TO BE

Daily Meditations for
Lesbians and Gay Men

AMY E. DEAN

BANTAM BOOKS

NEW YORK • TORONTO
LONDON • SYDNEY • AUCKLAND

A portion of the proceeds from the sale of this book will be donated to:

Lesbian and Gay Public Awareness Project (LGPAP) P.O. Box 65603 Los Angeles, CA 90065	The Gay and Lesbian Alliance Against Defamation (GLAAD) 80 Varick Street, 3E New York, NY 10013

PROUD TO BE
A Bantam Book / February 1994

Library of Congress Cataloging-in-Publication Data

Dean, Amy.
    Proud to be : daily meditations for lesbians and gay men / Amy E. Dean.
        p.   cm.
    Includes index.
    ISBN 0-553-37282-3 : $8.95
    1. Gays—Psychology—Miscellanea.   2. Self-actualization-
-Miscellanea.   I. Title.
HQ76.25.D43   1994
305.9′0664—dc20   93-38546
                                                                        CIP

Published simultaneously in the United States and Canada

Bantam Books are published by Bantam Books, a division of Bantam Doubleday Dell Publishing Group, Inc. Its trademark, consisting of the words "Bantam Books" and the portrayal of a rooster, is Registered in U.S. Patent and Trademark Office and in other countries. Marca Registrada. Bantam Books, 1540 Broadway, New York, New York 10036.

PRINTED IN THE UNITED STATES OF AMERICA

FGG   0 9 8 7 6 5 4 3 2 1

To Laurence Josephs, Professor of English
at Skidmore College.

As my teacher, you taught me to appreciate the world
of literature and to accept writing as a career. As a person,
you taught me to appreciate who I was in the world and
to accept my way of life.

INTRODUCTION

FOR YEARS THE term "gay and lesbian community" has been used to encompass *all* gay men and lesbians. The 1969 Stonewall riots are often credited with creating the foundation for the gay and lesbian community. Since that time, yearly gay PRIDE marches and celebrations strengthen that sense of community across the United States and around the world.

But what is it exactly that unites gay men and lesbians? There's no "right" answer; it often varies from lesbian to lesbian and gay man to gay man. What makes some lesbians feel connected with their gay brothers may make others feel disconnected; what makes some gay men feel empathy for their lesbian sisters may make others feel apathy.

While there are many issues, opinions, and feelings that can—and often do—*divide* gay men and lesbians, all gay men and lesbians can be united by this basic philosophy: "We are all in this together because of our sexuality." The understanding of same-sex love as well as the need to face the responses of family, friends, and society to this love automatically bond lesbians and gay men.

Sexuality *unites* gay people. The basic issues faced by a gay man every day of his life—family issues, career issues, issues surrounding coming out, relationship issues, issues regarding societal pressure, acceptance issues, self-esteem issues, the issues presented by violence, legal issues and rights, and so on—are no different from the issues faced by a lesbian.

How can gay men and lesbians, as individuals, strengthen themselves while, at the same time, strengthen their ever-growing community? By starting to focus, every day, on the issues that unite them—issues that are a direct result of loving someone of the same sex. For once the decision has been made to act on this loving lifestyle, like a pebble thrown in a still pond, *everything in a person's life changes*. All gay people must face such changes and deal with them. Alone, the changes can be overwhelming; shared with others, the changes can become more manageable.

This book focuses on the impact your sexuality makes on your life as well as on the lives of others. By exploring this impact, you can envision how the "coming out" pebble you threw in your pond that changed your own life is like the pebbles so many other gay men and lesbians have thrown in theirs. By becoming more aware of the needs and aspirations you share with other gay men and lesbians, you can start to feel more connected with them—connected with a community that includes brothers and sisters who all live under the same sky.

PROUD TO BE

The world is a new place, but it still needs to be remade.

—DOROTHY ALLISON

Imagine what it must have been like for the first explorers when they discovered new lands. What a wonderful experience it must have been—to see sights no person had ever seen before, to breathe in the unique smells, to hear the calls of unknown creatures, and to feel a different wind blowing on their faces. They faced a new world; they faced new beginnings—and they remade the new world into a place they could call their own.

You, too, can greet this first day of the new year as if you are an explorer who has found a new land. Today is the first day of a new beginning for you as a gay man or lesbian. No matter what last year's world was like, you've left it behind. All of its difficulties—the loss of a close friend or life partner, the breakup of a long-term relationship, disconnection with your family of origin because of your sexuality, hard risks and difficult changes you had to make because of who you are and how you live your life—are now distant.

Today, you can view this new year as a new world that you can call your own. What do you want to do with it? Think of at least one way you'd like your new world to be different from the world of last year. How can you make it happen? Spread your arms wide, open your heart, and face your new world with energy, hope, and vitality.

♦ How exciting—I have the opportunity to re-create the world for myself! Today I'll set one goal that will help me remake this world into a place that will be right for me and my sexuality.

Power is the ability not to have to please.

—ELIZABETH JANEWAY

Wouldn't it be wonderful if no one had any problems with the things you did, the words you said, the way you kept your house or apartment, the possessions that mattered to you, the causes that concerned you, or the sex of the one you loved? Yet isn't there always one person who seems to have a problem either with your sexuality or the way you express it?

When you strive to change yourself in any way for another person, you're making up your mind to live your life by someone else's standards. In doing so, you let another person govern your rules of behavior.

Why would you choose to give up such enormous power to another person? Perhaps you do so to avoid conflict, gather support, get attention, or earn respect, love, or affection. But what effect does that have upon you? Although you may gain one or all of those things, what you lose is far more valuable. For what you lose is your power to be you.

The next time you're confronted with someone who can't accept you and your sexuality, remember that you have a choice. You can strive to be what they want you to be, or you can strive to be yourself. One choice will be made solely for the benefit of another person; one choice will be made just for you. Which will you choose?

◆ Today I'll remember that when I interact with others, I always have a choice: I can weaken my personal power by pleasing someone else, or I can keep my personal power strong by pleasing myself.

A community is like a ship; everyone ought to be prepared to take the helm.

—HENRIK IBSEN

In every group of people, you'll always be able to find one individual who seems to have much more time, energy, and motivation than others. It's often this person who ends up chairing committees, organizing fund-raisers, coordinating mailings, juggling many projects at one time, and drawing everyone together for one common purpose.

Too often you and other members of a gay or lesbian group can become dependent upon one person to take care of everything. What would happen if that person was no longer available to handle everything or to provide the necessary direction? Would you and others be able to take over some of that person's responsibilities so your group would continue to function?

Letting one person take charge is like expecting only one pilot to fly every leg of a transworld flight. After several hours, sheer exhaustion will prevent the pilot from flying further. But if another pilot takes over the controls for a while, your flight can continue in safety and without interruption.

Think about one group you're involved with that has become important in your life. Then consider ways you can provide relief for another gay man or lesbian who has been ensuring your group's continuity and growth.

♦ Today I'll remember that a group's growth—as well as its survival—depends upon each member. So what can *I* do as an active member of my group to help out?

> *Sometimes, I feel discriminated against, but it does not make me angry. It merely astonishes me. How can anyone deny themselves the pleasure of my company?*
>
> —ZORA NEALE HURSTON

Discrimination because of your sexuality sometimes can be so painful, it's hard not to buy into it. You might think, for example, "Of course my company won't promote me—why would they want a gay man to head up this project?" or "My lover and I are so open about our relationship that it's no wonder my parents don't like us to be around them."

But when you buy into such discriminatory assessments, you only end up putting yourself and your sexuality down. Rather than seeing yourself as a worthwhile, important, lovable human being, you end up seeing yourself through their eyes: as an embarrassment, a source of discomfort, a less-than-whole, worthless human being who deserves very little respect, time, or attention.

Today, instead of seeing yourself as a reflection of what others see, look in your own mirror so you can see your own reflection. Let go of the judgments and assessments of others as you take a good look at yourself in the mirror. Then say aloud: "No matter what others think or say about me, I believe that I am a worthwhile, loving, wonderful human being who deserves to be treated with consideration, kindness, and respect." Then treat yourself that way!

♦ Today I won't accept the unkind and untrue beliefs others may have about me. No matter what others believe about me, I will believe this about me: that I am gay and I am a wonderful person.

Don't make friends who are comfortable to be with. Make friends who will force you to lever yourself up.

—Thomas J. Watson, Sr.

Imagine that you're at a party. In the large living room are several groups of people. Some look, act, and dress like you; you know they share common interests with you. Others look, act, and dress differently; you know they enjoy things in which you're not interested. Which groups of people will you choose to socialize with while you're at the party: those who are most like you or least like you?

Too often you may gravitate toward those who are familiar—people with whom you're comfortable or groups you easily connect with because of shared interests or tastes. But the world isn't always one big softball field or one enormous country-western dance. Not everyone has the same hairstyle, the same taste in clothing, or enjoys the same pastimes. And not all gay men and lesbians share the same political, philosophical, and spiritual ideologies.

Hanging out with "you-clones" all the time may feel comfortable because it's safe and familiar, but it lacks the challenge that comes from learning new things from "unlike-minded people." Today, dare to be different! Hang out with someone new and different or check out a new group. You may discover new friends who encourage you to learn more about yourself.

◆ Today I'll believe that each new gay man or lesbian I meet is a new chapter in my life. I can't wait to see the story of my life unfold!

Nothing so much needs reforming as other people's habits.

—MARK TWAIN

Do you find yourself constantly criticizing other gay men and lesbians for their faults? Do you often take inventory of your friends' character defects? Are you short-tempered with your lover because you feel he or she is incapable of living up to your expectations?

When you criticize others for their faults, it may mean you have similar problems to work through. For example, if you find yourself getting angry with a lover you believe to be thoughtless and self-centered, in reality your anger may stem from the fact that those are qualities you dislike about how you behave in a relationship.

Today, examine yourself carefully. Take a close look at your actions and behaviors. Ask, "Are the things that I criticize in others really qualities I embody from time to time?" Strive for honesty in your self-assessment. Then think about ways you can change what you don't like about yourself. Focus on improving yourself, not anyone else. You might be surprised to find out that your anger, irritation, and faultfinding is lessened once you make changes in yourself.

◆ Today I'll keep in mind that I may be slower to recognize and address the problems in myself and a lot quicker to identify those things in others. I can stop being so judgmental of other gay men and lesbians and work through my own problems.

Any magazine on the cutting edge of taste or fashion is going to recruit—either consciously or unconsciously—a gay sensibility. We were born to create trends. That's what we do well.

—KEVIN SESSUMS

In 1992 the editors of Condé Nast Publications Inc. went on record in praise of gays as "a driving force behind such mainstream magazines as *Vanity Fair, Vogue,* and *GQ.*" These magazines, which have a combined circulation of almost three million each month, reflect the popular culture—the way we dress, the places in which we live, and the forms of entertainment we enjoy.

The "gay aesthetic" that is being embraced and glorified by such magazines serves as a reflection of the creative force behind the periodicals. *Vogue's* editor in chief, Anna Wintour, relates that "My features editor is gay, my art director is gay, and most of the fashion designers I work with are gay." As a result, her magazine can be seen as a product of the gay people who work for it.

Reading publications that capture an intrinsically gay sensibility on their pages or promote an openness and acceptance for gay men and lesbians on their staff is one way you can show your support for gay creative energy. In doing so, you're recognizing the impact gay people have in creating both culture and cultural change.

◆ Today I'll be supportive of the gay sensibility, sensitivity, and sexuality evident in many popular magazines. My support of such magazines can help to strengthen the power gays have in the industry.

I have been so afraid to be alone that I'm living alone now. It's not that bad. Somehow I feel safe and secure. Even when I wake up in the middle of the night, I feel okay—trusting.

—JAMAICA KINCAID, FROM *LUCY*

Sometimes the pressure not to be alone can be so great that the minute a relationship ends you're ready to form a new one. You may choose to avoid processing the ending of a relationship because it means that for a short time, you need to be alone as you heal your heart. And what lesbian or gay man wants to be alone?

Yet not much mending of a broken heart can be done when you immediately thrust yourself back into the dating scene or into a new relationship. Without the necessary time and space, the issues that may have terminated your last relationship never get dealt with. So what can end up happening is that you chase away your fears of being alone by embarking on a trail that leads you toward others, but away from yourself.

Whenever a relationship ends, it's a good idea not to try to fill in the emptiness right away. Although your heart may echo with the loneliness of loss for a while, that's part of the healing process; what you feel you need to heal. So just for today, stay with your feelings of loneliness and fear, and trust that you are the only one who can teach yourself how to feel safe and secure.

◆ In solitude comes my opportunity for personal growth. Today I'll learn to trust that my solitude is a safe space. It can strengthen me so I can enjoy a much stronger relationship in the future.

*I'd become fond of Lester, and I wasn't sure why . . . maybe
I just liked him. It was possible for a woman to just like a man,
wasn't it? I thought so, but I wasn't sure. My radical feminist
friends would probably disagree, but then they disagree with me
on almost everything.*

— LAUREN WRIGHT DOUGLAS, FROM *NINTH LIFE*

Do your interactions with friends sometimes feel like an
episode of *Cheers*, where you try to help your lesbian and gay
male friends get along with one another—even though
they're each completely different? You may know controlling
people like Diane Chambers who see the world in terms of
black and white, right and wrong, their way (the correct way)
and everyone else's way (the wrong way). And you may know
freewheeling "Sams" who can't seem to take anything—you,
your friends, or the difficulties in living a gay life—seriously.
You may even have a Norm and Cliff hanging around—gay
buddies who are sometimes fond friends and other times
frustrating foes.

While a crazy cast of characters you're watching on TV can
seem hilarious, it can be horrible when they exist in real life.
For even though you may like all your friends, not all your
friends will like one another.

What should you do when such conflicts arise? Nothing.
You can like whomever you like, no matter what your friends
think; your friends may dislike whomever they choose. Just
treat all of your friends as companions who add to your life,
not as nuisances you feel you need to deal with.

◆ Today I'll accept each of my friends for who they are and
ask that my friends do the same.

I drink only my own blood now. Drinking someone else's blood is better, of course, but I'm a safe-sex vampire.

—GAY VAMPIRE, JACK

In this time of AIDS, do you still have an attitude that "it will never happen to me"? Do you feel you're so intuitive that you can tell whether or not a partner is safe? Do you find yourself trusting in beliefs such as "Women don't lie," "We can be careful without using precautions," or "I believe him when he says he's been tested"?

The HIV virus isn't going to look the other way when you don't use a condom or dental dam or when you engage in sexual acts in which bodily fluids are exchanged or are able to enter your bloodstream through a cut or tear. All it takes is just one partner, just one night, just one orgasm from a brief encounter to destroy your entire life.

If you were looking for a place to live, you wouldn't tell a realtor, "Please find me a house in a high-crime location." You'd want to live in a safe neighborhood. By the same token, if you were saving up for a special purchase, you wouldn't leave your money lying around. You'd want to find a safe place for it. If safety is important to where you live and what you earn, then why wouldn't safety be a top priority when considering your health?

While unsafe sex may *feel* better, safe sex is guaranteed to *last* longer. Safeguard your life with as much consideration as you'd pay to your home and your savings; practice safe sex.

◆ I can make safe sex pleasurable with the right partner. Today I'll strive to be with someone who's ready and willing to make love with me in safety.

J A N U A R Y   1 1

I'd like to be able to suggest or to show the young people today that there's a wonderful world out there and regardless of your way of life or your religion . . . you try to make a place for yourself in the world and to contribute.

—DALLAS COORS

Dallas Coors, heir to the multimillion-dollar business of Coors Beer, came out as a gay man in late 1992. At the time Coors, seventy-five, spoke about his next project—writing his autobiography about coming out in 1950 in a world where "that type of thing is totally unacceptable."

While the attitudes toward being gay have definitely shifted since the 1950s, it still isn't always easy for young people to come to terms with their sexuality. Coming out to family members, friends, and others always contains the risk of possible rejection; being open in a high school, college campus, or job can result in harassment, expulsion, or even violence. Even the decision not to come out to others, while it eliminates the risk of rejection or ostracism, still conflicts with the need to be honest.

Yet, despite the hardships involved in declaring one's sexuality and living openly as a gay man or lesbian, Coors still believes in openness and honesty. The best way to do this, according to him, is to trust that you should "just go on living."

♦ Today I can use the experience, strength, and hope of others who have come out long before me to gain the courage to live an honest, open life that's right for me. I'll believe in the philosophy "Live and let live."

My whole life is secrets. I could be the best spy in the whole world, because I keep secrets better than anyone.

—JEFFREY NICKEL

Do you ever say, "I just want to tell people about me, about my sexuality, about my lover," but then frantically tell yourself, "But they can't know. *They can't.* I've got to keep those things a secret." So you go into work each Monday morning and edit the pronouns you use as you describe the events of the weekend. Or you go to a family gathering with a gay friend, but keep your interactions "cool." Or you listen to the homophobic comments and degrading jokes about gays and lesbians made by your friends or coworkers and nod your head or laugh along at the punch line.

Yet even when you resolve to live with your secrets, they can eat away at you. They can prevent you from being more open with friends and family members. They can keep you from growing and moving on in your life. They can even destroy your self-esteem by leading you to believe that who you are and what you do is wrong, sick, or bad.

The best way to remove the unhealthy powers secrets have over you and your life is to divulge the truth to at least one person. Chose someone you trust—a spiritual adviser, sibling, professional, or a member of a gay and lesbian support group—who can be understanding as well as discreet. Once you find the courage to take this liberating step to release your secrets, you may experience a tremendous sense of relief.

◆ I'm not sick; keeping secrets is. Today I'll unburden my secret to someone so I can open the door to let greater freedom into my life.

Here is a mental treatment guaranteed to cure every ill that flesh is heir to: sit for half an hour every night and mentally forgive everyone against whom you have any ill will or antipathy.
—CHARLES FILLMORE

How willing are you to forgive an ex-lover who mistreated you, a family member who spoke harshly to you, a friend who wasn't there for you in a time of need, or a company that rejects your sexuality? You may feel it's easier to hang on to your feelings of anger, pain, and resentment than to forgive, for the feelings serve as a constant reminder of how you've been wronged.

But what good comes from being reminded of negative feelings? The unforgiving mind is like a pot of coffee that's been on the burner too long; it's dark, unpleasant, and full of bitterness. A forgiving mind is like a fresh pot of coffee: enticing, refreshing, invigorating, and rich with pleasant aromas.

Today you need to ask yourself: "Can I forgive someone who has wronged me?" Forgiveness is the ability first to let go of the negative feelings you have toward others. To do so, try to understand that the people who wronged you may have done so through a lack of understanding, through an inability to be honest with themselves, or through an inability to fully understand the impact their actions would have upon you. Such understanding can provide you with the key to unlock the door of forgiveness.

♦ When I'm unforgiving, I have a heavy burden to bear. Today I'll let go of some of this burden by forgiving someone. In doing so, I can lighten my load and enlighten my heart.

Remember that death is not to be postponed. The hour of your appointment with the grave is undisclosed. Before you die, do good to your friend; reach out as far as you can to help him. Do not miss a day's enjoyment or forge your share of innocent pleasure. . . . Give and receive. . . .

—ECCLESIASTES 14:12–19

Often death goes hand in hand with the phrase "If only . . ." It's so common to hear someone declare after losing a loved one, "If only we had been able to spend more time together," "If only I had treated each of our moments as precious," or "If only I had said all the things I wanted to."

Yet relating a litany of "if onlys" does no good once someone is gone. What should matter more is not thinking about all the things you would have liked to have done together, but taking action in the present—doing all the things you want to do *now,* before your loved one is gone.

Today is a day you can fill with giving, sharing, nurturing, loving, laughing, and conversing with someone who is dying. Read a favorite book aloud; share your memories as you flip through a photo album; play a game together; sit outside in the fresh air and sunshine; provide a nourishing soup or make a soothing cup of tea; cuddle together; tell not only what's on your mind, but also what's in your heart.

Do all these things while your special friend is alive so when he or she leaves, your mind won't be filled with "if onlys" or your heart bursting with regrets. You'll be able to mourn the death but know you were there in life.

♦ Today make up your mind that you won't miss a day's enjoyment with a loved one. Treat each moment as a precious gift you've been given to share together.

Before the Colorado election, as I began a 24-plus-city book tour, I struggled with the boycott concept myself. Should I not go to Alabama? The Ku Klux Klan there calls we Latinas "mud-women," a hate-filled name. I think it is critical to go to Alabama. Should I not go to Utah because they have the most oppressive law against women's right to abortion of any state in the nation? I think it is essential to go to Utah . . . the best medicine we possess must be placed on the worst of the wounds. The best medicines we have are our voices.

—CLARISSA PINKOLA ESTES

Sometimes silence can be an appropriate—and very powerful—form of communication. It is advisable to remain silent so you can listen to the thoughts and feelings of others. It is beneficial to remain silent when the words you would say might inflict hurt. It is effective to remain silent so the ridiculous and absurd words of others can be heard and judged as such.

Yet it is self-defeating and weakening to be silent just because someone wants you to. Silence that's based on such oppression gives the oppressors what they want. Clarissa Pinkola Estes—a Jungian psychoanalyst, award-winning poet, *cantadora* (keeper of the old stories), and author of the best-selling *Women Who Run with the Wolves*—believes gay men and lesbians should raise their voices when confronted by such silencing oppression. She says: "Bringing people alive, awake. Setting them free . . ." is what raising your voice is all about.

◆ Today I'll remind myself that there are times when silence can be ineffective. My silence can inadvertently punish me, as I am part of a group that's already disempowered.

I find it hard to accept anyone's death. I watched my mother die from cancer. I was overcome with grief and rage. I was told by someone trying to comfort me that we must all face death some day. "Some day, not now," I thought.

—DAVID KEATING

Is today another day you fear because you're facing death—not the death of someone close to you, but your own? Perhaps you're living with AIDS, diagnosed with cancer, elderly, or suffering from a debilitating medical condition. Are you wondering, "How can I do this for another day? I hurt. I'm tired. I'm scared. How can I find the strength, hope, and courage to get through another day?"

Today is not just another day to get through. Living while you're dying doesn't mean you have to continuously swim against the current of life until you're too weak to fight anymore. Death should never be thought of as such a battle—for no matter what you do, you'll never win.

Rather, seek to discover that the greatest reward in living with the presence of death is to become one with the current of the river of life. *Let go and go with the flow.* Even though you may be led toward still waters, you can enjoy the journey. Today, let go and simply let this day happen. Relax your emotional and physical tension and tightness; become one with the waters of life. Let your spirit flow today, and you will be strong and unafraid.

♦ Today I'll show my strength by surrendering and becoming part of the river of life. No matter where I flow today, I'll trust that I'm safe, secure, and never alone.

JANUARY 17

We have all grown up on the same sitcoms, eaten the same fast food and laughed at the same jokes. We have practiced the same religions, lived under the same political system, read the same books and worked in the same marketplace. We have the same dreams and aspirations, as well as fears and doubts for ourselves. . . . How, then, can our differences be so overwhelming?

—SHELBY STEELE

What makes you different from 90 percent of the population is the fact that you are physically, emotionally, and spiritually attracted to members of your same sex. Other than that simple distinction, everything else about you in relation to others comes from similar experiences. Yet it is that simple distinction—the choice you've made to identify and express your sexuality—that can make others reject everything about you, even the things you have in common with them.

Why should that hurt you so much, to have others reject you? Living as a gay man or a lesbian, you've learned tolerance; it may be a concept you wish others had. You know what it feels like to be different, to feel like you're an outsider, to feel that lack of connection with others. You may be tired of feeling those feelings again and again whenever others reject you because of your sexuality.

Today, exercise patience with others. They're not all going to accept you in the same way you accept them. Tolerate what you can; let others do the same.

◆ Today I'll strive to be patient and accept that the opinions others have about me may or may not change. Everyone is going to move at a pace that's right for them; I need to move at my own pace, with or without their approval.

Preference implies choice, and it is well established that the very large majority of homosexuals do not choose their sexual orientation any more than heterosexuals do. . . . it is highly unlikely that 10% of the population would choose homosexuality in a society so homophobic that it severely restricts the lives of lesbians and gays and exposes them to hate crimes of violence and even death.

—LEON J. GOODMAN

Authorities on human sexuality generally agree that sexual orientation results from a combination of genetic, hormonal, and environmental factors. You probably already know that. But how can you convince others who care about you—who believe that you've chosen a way of life that sentences you to years of unhappiness—that being gay is something that isn't so much a matter of choice, but simply *is*.

If you had chosen a career that involved the fight against child abuse or abuse of the elderly, those who care about you would probably be highly supportive of your chosen profession. After all, it's easy to understand why you would want to protect those who need such protection, for they have no choice about who they are: a child is a child and an aged person is an aged person.

By the same token, you are who you are. Let those who care about you know that being gay is simply one part of what defines you; it is as much an essence of your being as your height or the color of your eyes.

◆ Today I'll convey to those who care about me that being gay is not an option I chose; it is genuinely part of who I am.

We can't be who we are if we have to leave our culture behind.
— MARIANA ROMO-CARMONA

Walking the streets in any major U.S. city will bring you in touch with the cultural diversity evident in this predominantly white, English-speaking country. You'll see shops and restaurants that cater to ethnic backgrounds. Take mass transit, and you'll hear many different languages being spoken by passengers. Flip through radio stations or cable channels, and you'll see and hear programs geared toward those from other cultures. All these things symbolize the pride of people who come to America from other countries.

Just because you have gay pride doesn't mean that you can't also have cultural pride. You can be gay and Jewish, gay and Italian, gay and Afro-American, gay and Native American. You can celebrate gay events such as PRIDE and also times of importance to your culture, such as Orthodox Lent, St. Patrick's Day, Yom Kippur, the Chinese New Year, or Martin Luther King's birthday.

Being gay doesn't mean you have to turn your back on the holidays, beliefs, language, style of dress, or history of your cultural background, even if being gay is unacceptable in your culture. Today, seek out one of the many support groups, churches, or organizations that can help you maintain pride in your sexuality as well as pride in your culture.

◆ Today I won't let the cultural barriers to my sexuality force me into making a choice between the two. I can choose to remain true to myself as well as to my heritage.

Sticks and stones may break our bones, but words will break our hearts.

—ROBERT FULGHUM

Wouldn't it be wonderful if you could turn a deaf ear to every degrading label used to describe a member of the gay and lesbian community? Yet how many times do you wish you could've done the same thing when you were growing up—to a parent who called you stupid or no good, to schoolmates who labeled you sissy or fatty, or to so-called friends who whispered behind your back about the feelings you had for a teacher or classmate?

Although words are, in reality, just a series of alphabet letters strung together, it's their meaning and the venom with which they're delivered that can destroy family relationships, sever friendships, force alienation or self-imposed isolation—and break your heart.

It has been said that "Words are the freezing of reality." Once spoken, their impact is incredible and their meaning irrevocable. Yet it's important that you keep the words you hear today in today, and not in some past time that evokes painful memories. And it's equally important to be able to keep in mind that words used to inflict hurt reflect the reality of the speaker rather than the reality of the meaning of the words. So look closely at who delivers degrading epithets. Chances are you'll see an insecure and unfortunate human being.

♦ Today I'll keep in mind that name calling can disrupt inner peace. Rather than let the harsh words of another incite me, I'll use them to gain insights into why the speaker is saying them.

Why are so many of our young children gay bashers, who target gays and lesbians for violence? As a result, gay children have high rates of teen suicide and alcoholism. Your "values" are killing many of our children.

— A LESBIAN MOTHER OF A FOUR-YEAR-OLD

Media coverage of New York City's Rainbow Curriculum, which includes material on sexual orientation, gay family relationships, and respecting gays and lesbians, evoked highly charged responses. Those who were against the program expressed outrage that the time for children to learn about math and science was being taken up with information on homosexuality and "Daddy's companion, Frank."

But one of those who expressed praise for the program was a gay teen. He said, "I constantly hear about gay bashing, and it makes me crawl back further into the closet that I am protected by. Young students need to learn about the diversity of life."

Family values that include acceptance of *all* family relationships are rarely taught in the home. Instead, the home is often where lessons in prejudice, racism, and sexism are given. So what better place for children to learn about family diversity than a space for education, enrichment, and enlightenment?

Today, show your support of schools that promote learning about nontraditional families and homosexuality. Donate gay-and-lesbian-themed books to their libraries or contact guidance departments and volunteer as a peer counselor to gay teens in need.

♦ Today I'll support any school system that teaches its students that nontraditional families are based on loving support, kindness, respect, and acceptance.

Freedom means choosing your burden.

——HEPHZIBAH MENUHIN

Do you sometimes wake up, go through your day, or get ready for bed at night with the feeling that you're like a pack mule, dragging around a heavy burden? You might not even be able to identify your burden, yet you know it's there because you may feel no joy, no peace, and no security in your life.

But no painful burden—be it immobilizing anxiety about coming to terms with your sexuality, incredible fear of disclosure about your lifestyle, an unfulfilling job, an unhappy intimate relationship, or an addiction to drugs or alcohol—is experienced without a reason. They are your burdens for whatever healthy or unhealthy reason; more likely than not, they are there because you need to finally come to terms with them.

However, you are always free to reject dealing with any or all burdens or to deal with them so you can change the unhealthy conditions they cause. Today, look at the burdens that confound you. Remember that you're not a powerless, worthless, helpless individual who's at the mercy of society, friends, family members, or coworkers. You can change your burdens. *That's* what freedom is all about.

◆ Today I'll realize that while I may not appreciate my burdens, they are there for a reason. I can experience joy when I accept the freedom I have in choosing to deal with my burdens.

> *I think I must let go. Must fear not, must be quiet so that my children can hear the Sound of Creation and dance the dance that is in them.*
>
> —RUSSELL HOBAN

The child who crushes a kitten tightly to her chest is a child who is afraid that if she releases the kitten, it will run away from her and she will be left alone.

Telling the child that it's okay to let go of the kitten is the right thing to do, but so is your need to release the tight hold you may have on your child. As a parent, you may find it hard to stand back and let your child go freely through the good times in life as well as the bad. While life's ordinary rhythm carries *everyone* through good times and bad, sometimes you may fear the bad times so much for your child that you may try to hold back life's forward motion.

But when you do so, you prevent the forward motion that can carry your child out of the bad times and into the good. While you may want to spare your child the hurt and pain that may be faced because of your sexuality, remember that a child learns and grows from pain. It's always hard to watch a child stumble and fall, but sparing your child that tumble doesn't teach anything about balance, about confidence, about getting back up again, and about dancing the dance of life.

◆ Today I'll keep in mind that holding fast to my fears only keeps those fears close to me. I can release my fears about my child's well-being by trusting that the best learning often comes from mistakes, hurt, and pain.

You can't test courage cautiously.

—ANNIE DILLARD

What have you done lately that you believe took courage? Perhaps you came out to a close friend. You may have ended an unhealthy relationship. You may have informed your parents that your lover would be with you next holiday season. Or you may have asked someone you've been interested in out on a date.

Or perhaps you've done none of those things. Instead, you may have kept your sexuality hidden from a friend. You may have chosen to stay in a difficult or unbearable relationship. You may have avoided any discussion about you and your lover's future holiday plans with your family. Or you may have avoided letting someone know you're interested in them.

The definition of courage is the ability to conquer fear or despair. So courage isn't putting yourself in stressful or unpleasant situations. Courage isn't controlling your emotions. Courage isn't holding back, giving in, remaining silent, or minimizing personal needs.

Courage is the ability to strengthen yourself against the fear and despair of life rather than be drowned by it. That means you can't just dip your toe in courage. You need to dive in all the way. So today, identify an area of your life that causes you fear or despair. Then do something that helps you face those feelings.

♦ Today I'll take the plunge and be courageous. I won't walk away, hold back, or ignore; I'll confront, release, and deal with something that truly matters to me.

In love you must give three times before you take once.

—BRAZILIAN PROVERB

How much do you think you know about healthy love? Take a moment to reflect on a past or present relationship. Then think about the misconceptions you may have about love—misconceptions that often lead to disconnected relationships.

Love isn't based on competition; that is, finding the best "catch," the one who's the greatest in bed, the one who's the best looking, the best dressed, or who makes the most money. Love isn't based on expectations that a lover is going to make all your problems go away, ease the effects of a childhood dysfunction, or be a mind reader so you never have to voice your needs. Love isn't self-seeking, where you establish a relationship for the sole purpose of what you can get out of it.

Throughout the years, you may have looked forward to falling in love, to meeting the "right" person with whom love would bloom and endure automatically without any effort. But real love is not based on how much you can get or the right one to give it to you. Real love is about what you can *give.* If you are prepared to impart trust, acceptance, honesty, and generosity to another—without any expectation or desire to have such things returned to you—then you are ready to experience healthy love.

◆ Today I want an intimate relationship to go far beyond superficialities. I'll strive to create bonds with someone I love that are mutually enriching, deep, and lasting.

Faith is the bird that feels the light and sings when the dawn is still dark.

—RABINDRANATH TAGORE

The bird that sings long before the sun has risen is strong evidence of faith. For that bird trusts the sky will soon lighten, the sun will rise, and the world will come alive. It is when the bird won't sing that you know it has lost faith in the great continuum of life.

Are you a bird who can't feel the light right now? Perhaps you're dying and feel alone and frightened. Maybe your relationship is in trouble. You might be feeling disconnected with your friends or unhappy with your career. Perhaps you're feeling ashamed of your sexuality. Maybe you've lost your direction in life.

Yet when things seem darkest, that's the time you need to have faith that all things change, all wounds heal, all is eased through the passage of time. Things *do* get better.

When you find yourself thinking about your difficulties today, interrupt your thoughts by saying aloud, "But this, too, shall pass." Then remind yourself that there isn't a day that won't have lightness, there isn't a night that won't have a rising sun at its end, there isn't a problem that won't have a solution, and there isn't a weary soul that won't be energized again.

◆ Today I'll sing, for I have faith in the rising sun. Things aren't as bad as they seem; there is hope, for there is always change.

Always do what you say you are going to do. It is the glue and fiber that binds successful relationships.

—JEFFRY A. TIMMONS

When you say you can be there for a friend, how much do your actions back up your words? Would you use the word "dependable" to describe how you are in your friendships? Do you always mean what you say and say what you mean with your friends?

While you may believe you have many friends and that you're a friend to many, the true test of friendship comes when you are needed or need someone—not when there's a party to go to, a bar you want to check out, or a free evening where you don't have anything to do. For it's then, when you or others are most vulnerable and dependent, that friends are needed for help and reassurance.

But saying you're going to be there for someone and then actually being there are two different things. How often could you or a friend drop everything and be there for one another? Or would there always be another priority or a convenient excuse that would prevent that from happening?

Sometimes it's a lot easier to make a commitment to a lover than it is to a friend. But although lovers come and go, friends are often the most stabilizing, consistent part of a person's life. So today, be there for a friend—no questions asked, no matter what he or she needs you for—because that's what gives friendship its extraordinary power.

◆ Today I'll back up the promises I've made to a friend and show that I really can be there. The efforts I make in our friendship will only strengthen it.

What most of us want is to be heard, to communicate.

—DORY PREVIN

There are four simple words that can resolve conflicts, develop intimacy, clear up misconceptions, reveal innermost thoughts and feelings, and open dialogue. They are: "Let's talk about it." Like a green light on a traffic signal, your willingness to communicate encourages forward progress rather than keeping you from moving forward.

But what happens next, after you've expressed a desire to talk? Then you and the person you're speaking with need to become active listeners. First, that means that when one person is talking, the other is listening—really listening—not just formulating a response, daydreaming, or passing judgment. Second, it means that once one person is done speaking, the other gets a chance to be heard. It's only after these two steps have been completed that a response can be made to what the other person has said.

Good communication—one that allows both parties an opportunity to have the floor—is like a tennis match. Each person has a chance to serve the ball (share thoughts and feelings) and a chance to return the ball (respond or react).

Today, let others be heard and make sure that you, too, are heard equally. A willingness to listen is as important as the willingness to share.

◆Today I'll remember that communication involves two components: speaking as well as hearing. I'll remember that others—gay and straight—need my willingness to listen as much as I need theirs.

A nuclear physicist could meet a plumber. Bathhouses were a great leveler, a common denominator, a place where people did not have to be of similar social backgrounds.

—BRUCE MAILMAN

No matter what your profession, your income, your education, your interest and hobbies, your family background, or where you live and what you own, your link with all gay brothers and lesbian sisters is your sexuality. Being gay is a great leveler; it places you on equal footing with other gay people, even if you're not equal in other ways. And because it makes you an equal, it can help to soften class distinctions, social attitudes, and financial differences between gay men and lesbians.

When you're on equal footing with other gay men and lesbians, you don't have to apologize for the way you choose to live or feel ashamed at the success you've achieved. What you share far outweighs where you've come from, where you're going, and what you've got right now.

So does it matter whether you're a doctor or a dog walker, a secretary or a student, a programmer or a produce manager? Is it important what you make per hour, per year, or per client? How significant is the make and year of your car, where you live, where you shop, or how you dress? What matters when you're around other gay men and lesbians is your common bond—not your stocks and bonds.

♦ Today I'll remember that I am as good and worthwhile as every other gay man and lesbian. Our common bond equalizes us and makes me feel that I belong.

The tragedy of life is that people do not change.

—AGATHA CHRISTIE

Are you driving yourself crazy trying to change another's opinion or get them to accept you for who you really are? You are if you find yourself frequently complaining, "She just doesn't understand," "He doesn't listen to how I really feel," or "They can't see my point of view."

Sometimes, no matter how much you may argue or how sane and clear your argument is, you may never be able to change another's opinion or get them to see things from your position. Perhaps you're trying to talk to your parents about your lover. Are you trying to force their approval on an issue they'll never approve of? You may be trying to explain to your boss the importance of including "significant others" in the company outing. But is your boss able to conquer his own homophobia to deal with the issue rationally?

Before you become tense and angry, look at the people with whom you're arguing. Ask: "Do I respect these people? Are their opinions beneficial to me? Are they interested in my best welfare?" Then be ready to walk away from those whose opinions really don't matter and who won't care anyway—no matter what you do or say.

♦ Sometimes I struggle to change the opinions of those who have never supported me, rather than talk with those who have always been there for me. Today I'll distinguish between the two and seek those opinions I value and trust.

>   . . . *lives without spouses or children didn't count; didn't*
> *register on the meter of meaningfulness.*
> —ELINOR LIPMAN, FROM *THE WAY MEN ACT*

Some of the questions posed most frequently to gays and lesbians—often by well-meaning family members, straight friends, and heterosexual coworkers—are: "When are you going to get married?" "Don't you think you just need to meet the right man/woman?" "Don't you want to have children?" "Don't you like children?"

Such questions belittle your sexuality, ignore your significant other, and pass judgment on the way you live your life—all of which matter greatly to you. And such questions also suggest that living in a nice home, having a good job, and being happy don't matter if your life doesn't also include what society deems important: heterosexual marriage and raising a family.

While it would be terrific if there came a time in your life when no such questions were directed at you, the reality is that for as long as you don't live a straight way of life, those questions will probably be asked.

So today, accept the fact that even if you came out to all of those people who posed such questions, it probably wouldn't stop them from asking. What you *can* do is ignore their questions, change the subject, or simply respond: "As soon as anything in my life changes, you'll be the first to know."

♦ Today I'll remember that just because I don't live a straight way of life doesn't mean my life has no meaning. My happiness is more important than fulfilling a role others want for me.

I'm afraid of gay people. Petrified. I have nightmares about gay people . . . AIDS petrifies me 'cause girls be hanging out with gay guys. They could be in a club with their gay friend, give him a little kiss, and go home with that AIDS on their lips. . . .
—EDDIE MURPHY

In his 1983 concert film *Delirious*, Eddie Murphy swaggered onstage in a red leather outfit and, five minutes into his act, insulted the entire gay population with his crass humor and ignorance. But he's not the first comedian to do so; using gay men and lesbians as the basis for demeaning humor seems to be popular not only with straight comedians, but also with their audiences.

There is a fine line between when humor is appropriate, timely, and tasteful and when it is not. What offends one person might amuse another. Additionally, who tells the joke becomes critical: gay or lesbian comedians often joke about themselves or gay men and lesbians as a whole and succeed because they are laughing *with* others who share their lifestyle; straight people who tell the same jokes alienate gay men and lesbians because they are laughing *at* them.

Today, think about comedians you support by watching their films or videos or attending their concerts. Ask yourself: "Are the comedians I'm supporting offensive to me as a gay man or lesbian? Should I continue to support them?"

◆ Today I need to really listen to jokes told about members of my community. Will I laugh at them—even though they may be offensive to me or those I care for—just to join in with others?

It took me 11 months to get another job. Of course, since I was fired [for being gay], I had to come out at every job interview, and then I'd never know why the person didn't hire me.

—JULIE BRIENZA

A Christian broadcaster whom Julie Brienza interviewed for *The Washington Blade*, a gay weekly, found out Julie worked for UPI and urged his listeners to pressure the news organization to fire her. UPI complied, citing "professional infractions." Since November 1990, Brienza has been fighting the decision, but just wants "to get back into wire service or newspaper reporting."

Horror stories such as Brienza's may convince you not to come out at work to a supervisor or other person in a position of power. Yet you may also be hesitant to come out to coworkers who have become your friends outside of work. Mistrust that a work friend will knowingly or unknowingly out you can limit the level of openness in your friendship. The dilemma for you may then be between how much you value your job and how close you can be with your work friends.

Whatever secrets you keep from any friend prevents true intimacy, yet whatever secrets you keep from your employer about your private life may be necessary to maintain professionalism and job security. So today, exercise caution in your openness. Be certain that if you decide to come out to someone at work, a strong basis of trust is already in place.

♦ Coming out to family and nonwork friends is one thing; coming out to work friends is another. Today I'll remind myself that not everyone should be entrusted with an issue as personal as my sexuality.

In a time when you're focusing all of your personal resources, especially financial resources, on maintaining your health care, you tend to forget about what you love about life, whether it's going out to dinner with an old friend or going to a Bruins game or seeing a play.

—PATRICK FRANCIS MURPHY

When Patrick Francis Murphy was diagnosed as HIV positive, at first he denied he had the disease. When he finally began to take his condition more seriously, he became depressed, decided to have "a giant self-pity party," and started to abuse alcohol.

But he soon stopped drinking himself into oblivion and began to turn his life around. In 1992 he founded For the Love of Life (FLOL), a wish-granting organization for people living with HIV and AIDS. Like the Make-a-Wish Foundation, a national organization that grants wishes to terminally ill children, FLOL is designed to help people with HIV "live fuller, more complete lives [and is] committed to meeting the emotional needs that will . . . enhance the quality of their lives."

Today, think about a wish that would make you feel emotionally stronger or bring enjoyment to your life. Perhaps it's dining out with a friend, spending a weekend at a cozy New England bed-and-breakfast, or exploring a hobby that's always interested you. Share your wish with your partner or friends, and let them help make your wish come true!

♦ Today I'll think of treating myself well. What can I do that will help me feel happy and positive?

Every time I don't say it, I think about it. When I say "I" and not "we," I think about it.

—KEVIN M. SMITH

How often do you acknowledge the partner with whom you're in an intimate relationship? Do you often speak in terms of "us" rather than "him/her" and "me"? Do you think silence about your relationship might be construed as shame—how you feel about loving someone of the same sex—rather than fear—anxiety about what others might think, say, or do?

For Mitchell L. Adams and Kevin M. Smith, top officials in Massachusetts Governor Weld's administration, speaking publicly about their twelve-year relationship brought relief. They hoped speaking out would "set an example for other high-profile professional gays."

No matter how long your current intimate relationship may be—two months, two years, or two decades—you're always faced with a choice: to share the existence of the relationship with other people who may not be part of your accepting, supportive circle of friends, or to maintain silence even when close family members may question the truth about what's really going on.

Today, consider first the reasons that would make you acknowledge your partner and your relationship with others. Then, with your partner, decide whether you're both comfortable with such a revelation and how best to go about it.

◆ Today I'll remember that acknowledging my intimate relationship can be very liberating but, at the same time, very frightening. It's also a decision that's not mine alone to make, but mine and my partner's.

My experience has been that in the end when you fight for a desperate cause and have good reasons to fight, you usually win. I have experienced that more often than once, and you may object to my statement by calling me an optimist.

—EDWARD TELLER

How you deal with your sexuality shows whether you're a pessimist or an optimist. If you're a pessimist, you may yearn to live as an openly gay man or lesbian but feel constantly burdened by the disapproval of family members, the homophobia of straight friends, or society's rejection of your sexuality. You may believe that being gay means walking hand in hand with such burdens and therefore resign yourself to the belief that there is nothing you can do to change things or make them better.

However, if you're an optimist you're willing to admit you don't know what lies ahead politically, legally, professionally, morally, and personally in terms of your being gay. Yet what you do know is that no matter how you are viewed and treated by society or those who are close to you, you determine whether such things will influence how you live your life on a daily basis. As an optimist, you're willing to do something about the attitudes, behaviors, and judgments that confront you as a gay person and as a member of a gay and lesbian community.

To become more of an optimist, seek ways to ease the pressures placed upon you as a gay man or lesbian. Work to help family members accept you and your sexuality and enlighten your homophobic friends. Or protest injustices that affect your entire community or members of your community.

◆ Today I'll be an optimist. I believe I have good reasons to fight for acceptance of my sexuality, and I'll do all I can to achieve this end.

When a straight guy meets a gay guy, right away he thinks to himself that the gay guy wants to suck his dick. I say, "Doll, don't flatter yourself!"

—SCOTT VALENTINE

One of the most frustrating aspects of being a gay man or lesbian is dealing with straight society's stereotypical belief that gay men and women want only three things in life: sex, sex, and more sex. Anyone who is seen with you is considered a current bedmate; straight friends may fear to spend time alone with you because of possible sexual overtures; family members may not visit you for fear of "interrupting something."

While you can't change the attitudes of society as a whole, you can change what those who know you think about what it means to be gay. Ask your straight friends if they want to sleep with everyone they meet of the opposite sex. Then let them know that, like them, not all gay people want to sleep together just because they're gay. Point out to your straight friends that they have friendships with members of the opposite sex. Then tell them that gay men can be friends with other gay men just as lesbians can be friends with other lesbians.

Finally, point out that their intimate relationships involve more than just physical intimacy. Then explain that intimate gay relationships are also made up of all levels of intimacy: physical, mental, emotional, and spiritual.

♦ Today I can be a teacher who can educate those who think of my sexuality only in terms of sex. I'll let them know how meaningful my interactions with other gay men and lesbians are and how they enrich my life.

It matters not what you are thought to be, but what you are.
——PUBLILIUS SYRUS

There's a story about a man who owned a pair of eyeglasses that had only one lens. Through one eye he saw a world filled with clear, crisp images; the other eye saw only blurred, indiscernible shapes. "But that's okay," he commented. "Because most of the time I feel like I'm only half a person anyway."

Anyone who experiences low self-esteem knows that it can affect all areas of your life until you end up feeling like you're never a complete, whole person. Add to low self-esteem a low self-image that can result from reactions to your gay lifestyle, and you may rarely feel that you're a complete, worthwhile person.

Yet you can change your low self-image just as you can change to a new pair of glasses. If you *perceive* yourself to be only half a person——if you buy into the belief some have that gay men and lesbians are less than healthy, less than happy, less than whole people——then you may start to believe it about yourself. But if you keep in mind that perceptions are not facts, then you can take honest pride in who you are. Today, look at yourself and the world through two good lenses. Make an honest assessment of your good qualities and the positive progress and changes you've made in your life. Such things can help you see that you truly are a good, worthwhile, complete person.

◆ Sometimes I find it difficult to look at the world and myself because of my low self-image. But today I'll believe in myself without doubt and with clarity and honesty.

I find that I like the energy of women in a concert. But they can be the most over-bearing and disturbing fans, because they feel like they have a connection with you: "You're a sister. Gimme something."

—K. D. LANG

Imagine that you're a success in some highly visible profession—the arts, the movie industry, politics, or sports. Do you come out, or do you keep your sexuality a secret?

Often, when someone in a position of high visibility comes out as a gay man or lesbian, other gay men and lesbians then feel it is that person's responsibility to assume all the burdens of every gay man and lesbian and strive to correct them. Rather than recognize that the person has priorities and commitments to his or her own private life, the pressure and expectations gay men and lesbians may place on the person ignore that he or she has a life that exists out of the spotlight.

Before you place high expectations on respected role models to use their popularity to ease your struggles, ask yourself: "Do I make the issues of all gay men and lesbians my priority every day—in my job, at home, within my circle of friends, and in my moments of solitude?" Then look at your role models as people who you can admire, respect, and enjoy, but who need to make choices that are right for them.

◆ Today I won't place the label of "brother" or "sister" on one of my role models. I'll appreciate who he or she is rather than expect that he or she will become an active part of the gay and lesbian community.

> . . . *abusive lesbians are mindful that their partners are unlikely to call the police and use that as another control tactic. They will say "call the police. Do you think they're going to help the dyke?"*

—BETH LEVENTHAL

An estimated 500,000 gay men and between 50,000 and 100,000 lesbians are believed to be battered by their partners each year, according to statistics cited by activists. Yet most gay men and lesbians have been slow to acknowledge the violence in their midst—even when they may be a victim of domestic violence themselves.

Often, you may attribute a partner's abusive behavior to alcohol, drugs, or stress. Or you may blame yourself, thinking that if you only listened more, did more of your share around the house, were more patient, or handled things differently, the physical, emotional, or verbal abuse wouldn't occur. You may even make up your mind to try harder as you hope that when work pressures ease up or the other stresses in life become more manageable, your partner will no longer treat you so cruelly. Then you wait for things to get better.

But when things don't get better, what will you do? Today, rather than endure another minute in an abusive relationship, do something about it. Call a battered woman's shelter or hotline, seek help from a professional, or simply open up to a close and trusted friend. Waiting any longer for things to improve will just be a waste of your time, and could be dangerous.

♦ Today I'll make up my mind to take care of myself. I won't hold on to my terrible secret of abuse any longer. I'll acknowledge the reality of my situation with someone who can help me.

Relationships are real hard work. Commitment is hanging out in the fallow periods of the relationship, when we are not talking the same language and we feel like we are on different mountain peaks and being able to maintain some kind of commitment through those periods until we can get to the good times again. I think I grew up with the illusion that if you love someone that is enough.

—MARTY JOHNSON

Do you ever begin a discussion with your intimate partner by saying, "If you loved me, you would/wouldn't . . ."? Expecting that the *emotions* of love will handle the *realities* of a love relationship is like expecting that carrying a spare tire in your car trunk means you'll be able to put it on when you have a flat. But when your tire-changing skills are finally put to the test, that's when you'll see whether you're capable of doing the work.

No matter how much you love someone—or how much he or she loves you—that love isn't going to help you work out any of your relationship issues. Your love will give you the reason to want to work on those issues, but it won't show you how to compromise, communicate, or resolve conflicts. Your love will give you the responsibility to bring about solutions, but not the answers.

Today, strive to be a tire-changer in your relationship. Roll up your sleeves, identify one area of conflict that needs to be addressed, then schedule a time you and your partner can sit down and talk about it.

◆ Today I'll let go of the fantasy that "Love conquers all." Instead I'll believe in the reality that "Love can give me the strength to make changes in my relationship."

I have nothing against them [gays], but I certainly see no reason to jump with joy about it.

—JOHN WAYNE

Imagine you're at a party. You're being introduced to a group of straight men and women of different ages and backgrounds. The person who's introducing you says, "This is ——. And by the way, she is gay." All the faces around you beam broad smiles; a few begin to shake your hand or slap you on the back. "Splendid! Splendid!" one might exclaim. "I've only heard good things about you people. And now I actually get to meet one. I am honored!"

Straight people often receive such enthusiastic support when they're introduced as married, as a parent, as engaged, or with their partners. But someone who's introduced as gay would probably evoke silence, nervous mutterings, or even make people turn away in disapproval or disgust.

Not everyone will love you, approve of your sexuality, or accept you for who and what you are. But just because everyone can't be happy for you doesn't mean *you* can't be happy for you. Today, think of ways your sexuality makes you happy. Maybe there's the feeling of connection when you're at a pot luck, of euphoria when you're dancing to terrific music in a crowded gay bar, of safety and security when you hold your lover in your arms—or of peace and comfort simply being you.

♦ Today I won't let those who can't provide me with enthusiastic approval about my sexuality dim my enthusiasm for who I am. I can jump for joy over the things in my life that make me happy I'm gay.

It's great when gays and lesbians are visible. I'm happy my life is in a position where I can be out.

—DEBORAH CHASNOFF

Someone who suffers from chronic asthma has an invisible medical condition; unless you know the person is an asthma sufferer, you probably wouldn't be able to guess. But you would if this person was walking with a group of people that suddenly decided to break into a sprint. The asthmatic would soon begin to lag behind and gasp for air. When an inhaler was finally used, the rest of the group would know the person had asthma.

When you're a gay man or lesbian, you are similarly invisible. It is a "hidden condition," unless others know your sexuality. Sometimes this may feel comfortable to you, particularly when sexuality isn't an issue—such as at work. But other times you may wish others knew so they could be aware of your feelings, your limits, or your needs—such as times when you're invited to attend a straight function and it's assumed you'll bring a member of the opposite sex.

How you choose to live your life—as visible or invisible—is up to you. For Debra Chasnoff, director and producer whose film *Deadly Deception* won an Academy Award for the Best Documentary Short, being out has given her the freedom to combine her career with her lifestyle. Today, think of ways becoming more visible can give you new—and perhaps different—freedoms in your life.

♦ In what ways can my life change if I choose to become more visible? Today I'll increase my visibility for a positive outcome.

*When we think of cruelty, we must try to remember the
stupidity, the envy, the frustration from which it has arisen.*
— EDITH SITWELL

When you're made to feel less than adequate because of who
you are and how you live your life, what do you do? Do you
accept such feelings as the truth? Then do you try to change
how you look, act, or feel in order to elicit a more positive
response?

Today, rather than look inward when someone treats you
badly or makes you feel inadequate, look outward. Look
closely at the source of such treatment. How someone treats
you is often an indication of how that person feels about
himself or herself. What you may find, in examining the
person who takes great pains to shoot you down, is someone
whose shots could just as easily be aimed at himself or herself.

Self-love is often lacking whenever a person criticizes
another destructively, behaves irrationally, or withholds support and nurturing. Until self-love is developed, it's nearly
impossible to offer love to anyone else. Even your loving
behavior toward that person won't help self-love grow.

So how should you respond to people who treat you badly?
Don't take what they say or do to heart. That's part of their
agenda. Then limit the time you spend together. Choose to
spend your time instead with self-loving people.

♦ Today I'll understand that how others respond to me is
often a reflection of how they respond to themselves. I'll try
to gravitate toward people who are filled with self-loving
rather than self-loathing.

> *Love is what you've been through with somebody.*
>
> ——JAMES THURBER

Love is not something you express in words or writing to your loved one; it's not just a card or bouquet of flowers you send on Valentine's Day; it's not just a feeling you have in times of passion or moments of tenderness.

Love is a truth you share with someone—a truth that's based on forgiveness, kindness, generosity, and honesty. It's the willingness you have to cherish and respect another and to offer that person your strength and protection. It's the unspoken promise of honor and commitment you give freely—a timeless gift you willingly choose to share with someone. It's what exists through bad times as well as good, through times of disconnection as well as bonding, through instances of conflict as well as of resolution.

Remember that love is separate from the feelings of falling in love. Love is really what you've been through with a special person that's brought you to where you both are today. Perhaps this love is for a parent or sibling, for a best friend, for an ex-partner, or for your current intimate partner.

Today, on this day of love, ask yourself: "Have I shown love to the special people in my life? Have I bared my very heart and soul and conveyed that the love we share is a great thing, something that makes every day special for us and every burden we must bear together lighter?"

♦ Today I'll honor the love I've been through—or am going through—with a special person. I'll think fondly of all the ways I've benefited from the love we've shared.

I'm a teacher, and that probably saved me. As a teacher, you look for teachable moments in the classroom. For whatever reason, this case is a teachable moment. Not to use it to help people try and understand these issues and their interconnections would be criminal. But everybody shouldn't have to go through what we've gone through to learn.

—KAREN THOMPSON

In November 1983, Sharon Kowalski was left brain-damaged and physically impaired by an automobile accident with a drunken driver on an icy Minnesota highway. Ten months after the accident, a bitter legal battle began between Sharon's lover, Karen Thompson, and Sharon's parents, after they learned about their daughter's relationship with Thompson. They barred Karen from visiting Sharon even though Sharon indicated she wanted to see Karen and despite reports from medical caregivers that the visits were beneficial. But in February 1992, the Minnesota Supreme Court refused to hear an appeal of a lower-court decision that called Thompson and Kowalski "a family of affinity which ought to be accorded respect."

Whenever you feel your struggles as a gay man or lesbian are difficult, use the Thompson-Kowalksi case to put your difficulties in perspective. Could you go through waking up every morning for eight and a half years thinking you might never see your lover again, having your sexuality revealed to the world, or seeing your life turned into a public spectacle?

◆ Today I'll put into perspective the problems in my small world and remind myself of the seemingly insurmountable difficulties others are going through. I'll stop wasting my time complaining and get on with my life.

Every gay activist I talk to has their own version of "family values." My father is a lieutenant colonel in the Army Reserves; my mother is a mortgage broker, but my parents have stood by [me] for what is right—unlike the Boy Scouts. . . .

—JAMES DALE

To what social organizations do you belong that make you feel like you're connected with a family? Perhaps you're a member of a church choir, serve on a town or city committee, or volunteer your services at a gay youth organization. You may feel a real sense of belonging with the other members. But what would happen if your organization suddenly discovered your sexual orientation?

Twenty-two-year-old James Dale found out what might happen the hard way, after the Boy Scouts of America learned in 1992 that he was gay. A highly decorated Eagle Scout, Dale was expelled from his position as an assistant scoutmaster. He has since filed a lawsuit against the organization under New Jersey's law protecting gay men and lesbians against employment discrimination.

As you think today about organizations you belong to, consider their values and the values of their members. Would you still be able to experience the same sense of belonging and connection if others knew about your sexuality? Consider your response so you can accurately assess the organization's place in your life.

◆ When I feel like I'm part of a "family," I sometimes expect the "family values" to be there, too. Today I'll make sure that I'm not placing unrealistic expectations about values on a group to which I belong.

The greatest danger, that of losing one's own self, may pass off quietly as if it were nothing; every other loss, that of an arm, a leg, five dollars, etc., is sure to be noticed.

—SØREN KIERKEGAARD

Codependent behavior is exhibited by a loss of self within a relationship—a loss that's replaced by focusing on, reacting to, and taking care of all the thoughts, feelings, and behaviors of another. When you're codependent, another person's wants and needs—not your own—become all-important.

Such a loss of self can threaten you at every juncture in an intimate relationship—from the "honeymoon period," to the "let's move in together" stage, to the commitment ceremony. What you want is to share love and attention with another, but what you do is give those things away.

If you're codependent, you may feel inadequate or unsure of yourself. Yet when you look outside yourself to another to provide you with security, what you end up with is a false sense of security—one that's based on another needing you, rather than you needing you.

Today, take the first steps away from codependency by using positive self-talk. Tell yourself that just for today, you can be a secure person—someone who doesn't need to be needed.

♦ Today offers me plenty of time to practice becoming a much stronger, much more secure individual. I'll use positive, growth-enhancing words and thoughts to limit my codependent behaviors.

There's a lot of rebirth going on. There's only so long you can stay depressed before you realize that the best memorial to your friend is living a happy life.

—PETER D'AMATO

Sometimes it may feel like you're spending a lot of your time watching too many people you love die. It can be devastating not only to lose someone close to you, but also to process at the same time the inevitability that others you know will meet the same fate.

How do you get on with your life despite the constant reminder of death? You have a choice. You can choose to sit back and watch your friends die, putting your life on hold as you immerse yourself in their imminent passing. Or you can decide, "To hell with it! I'm not going to waste my life being depressed and standing hopelessly by waiting and watching. I'm going to make the most of my life and do what *I* want to do."

It's not selfish to want to live when others you know are dying. It's part of nature. The cycle of seasons tells you that death is never the end; it always marks the beginning in the process of rebirth.

Today, think of the losses in your life as reminders that you need to appreciate the time you've been given. It's all you have.

♦ While I know I need time to mourn, I also need time to move on in my life. Today I'll strive to balance my time between looking back and looking ahead.

> . . . *sexual orientation is only one aspect of homosexuality, which is really a personality, a sensitivity. A spirit. It cannot be ignored like a pimple or repressed like the urge to eat a chocolate-covered cherry; it cannot be isolated from one's personality. It is an inexorable part of what makes one an individual.*
>
> —RICHARD FRIEDEL

Are you someone whose same-sex attraction initially frightened you so much or became so difficult for you to handle that you tried to repress or deny it? Did you then frantically date or sleep with members of the opposite sex—or even get married and raise a family—in order to convince yourself that you were "normal"?

Many heterosexuals will contend that attraction to members of the opposite sex is normal and that its primary purpose—propagation—is part of the natural order of things. The fact that other people may be attracted to members of the same sex creates an incredible dilemma for them; they don't understand how something that's so natural and normal for them isn't what everyone else wants, too.

But, as you've discovered after unsuccessfully suppressing your same-sex sexuality, being gay *is* right for you. Today, recall the times of struggle in the past as you tried to reject your own homosexuality. Then think about how you feel right now, about how being gay has become an undeniable part of who you are.

◆ It hasn't always been easy for me to accept being gay. But today I'll be grateful for the years of struggle that have led me to a more fulfilling and natural way of life.

As the old man walked the beach at dawn, he noticed a young man ahead of him picking up starfish and flinging them into the sea. Finally catching up with the youth, he asked why he was doing this. The answer was that the stranded starfish would die if left until the morning sun. "But the beach goes on for miles and there are millions of starfish," countered the other. "How can your effort make any difference?" The young man looked at the starfish in his hand and then threw it to safety in the waves. "It makes a difference to this one," he said.

—MINNESOTA LITERARY COUNCIL

Your support to others in need in your community can make a difference. Perhaps someone who's dying of AIDS could benefit from a daily phone call or occasional visit. Maybe a teenage friend of the family is struggling with issues of sexuality and acceptance and would benefit from hearing about your own struggles. Perhaps a friend whose long-term relationship just ended would feel less isolated and alone by being included in your social plans. Or maybe you could give a newcomer to a support group your telephone number.

How you treat the many in-need "starfish" today will not only make a difference to them, but also to your own growth. For when you reach out to others in need, you're giving of yourself in a positive way that connects you not only with others, but also with the world around you.

◆ If I can reach out today to people who need me, I'll have made a difference to their lives as well as to mine. My efforts can help let in the positive feelings of life.

If you want your dreams to come true, don't sleep.

—YIDDISH PROVERB

Dreams are subconscious views of your hopes. A bad dream is something you hope won't happen; a good dream is something you can't wait to happen. But unless you act on your hope for a good dream to come true, it will always disappear in the morning.

Perhaps you have a dream of one day being settled in a long-term relationship. Maybe you have a dream of being a co-parent with your lover. You might dream of someday opening your own business, taking time off to write a book, or going back to school. Perhaps your dream is to be out to your parents, to march in a PRIDE parade, or to ask someone you have a crush on for a date.

You're the only one who can make such dreams happen. So what's stopping you today from taking the steps necessary to help you reach a dream? If the dream is something you believe will never happen because it will take too long, then break it down into small, manageable steps. You can take that expensive but long-dreamed-about gay cruise if you begin a weekly savings plan today. If a dream involves something you don't know much about—opening your own business, for example—then begin researching it or contacting those who are knowledgeable.

Future dreams *can* come true, but only if you start working on them today.

◆ What will help me most to realize my dreams is the work I put into achieving them. Today I'll visualize a dream and then take the first step toward making it happen.

> *Besides, we adopted these two kids. We saved them from abusive, neglectful straight parents.*
>
> —Dusty Arujo

Jason Anderson and his lover, Dusty, live in a quiet, but mostly straight section of San Francisco and are the proud parents of Daniel and Gabriela. The men endured months of legal battles to legally adopt their two children, but now have to deal on a daily basis with the straight community's shock and homophobia at a same-sex couple happily raising two happy, well-adjusted kids.

For many gay and lesbian parents, part of the motivation to raise children is a dream to get things right—to prevent the problems and difficulties they faced as children growing up in dysfunctional childhood homes. The impact your family's dysfunction—alcoholism, drug addiction, eating disorders, physical, emotional, or sexual abuse—had on you while growing up may be a contributing factor in your desire now to raise children of your own, to support same-sex couples who choose to have children, or to be concerned that your nieces and nephews are raised in healthy, happy homes.

Today, take an active role in the life of a child you care about. You can talk to your siblings about the impact of childhood dysfunction, or participate in teaching the child one basic, positive skill.

♦ Today the biggest contribution I can make to family values is to have a positive impact on the life of a child I know. My support can make a difference in that child's future.

Gays should not be allowed in the military. That would compromise good discipline and uniformity. Many people outside the military say that attitude is discriminatory. They are correct. But the military discriminates every day. It discriminates between an acceptable and unacceptable haircut, between physically fit and unfit, and between acceptable and unacceptable behavior. Allowing homosexuals to serve alongside normal males and females is unacceptable.

—GREGG M. NAKANO, FIRST LIEUTENANT, USMC

Is there a day that goes by in which you don't have to deal with people who use your sexuality to determine that you are unacceptable? Rather than reject a concept, idea, or belief, these people are rejecting you as *a person*—another human being—because of the concepts, ideas, or beliefs you live by. They are using your basic personal philosophies to determine such things as your ability to teach a class, to treat the sick and dying, to be a spiritual resource, to coach athletics, or to serve and protect your country.

How can you deal with such discrimination? In many states there is a legal system with laws in place that can protect your right to employment. Use such resources when they are available to you; when you don't, you're saying that it's acceptable for someone else to determine that you're unacceptable.

◆ Today I won't allow anyone to prevent me from doing the work I want to do. It's up to me to stop job discrimination against gay men and lesbians.

> *Love is love. We're told little boys should love little girls and little girls should love little boys. We know it's not so.*
>
> —JULIE HARRIS

Life without loving someone of the same sex may seem unimaginable to you today, but looking back, you may be able to identify ways you avoided falling in love with someone of the same sex: by thinking in terms of friendship rather than love, by having secret sexual encounters, by limiting intimacy through isolation, or by denying your true sexual feelings.

Although you may have been unaware at the time, you were probably afraid of the vulnerable feelings such a loving relationship would create. You may have protected yourself so you wouldn't have to deal with having to accept an intense, passionate, deep love that society rejects.

Today, are you ready to let yourself experience such true love? Are you ready to let such love into your heart and not push it out—no matter what others think, say, or do?

One way to do this is to be willing to take a risk. Perhaps the love is even there right now, but you're afraid to let it in. Today, try not to draw back when someone you care about is reaching out to you. By allowing yourself to stay in the feeling and the moment, you can gradually let the love in.

♦ I've denied myself a true love for so long that sometimes I forget how to let love into my life. Today I'll take a risk and make myself available so I can establish a connection with someone I care about.

Simply to live is a wonderful privilege in itself. . . . But to what are you alive? Is it merely to a daily routine? . . . How much do you really live outside of your chosen profession or occupation?

—HENRY WOOD

How willing are you to devote time and attention to all areas in your life? Think about the tree farmer who must cultivate evergreen trees for next year's holiday sales. Obviously the farmer wants all the trees to grow as strong, tall, and full as possible. Yet if the farmer focuses on the growth of only one or two trees, the rest of the trees will suffer.

You have within you a similar "forest" made up of individual trees that require your attention for their growth: a career tree, a family tree, a friendship tree, a sexuality tree, a gay-and-lesbian-politics tree, an intimacy tree, and so on. But if you spend more time and attention on one, the neglected ones will not grow strong.

Every part of your life needs attention. Today, think about where you devote most of your time and energy. Are you more concentrated on your career, striving for success and promotions, than you are on your health and exercise needs? Are you so focused on an intimate relationship that you're neglecting your friendships? Begin to balance your time by subtracting an hour from one area and adding it to another.

♦ Every part of my life needs attention for me to be happy. Today I'll begin to balance my time so all areas get the attention they need.

The reason we are asking Gomes to step down is not because he is homosexual, but because he teaches that homosexuality is not sinful within the Christian church.

—SUMNER ANDERSON

When Harvard University minister and professor Reverend Peter John Gomes declared, "I am a Christian who happens as well to be gay," he set off a public furor and placed his career on the line. His coming out was prompted by an article in a conservative student magazine that denounced homosexuality as destructive for individuals and society and cited Jewish, Christian, and Muslim scriptures. Following Gomes's declaration, Sumner Anderson founded a student group called Concerned Christians at Harvard for the specific purpose of causing Gomes's resignation as chaplain.

Should it matter that a chaplain or religious leader is gay? Should one's homosexuality be judged by theologians? Does being a gay man or lesbian preclude being a faithful, good, believing, and devout person?

What you believe, the faith you have, and the way you express your spirituality should be personal and private. Your choice of religion, the place where you choose to worship, the prayers you say, and the spiritual meditations that guide you need to come from within. Today, trust your own judgment about what's spiritually right for you.

♦ I want to live a healthy and meaningful life—one that includes a belief in the existence of a power greater than myself. Today I'll connect with this power and use it as my spiritual guide.

Perhaps someday it will be pleasant to remember even this.

—VIRGIL

When you're in the midst of a particularly difficult situation—your lover has left you for someone else, you've tested HIV positive, you've just come out to your parents, or your company is beginning a series of layoffs—do you find it hard to trust that things will eventually work out for the best?

Yet there's nothing that a little time and distance from a trying situation can't help. Sometimes it may take a day, a week, or even years to be able to reach a resolution. But gradually, as time goes by, your tears and fears will give way to acceptance. As you slowly begin to accept, you may even be able to look back at your initial responses and realize how far you've come. Then, when you've worked through the difficult time, you may even be able to reflect on it as a positive, beneficial, rewarding—and even pleasant—experience.

"This, too, shall pass," can be a helpful statement to keep in mind when you're confronted by an unpleasant situation. Keep in mind that birds always gather enough food to survive and animals grow a protective winter coat. You, too, can gather the strength and protection you need to get you through the tough times.

◆ Today, when I feel baffled and alone as I face my difficulties, I'll try to remember that my life will, ultimately, work out fine. I just have to have faith and remain calm and trusting.

The first three times you came with the same story [they] would listen and try to help. But if you showed up a fourth time and it was the same old tired things, the others in the circle would just get up and move . . . it was time you did something about it.

—ANNE CAMERON

Day after day, do you talk about the same problem over and over again—a problem in your relationship, on the job, with your family of origin, with your roommates, or with your finances? What are you looking for in repeatedly processing the problem? What are you asking for when you talk to others?

Chances are you're not asking for help, because the people you talk with are usually giving you good suggestions—which you reject. You're really not looking to make changes, because you keep holding on to the same problem and wallowing in your misery—and refusing to move on.

But think about a time when you've been in the opposite position, listening to someone talk endlessly about the same problem. After hearing that person for a while, wasn't it easy to tune out? Didn't you just want to scream, "Move on! Nothing's going to change unless *you* change!"

Today, you can take that advice. Stop hanging on to your problem and *do* something. Until you do, both you and the problem will remain the same.

◆ Do I need to repeatedly use my friends as sounding boards? Today I'll make up my mind not only to ask for help, but to try out at least one of the suggestions I'm given.

The best thing to give to your enemy is forgiveness; to an opponent, tolerance; to a friend, your heart; to your child, a good example; to a father, deference; to your mother, conduct that will make her proud of you; to yourself, respect; to all men, charity.
—FRANCIS MAITLAND BALFOUR

The best way to get something positive that you want is to give that same thing to someone else. This applies to love, hope, forgiveness, understanding, comfort, kindness, time, attention, concern, and respect.

But it may be hard for you to want to give out that kind of positive, healing, connecting energy to others, particularly when such people have treated you badly. Those who don't accept your sexuality, those who only have harsh words of condemnation for you, and those who say they love you but then apply conditions to their love may seem like the last people in the world to whom you'd want to be nice.

Yet the Prayer of St. Francis of Assisi relates: "Grant that I may not so much seek to be consoled as to console;/ To be understood as to understand;/ To be loved as to love;/ For it is in giving that we receive—/ It is in pardoning that we are pardoned. . . ."

Today, each time you give to another, remember that you're reaching out your hands to join with them in a circle of connection; what you give is also what you get.

♦ Today, can I be an instrument of peace and forgiveness rather than anger and resentment? I'll look at my actions toward others as sources of inspiration I'm creating for them, too.

My dog Treader loved being on tour. I got him when I got sober, and he's helped me keep my perspective, see life through a dog's eyes. You're doing all right if you've got food, a place to sleep and someone to pet you.

—IZZY STRADLIN

Maintaining sobriety in the gay and lesbian community can be an extremely difficult task, particularly when a great deal of socializing goes on at bars, and many gatherings and parties serve alcohol. Support for your recovery from addiction to alcohol may even be hard to find within your circle of friends and acquaintances; many won't understand what your problem is because they don't see their own problems with drinking.

But there are many options for staying sober while still socializing in the gay and lesbian community. There are numerous gay and/or lesbian Alcoholics Anonymous meetings; several social clubs that promote drug, alcohol, and smoke-free gatherings; athletic groups that aren't focused around after-workout brews; spiritual gatherings that restrict drugs and alcohol; and countless other recovering people like you who are struggling every day to be clean and sober.

Today, explore alcohol-free options you can participate in by contacting a gay and lesbian hotline or looking through the calendar pages of an area gay newspaper.

♦ Recovering from my dependency on alcohol doesn't mean I can't go out and have a good time. Today I'll line up things I can do for the weekend that will help me maintain my sobriety.

You can be a child only once—but you can be immature forever.

—ANONYMOUS

Do you ever reflect on your behavior in a relationship and wonder why you sometimes act so immature and childlike? Maybe you depend on your partner to cook and clean, then you get upset when you're asked to take a turn. Perhaps you rely upon your partner's financial support or guidance in budgeting your personal finances that you feel financially insecure. Perhaps the suggestion that you spend some time apart makes you feel like a lost child, abandoned and alone.

Part of the reason why immature feelings may erupt in an adult relationship is the lack of acceptance of gay and lesbian relationships in society. The "normal" socialization process of meeting someone, dating, introducing this person to family members, and then eventually choosing to settle down together isn't supported by society. As a result, you're left on your own to struggle with difficult issues such as balancing responsibilities without the benefit of male/female role identification.

You can either give in to your immaturity or take the difficult step to become a more responsible adult in your relationship. Today, do something that will benefit not just you or your partner, but you *and* your partner. Cook a meal together or make a special plan for the weekend. Such contributions can add to your own growth as well as to the growth of the relationship.

♦ Rather than feel childlike in my relationship, I'll take more responsibility for myself. Today I'll start to get in touch with my own needs and discover ways I can satisfy at least one need myself.

Death ends a life, but does not end a relationship.

—ROBERT ANDERSON

Although grieving is a process that involves a considerable amount of tears and sadness, it doesn't have to be the ruling influence in your life. Because a close friend, family member, or life partner has died doesn't mean you have to suspend feelings of lightness and joy in your life or suppress laughter.

Didn't the person you lost make you laugh? Didn't this person make you smile and feel joy in your heart whenever your eyes met, your voices mingled, and your hands touched? These are the things you can recall today—the good memories, the fun times, the shared experiences, and the things that made tears of laughter run from your eyes.

Today, take out a scrapbook or photo album and remember with a light heart the one you lost. Imagine he or she is sitting next to you as you flip through the pages and relive the wonderful moments you shared together.

◆ Today I'll speak to the one I lost as if he or she were right beside me. I'll say, "Do you remember . . . ?" as I talk about a time that will always bring me joy whenever I think of it.

The idea behind the amendment was to drive us back into the closet. But it's not working. It's having the opposite effect.

—JIM THOMAS

Colorado's 1992 antigay Amendment 2 had an amazing impact on gay men and lesbians. Within twenty-four hours of the passage of the amendment, seven thousand gay men and lesbians from across the country had contacted activists to ask what they could do to help and mobilized within the state to take public action.

The overwhelming response motivated Coloradan Jim Thomas to come out at the workplace; first to a trusted co-worker, and then to his boss. Thomas and many of his friends had the same reaction to the amendment: they found the strength, through fear or anger—or both—to declare their homosexuality openly. When six hundred people showed up at a rally at the state capitol in Denver and linked hands around the massive, domed building in a show of solidarity, an older gay man who hadn't come out said, "I'm sure some people are going to spot me on the television tonight, and that's okay."

Because the amendment makes it illegal in Colorado for the law to protect homosexuals from repercussions such as being fired for homosexuality, the fact that so many people decided to come out publicly emphasizes their personal desire to place individual freedom over legal persecution.

Today, what can you do to ensure your individual freedom?

♦ Today I can choose to be energized by discrimination or view it as a slap in the face. My response will determine how committed I am to standing up for myself—or feeling ashamed of myself.

I suppose at one time the idea of a monogamous relationship seemed absurd to me. The idea of sticking together and working things out seemed too much trouble when there were so many possibilities out there. But as I get older, I realize that the world isn't full of unlimited possibilities at all.

—STEPHEN McCAULEY

Do you ever wish you could get back with an ex-lover? Do you strive to maintain a close friendship with a past lover because your new lover doesn't seem to take the time to know you or care about you as much as your ex did?

Think back to the reasons why your relationship ended. Was it because of an unresolved issue? Annoying habits? Difficulty in communicating? Boredom with the same old routine? A disinterest in sex? A yearning for something or someone new, different, and exciting?

Such things are part of every monogamous relationship. There's always a certain amount of conflict, of settling into routines, of restlessness that occurs. Yet just because such things happen doesn't mean the relationship has to be over. Identifying issues so you can work on them—and then through them—can sometimes help you and your partner move into a more fulfilling and rewarding interaction.

Today, concentrate on ways you can stay in your relationship. Don't be afraid to talk about an issue that concerns or upsets you; communication can make the path you take together smoother and more enjoyable.

♦ I don't want to let go of someone I may regret losing later on. Today I'll help open the channels of communication so we can hear each other loud and clear.

> *Gay males, who in the stereotype are labeled effeminate, and lesbians, whom the stereotype describes as manly, turn traditional dualistic notions of male and female upside-down. . . . Homosexual men and women, in fact, have been crucial to [the] process of shaping more humane ideals of the masculine and the feminine.*
>
> —JAMES CARROLL

In this century, the entire human race is struggling to free itself from outmoded stereotypes and metaphors. Emerging ideas of manhood have enlightened men and enabled them to acknowledge less macho, more sensitive natures. Challenges to feminism now allow women to be aggressors, competitors, and breadwinners.

Gay men and lesbians have always been at the forefront of such gender challenges. Effeminate gay men, who explode with emotion, wear makeup and women's clothing, and view bake-offs as more exciting than play-offs, and "super-macha" lesbians, who prefer the label "dyke" as they don leather jackets, lace their work boots, and rev up their motorcyles, have made every gay man and lesbian become more conscious of "the other side" of their sexuality.

Today, gay men are also developing a nonstereotypical macho side—through body building and gay athletic competitions—while lesbians are exploring their nonstereotypical feminine side—with fashion, makeup, and motherhood. Such modifications lend a more balanced ideal to the overall definition of gay and lesbian.

◆ Today I'll explore "the other side" of my definition of myself as a man or a woman. In what ways can I explore masculine behaviors or in what ways can I be more feminine?

Gay consumers are spending increasingly large sums of money on clothing. Fashion is a top spending priority. So are gym memberships, vitamins, health care products, and out-of-the-home dining.
—HOWARD BENNET, MANAGING EDITOR OF SAN FRANCISCO GAY
BOOK BUSINESS DIRECTORY

How do you spend your money? Do you set aside a certain percentage of your earnings to support the gay community? Perhaps you spend money on products and services offered by gay and lesbian businesses. Maybe you purchase books by gay and lesbian authors; you may encourage your friends not to lend or borrow such books in order to support the publishers and authors. Perhaps you seek out the work of gay and lesbian artists, attend gay and lesbian festivals or functions, or donate money to worthy gay and lesbian organizations.

Being a supportive consumer in the gay and lesbian community means you're taking part in ensuring the existence of the work, energy, dedication, and creativity of your brothers and sisters. But it's not only gay men and lesbians who can benefit personally from the financial decisions you make. You also can support companies whose policies benefit gay men and lesbians in the workplace. For example, Levi Strauss's 1992 decision to extend full medical and dental benefits to all employees' domestic partners—gay, lesbian, and heterosexual—might factor in to the decision you make when you need a pair of jeans.

◆ Today I'll become more conscious of which companies, nonprofit organizations, and individuals benefit from my spending. I'll make sure that at least one purchase this week directly benefits the gay and lesbian community.

*I've known gay and lesbian people all my life. . . . Some of
my most brilliant teachers and some of my classmates were gay.
They were just a part of the community of people. I think that is
what is important to understand.*

—JESSE JACKSON

How diverse is the community of people you know? Does the
world of people you interact with include gay men and
lesbians as well as straight people, people of color, Asians,
Native Americans, Latinos, people with different religious
beliefs, those who are physically challenged, and children?
How closely does the fabric of people in your community
resemble the fabric of people in the world?

Just because you're gay doesn't mean you should spend the
majority of your time associating solely with those who are
most like you. When you do, you narrow your focus to
include only gay and lesbian issues, limit your experiences,
and restrict your education about the world and its people.
But when you expand your world of interactions to include
those whose experiences, cultural backgrounds, beliefs, and
knowledge differ from yours, you broaden your awareness
and enrich your life.

Today, strive to become part of the community of
people—rather than apart from people in order to be in your
own community. Seek to discover and understand how those
different from you think and feel, how they celebrate special
events, and what matters to them. Such understanding can
make your world just a little bigger—and better.

◆ Today I can broaden my horizons by striving to see the
world through the eyes of those who are different from me.

Some friends of mine were hustling and they told me all you had to do was mess around with these guys and they'll pay you some money. I thought that was pretty cool 'cuz I was fooling around with guys for free.

—TONY, A BISEXUAL HOMELESS YOUTH

Gay homeless youth are a growing population in cities. Their life on the streets, which often begins by family rejection when they reveal their sexual orientation, is harsh. For some boys, the nights are a continuous barter of drugs, money, and sex. They talk flatly of multiple sexual encounters with strangers as if they were giving directions to a transit stop. Some may score a "sugar daddy" who'll provide them with a bed for a week or more; many, however, sleep in subway tunnels, on grates, or under bridges and highway overpasses.

While some young boys find temporary solace in churches, drop-in homeless centers, and shelters, both homophobia and disgust for prostitution make few sympathetic to their plight. What can you do to help these boys? Contact a gay and lesbian hotline or youth organization to find out what services you can provide. Encourage a church to open its basement a few nights a week to provide shelter, counseling, and food for them. Purchase condoms and distribute them to the youth. Or when you see a young, homeless boy in trouble, buy him a meal and give him some friendly support.

♦ Today I won't turn my back on a homosexual homeless youth who needs financial, emotional, and spiritual support. I'll help him in any way I can to make his life a little easier.

> *We cannot allow organizations to dictate what can and cannot*
> *be printed in this country. If we allow the religious right to*
> *determine what major printing companies can and cannot print,*
> *can we be sure that only erotica will fall under the censor's eye? Or*
> *will we see printers declining to manufacture books that are*
> *pro-choice? Or books that promote gay and lesbian rights?*
>
> — WENDY STROTHMAN

What compels some publishers and printers to produce for sale explicit pornographic books that degrade women, show the abuse of children, and condone rape, yet not books that disseminate lifesaving information on gay and lesbian safe sex, AIDS awareness, or education about sexuality that can prevent gay teen suicide?

Wendy Strothman, the president of Beacon Press, posed a similar question when a book her company wished to publish by a tenured philosophy professor at the University of Illinois was refused by twenty-three printers. Their refusal came at the same time Madonna's *Sex* had a first printing of 500,000—a run that sold out faster than any book in history.

You might feel that censorship of gay- and lesbian-themed works would be more equitable if all sexuality-based works were similarly scrutinized. Or you may feel there should be no censorship. But whatever your true feelings, you can "voice" them with your pen and wallet. Write to publishers and printers who refuse to produce gay literature; refuse to purchase materials they do print.

◆ Today I'll express my feelings on gay censorship by "talking" with my wallet. In addition, I won't buy materials that I find personally offensive.

I grew up thinking I was nothing out of the ordinary. I played with Matchbox cars, squirt guns and Star Wars figures like any other good little tomboy. I was confronted with images of Ken and Barbie, not Barbie and Christine. I was led to believe that I would live in a dream house and drive a pink Corvette when I met and married Mr. Right.

— LEE FEARNSIDE

What are the myths you learned about heterosexual love when you were growing up? That true love conquers all? That you'll know who's right for you the moment you set eyes on each other? That there's only one true love for you in the world; if you lose this person, there will never, ever be another opportunity to experience true love? That the "perfect" partner is someone who satisfies all your wants and needs? That great sex means great love?

Despite your same-sex preference, you may still believe such myths. As a single person, you may be in hot pursuit of Mr. or Ms. Right—the one who will make all your dreams come true. As a partner in a couple, you may push your lover to be "perfect."

Yet today it's important to realize the true definition of "myth"—just an imaginary person or thing. Knowing who's right for you means choosing a partner with whom you're compatible, with whom you get some of your needs met, and who is willing to make a commitment to working on a relationship with you. Those are the true components of true love!

♦ Today I'll keep in mind that good sex just means good chemistry; infatuation is short-lived but true love grows over time; and no one will ever give me *everything* I want and need.

It seems to me that since I've had children, I've grown richer and deeper. They may have slowed down my writing for a while, but when I did write, I had more of a self to speak from.

—ANNE TYLER

The decision to bear a child, adopt, or become a foster parent is a weighty one for gay men and lesbians. Not only does such a decision have an impact on your life, your partner's life, and your immediate family's life, but it also has an enormous impact on the life of the child. You and your partner may be overwhelmed by hundreds of questions about your child's upbringing and growth in relation to your sexuality. Many questions will have no immediate answers; some will be discovered as you travel along the road of parenting; some will change over time through circumstances and experiences you'll share with your child.

There are endless considerations to come to terms with in choosing to raise a child. But what can never be chosen or prepared for beforehand is the impact a child will have on your life. For gay men and lesbians who have children, that impact can often be seen in the way their children deal with their parents' sexuality—often in mature and instructive ways. You can learn a great deal from your child, and as your child grows, he or she can learn from you.

♦ Today, when considering children, I'll consider the ways parenting can help me learn and grow. While I know having a child won't always be easy, there are benefits that will enrich my life, my partner's life, and the life of our child.

No one can make you feel inferior without your consent.
—ELEANOR ROOSEVELT

A secure self-image and unwavering self-confidence are characteristics everyone longs for. However, being a gay man or lesbian in a society that denounces, distrusts, and condemns your sexuality can affect how you feel about yourself.

Doubting what you know in your heart is a valid way of life is one way you let society's values challenge your belief in yourself. Questioning what is correct and comfortable for you is one way you let others' opinions chip away at your self-confidence. Focusing on weaknesses rather than strengths, negatives rather than positives, and incapabilities rather than abilities lets the opinions of others contribute to an inferior self-image.

Rather than allow your self-esteem to deteriorate and your self-acceptance about your sexuality to be challenged, today begin building a strong belief in yourself that will withstand all present and future assaults upon who you are and how you live your life. Use positive self-talk to bolster your self-esteem, nurture a healthy ego, and fortify the choices you've made in your life. Today say aloud, "I won't let any person, any employer, or any organization make me feel inferior. I am a good, worthwhile person who has a right to live my life in a way that's right for me."

♦ Today I'll be conscious of my self-talk. Is it what I believe or what others have led me to believe? Is it positive and motivating? Is it strengthening and empowering?

If I had to assess what I've done up to this point, I'm very proud that I represent the possibility for black gay men to write and create, that the possibility does exist, and that you may even be able to do it full-time.

—ESSEX HEMPHILL

A line from one of Janet Jackson's songs asks, "What have you done for me lately?" Too many people ask the same question of others in their life—a life partner, friends, family members, an employer—as if those people existed solely for their benefit.

Instead of asking what has been done for you lately, ask instead, "What have I done for others?" What achievement have you made in your life that makes you proud because of its benefit to others? Perhaps you scored the winning basket for your team in the league championship; maybe you volunteered at a soup kitchen a few months ago during the holidays; perhaps you devoted time one evening to delivering the latest issue of a gay newspaper.

When you do for others, you're showing them what they can do, too. Those who notice your drive and determination on the basketball court see how they can contribute in the next game. Those who hear of your experience in a soup kitchen may volunteer over a future holiday. Those who watch you devote time to doing a thankless job for the gay and lesbian community may someday do the same.

Today, forget about what others can do for you; instead, do for others so everyone can benefit.

◆ What can I give back to the gay and lesbian community that will show gay men and lesbians the difference one person can make? Today I'll strive to be a giver rather than a taker.

Is there any stab as deep as wondering where and how much you failed those you loved?

—FLORIDA SCOTT MAXWELL

There's nothing worse than seeing the look of disappointment and disapproval on the faces of friends or family members after you've come out to them, after you've introduced them to your new lover, or when you speak with them about issues of importance to the gay and lesbian community. Even though they may respond with acceptance, understanding, love, and support and treat you as well as they always have, it may be hard for you to escape the sinking feeling that you've let them down.

Feeling as if you've failed in the eyes of those you love is a difficult emotion to work through. You know you could make everything "right" again with them if you told them you weren't gay, if you brought home a lover of the opposite sex, or if you stopped discussing issues that affect your gay community.

But trying to be someone other than you are, hiding the truth, or not being open and honest will still make you feel like you're a failure—not to others, but to yourself. Today, be mindful that what you share with those you care for is said not purposefully to hurt them, but to help them understand you better. While a friend or family member may never be able to accept you or your sexuality, what they can accept is your openness and honesty.

◆ Today I'll treat those I love as I hope to be treated: without judgment, criticism, or rejection. While I won't expect them to accept everything about me, I hope they'll accept my honesty.

Our goals are to act as a new model for sex facilities and also as a model for ways people can be sexual with each other, be good to each other, and take care of themselves.

—BUZZ BENSE

Eros, the Center for Safe Sex in San Francisco's Castro district, was created for responsible, health-conscious people to participate in a clean, safe, same-sex club experience. Co-owners Buzz Bense and Bob West provide participants with sex etiquette brochures, encourage safe group-grope sessions, and offer workshops, training sessions, and meetings that focus on educating gay men about safe sex. For lesbians, Ecstasy Lounge is San Francisco's only sex party exclusively by and for women. Co-organizer Judith Cohen comments: "A lot of younger lesbians are ready for it. We want to show that safe sex is hot sex."

Today's sex "clubhouses" are committed to letting participants combine enjoyable sexual recreation with safe sex education. Are you similarly committed to actively, but safely, expressing your sexuality? Or are you hesitant to engage in passionate involvement because you're not really certain what constitutes safe sex?

Before you rely on the word of a potential partner about the safety of a certain act, or trust an assurance of a negative test result, find out what constitutes safe sex. Contact a gay and lesbian hotline or a nearby AIDS Action Committee. Read literature that's available. Educate yourself first, before you express yourself!

♦ If I don't know the answers to any of my questions about how to practice safe sex, I'll make it a point today to find out on my own. Protecting myself means respecting myself.

Nobody grows old merely by a number of years. We grow old by deserting our ideals. Years may wrinkle the skin, but to give up enthusiasm wrinkles the soul.

—SAMUEL ULLMAN

Today you may see more and more young gay men and lesbians at bars, in organizations, on the college campuses, and in the cities. You may look at them and think: "If only I could be their age and coming out now. I would have so many more years to live and grow in a time that's much more open and accepting than it was for me."

You may have heard it said, "You're as young as you feel." Although physically you may not feel so young today, you can use that statement to help rejuvenate your state of mind and your passion to experience all life has to offer. Why sit back and reminisce about the difficulties of coming out at the time you did, when you can simply be out right now? Why bemoan all the things you didn't have yesterday — bars, sex clubs, support groups, and so on—when all those things are available to you today? Why stay isolated and alone as you've done in the past when there are so many ways today to connect with the gay and lesbian community?

To feel younger, imagine today as the year in which you've been given a new life. So today you're one year old—and just coming out to this brand-new world! You can speak your mind, join any organization you want, meet new people, and be as gay as you want. You're not old—you're just a babe ready to learn and grow!

♦ Today I'll forget my chronological age and think about how young I am to this new, open world of being a gay man or lesbian. I *am* young, with lots of time to experience life and grow.

I knew early on I wasn't what they expected. Especially when I got near the age of competitive sports. Then I knew something was way wrong. That's when I really began to take a beating.

—DAVID GRUNDY

Growing up gay means that at one time or another in your young life you probably were subjected to abuse. It could have been simple name-calling—faggot, queer, lezzie, or dyke—by schoolmates. The abuse could have come in the form of rejection by your peers, a close friend, or family members. It could have been more blatant, such as losing a summer job after coming out, or being kicked out of private school or college. Or it could have been much more severe, such as being beaten or sexually violated.

Yet despite the abuse you received in the past, today you're able to stand tall, face the world, and not waver from living your life as a gay man or woman. What strength it took for you to remain true to what was in your heart! What courage it took for you to face adversity and adversaries and not submit to pressure! What faith you must have had to believe in yourself—that you could survive then so you could live today!

Strength, courage, and hope are what being gay is all about. You share these qualities with every gay man and woman who has gone before you and who is sharing this world with you today. Be proud of yourself, and be proud of them!

♦ What a joy it is today to see how far I've come from the past days of abuse! The little boy or little girl I once was has survived and no longer will take any abuse because of my sexuality.

The meeting of two personalities is like the contact of two chemical substances: if there is any reaction, both are transformed.

—CARL GUSTAV JUNG

Whenever you interact with someone, positively or negatively, you both come away transformed. You absorb a lesson about yourself, your behaviors, or your attitudes, and the other person does the same. So being unaware of the benefits of daily interactions with those who either accept you as a gay man or lesbian or reject you means that you may miss out on some of your greatest learning—and teaching—experiences.

Dr. Gerald Jampolsky, a well-known healer who started an organization in 1975 called the Center for Attitudinal Healing, founded the center on the principle that "We are students and teachers to each other." So interacting with someone who is accepting and nurturing of you and your sexuality can teach you that you are a good person. But you can also learn a lesson from someone who is rejecting and unsupportive of you and your sexuality; this person may challenge you to take a look at yourself and how openly you present yourself to someone who has difficulty with your way of life. You may discover that you need to be more understanding of that person's level of comfort and, in so doing, can transform interactions with that person from disrespect and discomfort into a newfound respect and ease with one another.

◆ The lessons in life that I learn from my teachers will help me to become a better teacher myself. Today I'll be both a willing pupil and a ready teacher.

Peace of mind is that mental condition in which you have accepted the worst.

—LIN YUTANG

When to come out and who to come out to are never easy decisions to make. But such decisions can be made easier by first asking yourself, "What's the worst possible thing that could happen if I came out to _____?" Identifying the worst-case scenario before identifying your way of life to a friend, coworker, or family member is the first step you must take in learning how to accept the consequences of coming out; with such acceptance can emerge an ability to deal effectively with any and all responses.

You can make your goal for coming out to accept *all* responses, rather than expect a certain response. When you "go with the flow"—no matter where that flow takes you—you have the ability to soften harsh responses and soothe fears.

Coming out to another with acceptance means you'll be more capable of remaining calm, objective, and understanding. Such peace of mind, in contrast to frustration, rigidity, and anxiety, shows not only your commitment to your way of life, but also your willingness to help another work through an understanding of why you are the way you are.

Today, practice acceptance when coming out to someone. Allow room for any response—positive or negative. Remember, acceptance is the *only* solution to working through confusion, adversity, conflict, and difficulty.

◆ When I'm calm, I'm a better listener. Today I'll use acceptance to lead me to a calm, peaceful frame of mind. Then I can be a resource who can help someone work through learning about my sexuality.

It's the adults who have been unable to take the sex out of homosexuality. These aren't books about sex or sex education. They're about families.

—LESLÉA NEWMAN

Lesléa Newman, author of *Heather Has Two Mommies* and *Gloria Goes to Gay Pride*, never expected her books to create controversy; she also never expected them to circulate outside the gay community. When a lesbian mother told her she couldn't find any books for kids on the subject of gay parenting, Newman wrote *Heather* as a favor. She initially published the book herself and sold it from her living room until Alyson Publications bought the book in 1990.

But when Newman's picture books for first-graders were included on an optional reading list in New York City's Children of the Rainbow curriculum to teach six-year-olds respect for minorities, the resulting controversy made headlines across the United States. The focus of the national debate has been on the books' clear goal to show nontraditional homosexual parent relationships as real complements to the traditional heterosexual parent relationships.

Such books can comfort a worried youngster and help his or her friends gain understanding that not all families are the same. Today you can support access to such books, which show gay families as positive and loving, by asking your local bookstore to order copies or by purchasing copies and donating them to your local library.

◆ Today I'll remember how useful books can be to children in validating different ways of life. I'll support the publishers of gay-positive books for children and do what I can to ensure access to such books.

No government has the right to tell its citizens when or whom to love. The only queer people are those who don't love anybody.
—RITA MAE BROWN

Has anyone ever said, about someone you love, "I just don't think so-and-so is right for you"? You may have resented their opinion, felt that who you loved was none of their business, or wondered what right they had to pass judgment on someone you chose to be with.

Should your bedroom activities or what you feel in your heart be similarly scrutinized by governments or ruling bodies? Laws that declare homosexuality wrong or illegal represent similar intrusions upon your personal life. Should you be turned away, turned out, or tuned out because of who you are and the sex of those you love? Discrimination based on sexual preference restricts your personal freedoms. Should members of the majority have free rein to treat you inhumanely and unfairly because your way of life is not the commonly accepted way of life? Gay bashing and hate crimes attempt to force adherence to someone else's ideal of happiness and fulfillment.

Today, don't let *anyone* try to tell you who's right and who's wrong for you. Write or call your congressional representatives to express your views on ensuring that the rights to life, liberty, and the pursuit of happiness not be denied to any gay man or lesbian.

♦ Today I won't remain silent about my way of life. I'll make sure my voice is heard among those voices who determine how I'm treated by my government and its laws.

Something serious had been said. Perhaps it was, "I no longer love you." . . . He would have said it in a kind way, because it is easy to be kind when you are in his position, the winning-hand position.

—JAMAICA KINCAID, FROM *LUCY*

Infidelity in the gay and lesbian community causes many long-term relationships to end, disconnects or severs friendships, creates conflict between team or group members, and forces family members to deal with awkward situations. Yet infidelity doesn't have to be the cause of so much heartache and difficulty; rather, if infidelity is treated as the *symptom* of a problem within a committed relationship, then dealing head-on with the problem may be the answer.

Certainly hurt and jealousy will stand in the way of immediate attempts at reconciliation. But after a short time of physical separation or not dealing with the problem, you and your partner may be able to sit down and discuss what went on. Strive to keep the focus on problems within the relationship that led to the affair, not on personal shortcomings. Caution your partner not to blame his or her actions on people or circumstances, but instead to take responsibility. Discuss outside resources you can use to work through your problems, such as a spiritual adviser or therapist. Finally, both you and your partner need to be open and honest about what you both want in order to know whether your visions of the future of your relationship are compatible.

◆ Today I'll make a serious effort to determine whether my relationship is worth saving. If it isn't, I need to walk away; if it is, I need to stay and work on it.

The person who fears to try is thus enslaved.

—LEONARD E. READ

Fearing to identify, acknowledge, accept, and then express feelings about your sexuality is a form of enslavement; through such suppression, you allow yourself to become a submissive victim to your fears. When you allow your fears to dominate how you think, act, and feel, the result is an inability to move forward and to explore what is in your true nature.

When you're so immobilized, you fail to think new thoughts, live new experiences, chance new interactions, and grow in new ways. All that you feel in your heart and soul is denied; all that you could enjoy in life passes you by. You give up on yourself by failing to try.

Today, remember that you have been given a gift of life—life that makes you a member of 10 percent of the population. You have also been given a gift of love—love that means you're attracted to members of your own sex. To put off living and loving in a way that's right for you because of fears—real or imagined—means you take away from who you are and how you'll grow emotionally, physically, and spiritually.

Look to this day as one in which you participate in life and love in a way that's right for your growth and development as a gay man or lesbian. Work through the fears that hold you back by telling yourself, "I don't want to live rooted in the same spot. All will be well in my life when I take action and do what's right for me."

◆ When fear crouches close at my heels, I'm never able to move ahead. Today I'll test my wings and participate in an activity that enables me to express my feelings as a gay man or lesbian.

> . . . *the gay community has become so much more aggressive. No one's going to take it anymore, the oppression and all the hate, for no reason.*

> —BILL VAN PARYS

There once was a television commercial that began with a close-up of an attractive actress who pleaded, "Don't hate me because I'm beautiful." What that line really communicated was: Don't dislike me because of who I am or the positive quality of beauty I have.

As a gay man or lesbian, you could speak a similar line to those who ignore you, mistreat you, reject you, abuse you, make fun of you, or discriminate against you because of your sexuality: "Don't hate me because I'm gay." Yet don't you often wonder why others become so negatively charged against you and your way of life when you aren't harming them in any way?

The answer to that question can be found in the belief that hatred is a disguise worn by fear. The things people hate the most are usually the things that make them feel threatened, uncertain, anxious, or stir up bad memories. So it may not be you or even your way of life that causes you to bear the brunt of a strong emotional response.

With this in mind, today challenge someone's negative response toward you by asking, "What is it about me that scares you so much? And why can't *you* deal with it?"

♦ Today I won't remain silent to the insults, oppression, or animosity expressed by others because of my sexuality. I'll turn their hatred back on them by asking them to take a long, hard look at themselves and their own fears.

Ozone and friendship will be our stimulants—let the drugs, tobacco, and strong drink go forever. Natural joy brings no headaches or heartaches.

—ELBERT HUBBARD

Do you ever play the memory game "Remember when . . . ?" with old friends? Often the memories you dredge up together center on the use of drugs or alcohol. Back then, you may have felt such events to be humorous and enviable; today, however, you may recall such times, shake your head, and comment, "I can't believe how much my life revolved around drugs or alcohol. Was there ever a time when I wasn't drinking or using?"

When you learn to live life without a primary addiction—to drugs, alcohol, cigarettes, food, or sex—you begin to see life in a whole different way. Fresh air, sunshine, and simple things like taking a walk in the woods or sharing a cup of coffee with a friend take on a whole new meaning. Weekend nights spent enjoying the pleasant company of friends, a romantic dinner date, or the serenity of your own solitude yield mornings after that are free from hangovers, guilt, depression, and fatigue.

When you free yourself from all addictions and replace them instead with pleasurable choices, such newfound freedom can give you a more serene outlook on life and a greater respect for yourself. Today, think about an addiction you'd like to get rid of. Then contact a support group that can help you let go of it.

♦ Today I'll look at some of the addictions in my life and the hold they might have on me—physically, emotionally, and spiritually. Then I'll reach out to a twelve-step group and ask for help.

If you start funding groups based on the choice that group has made, we'll be funding everyone from the left-handed club to the bestiality club.

——JON WAGGONER, STUDENT GOVERNMENT PRESIDENT,
AUBURN UNIVERSITY

On many college campuses gay men and lesbians are organizing for the purposes of support, activism, and demonstration about gay and lesbian issues. While Ivy League schools have had support groups since the 1960s and many have had formal campus groups since the mid-1980s, gay and lesbian groups have only recently begun to become a significant political force at many southern schools. Usually the response to gays on campus has led to increased tolerance and the inclusion of courses in gay and lesbian studies. But intense confrontations have been played out at Auburn University, where police arrested a student for firing at activists with a pellet gun. When gay students rallied after the attack, opposing students formed their own group against "the choice to practice the homosexual lifestyle."

How tolerant is your alma mater, the school you're currently attending, or a college or university in your area? Contact the college's administration and ask what options are available to support gay men and lesbians on campus. Depending on the response you receive, you may wish to address a letter to the president that outlines your feelings or reconsider financial support to the institution.

◆ Today I'll support any college or university that recognizes gay men and lesbians, their support groups, and the protection of their rights. I'll show my support in writing, through a financial donation, or by offering needed business services to a gay and lesbian campus group.

I was African-American. I was well-educated. I was from an upper middle-class, two-parent family. I felt an obligation as a person of color and someone who had positive role models. I wanted to return something to the community.

—DOUG ROBINSON

Doug Robinson, a computer programmer at a New York City bank, lives with his two sons and his lover in an apartment overlooking the Hudson River. One of his biggest concerns, before making the decision to become a parent, was how he could give of himself to others in need. The answer came to him when he decided to adopt. In 1986 he became a single father of an abandoned Haitian baby; four years later, he adopted a neglected African-American boy. Today, he has no doubt that the adoption of Justin and Zachary was the right thing to do; he has returned the love and positive upbringing to two children in need.

Do you have a similar need to give something positive back to the gay and lesbian community? Perhaps you can volunteer your services on a hotline. Maybe you can advise a gay youth group. Perhaps you can contribute to the fund-raising for a gay men's chorus or a lesbian traveling band. Or maybe you can start a support group to help others deal with difficult issues such as incest, adoption, battering, coming out, or parenting.

♦ Today I'll make up my mind to take the first step in giving something back to my community. What can I do that will show my gratitude to others who share experiences similar to mine?

It was really devastating—hard on me mentally. I never had any problems, and this was like someone spit in my face. Sandra and I had been out for a long time, and for them to tell me my relationship was wrong and that I don't deserve a job because of it, that's bullshit! I'm just as good as anybody else, if not better than some of 'em.

—CHERYL SUMMERVILLE

In January 1991 the management of the Cracker Barrel company announced it would no longer employ people who didn't have "normal heterosexual values." Cheryl Summerville was fired in February when she voluntarily came out in protest of the policy. She had no legal recourse to regain her job; employment discrimination against gay men and lesbians was legal in Georgia. She used her free time to do odd jobs and to travel across the country to promote passage of a national gay and lesbian civil rights bill.

Depending on where you live, you may feel freedom and protection as a gay man or lesbian or fear visibility and live in a closet. If you live in a state where your rights as a gay man or lesbian aren't protected, think about the reasons why you stay there. Perhaps you have strong family ties, a great job or one that requires you to live there, or something or someone else that makes you want to stay. But today take a moment to think about whether where you live right now is really where you want to be. If it isn't, ask yourself, "How and when can I make a change?"

♦ Today I'll examine my home state's laws regarding the treatment of gay men and lesbians. Are the laws acceptable to me? I'll think about ways I can deal with the laws for as long as I live where I do—or I'll choose to leave.

It may be different for gay women, but I think as a whole, gay men are very fucked up about looks. And I think they would agree with me, too.

—SANDRA BERNHARD

Are you too hung up on appearances? Do you feel that you or others you know drive themselves crazy and impose limitations in their lives based upon superficiality?

Superficiality can involve a compulsive drive to create an image-appearance: a way of looking, acting, dressing, talking, walking, or behaving designed solely to create an impression so others can't see who you really are inside. So you may search for months to find the right cologne or perfume in order to exude a scent others will find appealing. You may spend a large portion of your salary on clothes designed to create an impact on the dance floor. You may drive an expensive foreign car, buy sought-after tickets to sporting events or plays, or shop at exclusive stores in order to impress others. You may seek those things for yourself and look for such things in others. Yet in doing so, you're forcing others to focus on what's outside of you rather than what's on the inside.

Today, you can be happy with your body, your clothes, your job, and your possessions without being obsessed with them and how they appear to others. Ask yourself, "Which do I prefer: someone who finds me appealing because of what I have, or someone who's attracted to me because of who I am?"

♦ Today, rather than be conscious of my outward appearance, I'll identify a quality I have inside that makes me a great person. When I interact with others, I'll strive to look inside at their positive inner qualities.

The activist is not the man who says the river is dirty. The activist is the man who cleans up the river.

—ROSS PEROT

What does activism mean to you? For some, activism equals anger; it's a way of expressing frustration and channeling hostility through protest and demonstrations. For others, activism is a form of outreach—a way for gay men and lesbians to join together in their community for common purposes. Some people see activism as the hip thing to do—like wearing a red ribbon just to be part of a popular cause. For others, activism is a form of indirect action they can take by conducting research, surveys, and interviews.

John Woods, founder of Queer Scouts, a direct-action group opposed to the Boy Scouts of America's ban on gay scoutmasters, sees activism as fluid. He explains: "If the need arises, you create a group, because it's a hook for people, something the media can identify with, and it's serving the particular issue. Then you move on."

If you belong to a gay or lesbian activist group or are thinking of joining one, consider what it is that you expect to gain from being part of the group. Is it long-term good you're looking for, or simply touching the life of one gay person who needs help? Today, make sure your activist actions contribute in some small way to the good of the gay and lesbian community as a whole. In that way, you'll be doing something for yourself as well as for others.

◆ Today I'll choose to become more active in gay and lesbian activism. I'll use my energy, creativity, and voice to effect change for gay men and lesbians everywhere.

The tribal attitude said, and continues to say, that Gay people are especially empowered because we are able to identify with both sexes and can see into more than one world at once, having the capacity to see from more than one point of view at a time. And that is also an Indian way of seeing.

—JUDY GRAHN

When you consider all points of view about an issue that concerns you as a gay man or lesbian, do you ever stop to think that there can also be a spiritual outlook that could help you resolve the issue—an outlook that's based on faith, trust, and belief in a power greater than yourself?

Often the things that concern you the most about your sexuality—coming out and how others will respond to you, your relationship with your family of origin, being gay in the workplace, or developing an intimate relationship—can't be resolved in a short time, by taking action, or with rational, logical thinking. So how can you get through each day without worrying about what's going to happen next?

The things that confuse you, frighten you, or make you feel helpless are best resolved by looking at them through a more spiritual vision, such as through prayer and meditation, by connecting with nature, attending church, or consulting a spiritual adviser. By using your spiritual "eyes," you'll be able to see how faith can ensure that all things will work out over time.

♦ Is there anything today about my life that confuses me or makes me feel helpless? Today I'll find my answers by seeking guidance from a spiritual resource.

A P R I L 2

If Longtime Companion *had made $80 million, they'd come up with 10 more of them. Period. Things in Hollywood are about survival. It's the '90s. Hollywood doesn't owe a debt to anyone but itself right now, to stay healthy and robust. It's a difficult time to be different here. The old-boy network is trying to protect only itself.*

—HARRY GITTES

Inaccurate, stereotypical, and often degrading portraits of gay men and lesbians on-screen seem to have become a norm in Hollywood. Activist organizations have been trying to raise gay consciousness in major motion-picture studios by educating them about gay and lesbian issues, encouraging the development of scripts that deal with homosexual themes or characters, and assisting in the finer points of language and character. While some studios have become more sensitive to gay and lesbian cinematic portrayals, there are few gay message pictures and few real-life or humanistic gay scenarios in movies. For the most part, Hollywood remains a closeted industry that thrives on box-office clout.

But while film is a powerful medium, so, too, is the gay consumer. Why support movies that have a negative impact on gay and lesbian self-esteem or that encourage violence and hate crimes? Let your freedom of expression be heard by refusing to spend money on movies that are unsupportive of the gay and lesbian community.

◆ Today I'll rent or attend movies that don't degrade or demean gay men and lesbians and boycott those that do. I'll write a letter to a gay publication urging its readers to do the same.

I'm not interested in compassion that is focused on my death.
Real compassion supports my living and supports me when I
express my true gay self.

—PETER, PERSON WITH ARC

When you must deal with the imminence of your death because of AIDS, breast cancer, aging, or a chronic medical condition, the last thing in the world you want to be reminded of by others is the inevitability of your death. Well-meaning friends who now get together with you to take care of your physical needs rather than spend quality time with you, a caretaking partner who now makes decisions without consulting you rather than "bother" you, or family members who never came to visit before but now visit clearly show you that more energy is being exerted in support of your dying than of your living.

You need to surround yourself with people who want to support your living. Choose to be with friends who can still be friends—who want to laugh, share a meal, watch a video, play a game, or take a walk on the beach. Let your partner know that you still have a voice and a choice in things that affect your relationship. Limit interactions with family members who are acting out of guilt rather than love when they come to visit.

Today be honest with your friends, partner, and family members about what you need in order to make this day one that's full of reminders about life—not death. Speak your mind, set your boundaries, and ask for what you want.

◆ Even when others are trying to be loving and compassionate, I sometimes feel that their concern is based on my death rather than my life. Today I'll ask those around me simply to be themselves so I, too, can just be me.

. . . trust me. Nobody you know is going to be happy that you like women. They not only won't like it, but they'll try to convince you not to see me again. The pressure they put on you will be tremendous.

—DEBORAH POWELL, FROM *BAYOU CITY SECRETS*

It's not uncommon for teenagers who declare their homosexuality to parents to be grounded, to be forbidden from seeing a love interest, to have religious guilt piled on them, or to be sent to a psychiatrist to be "straightened out." But such tactics are not limited to parents and their gay children; often, in adulthood, friends and family members can inflict incredible pressure on you to reconsider your gayness by threats ("I'll take you out of the will if you keep seeing her"), bribery ("If you go out on a date with someone of the opposite sex, I'll buy you something nice"), denial of a future interaction ("It's either him or me"), or exclusionary tactics ("You're certainly welcome, but not if you bring her").

Such pressure to change your sexuality is designed to have a negative impact on your self-esteem, create added conflict in your life, inflict guilt, control your actions and behaviors, and force you to do what others think is right.

Today refuse even to converse with someone who is trying to pressure you in any way about your sexuality. Terminate such a conversation by saying, "This is not a topic open to discussion. When you're ready to talk to me about something else, let me know."

♦ There's no reason why I need to listen to someone who's not supportive of me or my way of life. Today I'll turn a deaf ear on any antigay pressure tactics by hanging up the telephone or physically distancing myself from the speaker.

Queer people are always looking for something to invigorate them. They explore the world in a different way from the rest. When traveling, they go places and see things that would scare the average tourist. They are not afraid of experimentation, of the bizarre, of the lunatic, of the new.

—ANDRÉ LEON TALLEY

Do you participate in what's called the "gay outlaw aesthetic"? This "outlaw outlook" is based on growing up gay, which presents you with a vastly different experience from growing up straight. Such a difference often forms the way you look at things as you grow older—a way that affects the things that interest you (movies, television, fashion, theater, photography, and design), the people who fascinate you (those who break the rules, who walk against the wind, or who take pride in shocking, startling, or shaking up the accepted norm), and the places you travel to (remote islands, rugged wilderness locations, or funky cities that teem with gay culture).

When was the last time you did something that other gay men or lesbians might not dream of doing? Did you take a gay friend to your school's prom, speak out against a well-known gay role model, hold hands or kiss your lover in public, or plant a Silence = Death sticker on a public restroom wall?

Today, be as gay as you want to be. Dare to do something different!

♦ Being a gay man or lesbian means I can not only create cultural change, but I can also reinvent my personal culture. Today I'll challenge a boundary or convention that keeps me locked in a boring, routine, or old pattern.

When you look at relationships that make it, the people are good friends and treat each other with respect; they have shared values and they trust one another. Trust is the foundation. Without it, you don't feel safe. If you don't feel safe, you can't be vulnerable. If you're not vulnerable, you can't be intimate.
—LONNIE BARBACH

What does intimacy mean to you? Although it can mean different things to different people at different times in their lives, basically intimacy stands for emotional closeness. Developing emotional closeness with a partner can be hard for you as a gay man or lesbian. For one thing, there's often an incredible amount of childhood baggage brought into relationships by each partner—abuse issues, abandonment issues, trust issues, and so on—that restrict intimacy. In addition, the impact past relationships may have had on creating the feeling that interactions are meant to be short-term can make it hard for two people to develop trust so they can be vulnerable with one another.

Yet there are ways you and your partner can create a foundation upon which healthy intimacy can be developed. Accept one another, including each other's inadequacies. Make each other feel important and special in a way no one else has. Share secrets. Try to resolve conflicts immediately. And, most importantly, show that you're committed to your relationship.

♦ Developing intimacy involves bonding, talking about feelings, being open and honest, and problem-solving together. Today I'll show my partner that I'm willing to develop intimacy in all of these areas.

Straight people have their own world set already, and they're rotting in it. Why would you want to be a part of it? Strength comes in developing yourself on your own two feet, in feeling the loneliness of it all, and in loving yourself enough to laugh your ass off at your mistakes.

—SUSAN TYRRELL

Do you see yourself as an outsider looking in—a gay man or lesbian who's living uncomfortably while trying to fit into the straight world—or an insider looking out—a gay man or lesbian who's living comfortably in a gay way of life that's real and right to you?

Too often you may feel pressure to fit in with the straight population, to blend in with it in order not to call attention to you, your sexuality, your politics, your beliefs, your issues, and so on. But when you attempt to do so, you become a chameleon—a creature who adapts to any environment it encounters so it doesn't stand out in any way.

Today, instead of being a creature of adaptability, why not strive to be a creature of change? To do so, create the environment that's right for you. This may mean that you make some waves, that you behave in ways others don't expect, or that you make choices that are based on *your* best interests. While you won't always gain approval and acceptance from others, you can approve of and accept yourself.

◆ Today I'll stop trying to disguise who I am and what makes me happy for the good of others. I'll be strong, confident, and self-assured as I create a way of living that's right for me.

> *You may have to fight a battle more than once to win it.*
> —MARGARET THATCHER

Wouldn't it be great if the first time you came out was the first—and only—time? So, no matter what age you were when you came out, once you identified your sexual preference and then told those friends and family members who were in your life at the time, you never had to raise the issue again.

But coming out isn't a one-shot revelation; it's an ongoing process. Who you need to come out to at particular times in your life is always changing as the people, places, and circumstances in your life change. This means that you may often find yourself faced with decisions about which people in your life you need to come out to at a given time.

Because coming out is a process that you may have to repeat many times in your life, how you come out to others can provide you with a measure of your growth, maturity, and level of self-acceptance. What you once may have blurted out to your parents in defensiveness and anger as a teenager may today be discussed in a calm, rational manner with a close friend or an employer.

Today you can view coming out as an ongoing process that requires persistence and patience. Yet each time you participate in this process, you're validating who you are in a positive, self-nurturing way.

♦ Today I'll view the act of coming out to someone as a wonderful way to reaffirm my acceptance of my sexuality. Each time I come out will increase the pride I feel about myself and my way of life.

He is a prostitute. They call him "Dead of Winter," because he goes out looking for men no matter how cold the weather gets.

—A MAN IN SHANGHAI

Liu Dalin, one of China's best-known sexologists, reports that overall, life for gay men and lesbians in China is still lonely, often bitter, and potentially tragic. But he hopes that the research he's doing in the communist country will help change social attitudes so gay men and lesbians can live without suffering prejudice. In 1992, his efforts seemed to be moving the country's leadership in the right direction; the first organized study on homosexuality conducted since the 1949 revolution concluded that China has a "sizable homosexual" population and that gay people are "normal."

How aware are you of the treatment of gay men and lesbians in other countries? While you may feel you have enough problems to deal with in the United States—with issues such as the AIDS epidemic, hate crimes, and discrimination—it might help you put your own difficulties in perspective by learning about how progressive or repressive other governments are toward their gay men and lesbian citizens.

Take some time today to read back issues of national gay and lesbian publications to get an idea of where other countries stand with their views and treatment of your brothers and sisters around the world.

♦ What can I learn about other gay men and lesbians if I focus solely on my small community, my state, or even my country? Today I'll expand my knowledge to include the struggles and triumphs of gay men and lesbians in other countries.

One often learns more from ten days of agony than from ten years of contentment.

—MERLE SHAIN

Pain pushes you, sometimes gently, sometimes forcefully, but always in the direction of healing and growth. Such pushing encourages you first to accept difficult changes in your life—the death of a friend, the loss of a parent, the termination of a long-term relationship, a physical injury or illness, an emotional trauma. Accepting *all* experiences as necessary—because you're gay as well as because you're human—is part of the ebb and flow of life.

After acceptance comes adjustment, or the changes you need to make, based on what you have accepted. You may need to work through the death of a loved one with the help of a support group or friends. You may choose to handle the ending of a relationship by relearning how to take care of yourself. You may have to work with a physical therapist or depend upon friends to help you recover from a physical injury or illness. You may need to deal with an emotional trauma with the guidance of a therapist.

As you work through the adjustment period and make changes, you may reach a point where you're able to look back at the painful times and feel a little less pain. Eventually you may even be able to celebrate such difficult times by recognizing their importance to your overall growth.

♦ Today I'll remember that a positive attitude will enhance the value of every experience, both good and bad. With this positive attitude, I'll find it easier to accept the pain and then learn to grow from it.

APRIL 11

I looked at a picture of the three men [gay bashers] who were arraigned. They were 16, 17 and 18. They didn't look like criminals. One looked like my son. Looking at that picture, I started wondering—where does hate come from? Some of it comes from booze and boredom. But the people I interviewed always came back to one source—the church.

—BETTE GREENE

In 1984 in Bangor, Maine, a twenty-three-year-old gay man was thrown off a bridge by a gang of gay bashers who ignored his pleas that he couldn't swim. The man died. Author Bette Greene decided to write a novel based on the incident, *The Drowning of Stephan Jones,* which tells of the violent death of a young gay man who is living with his lover in a small town in Arkansas and is drowned when two members of a gang are persuaded by a third to throw him in the water. In her conclusion to the book, Greene cites churches as an important source of the hate that motivates gay bashers; she proposes that religious leaders lead a coalition "dedicated to ending violence against gay and lesbian minorities."

Think back to what your religion taught you about homosexuality when you were a child. Were you led to believe that homosexuality was evil? Remember that young children now may be receiving similar teaching. Today, meet with a religious leader in your community and urge that he or she teach children to "love thy neighbor"—no matter who they are.

♦ Today I won't let young children grow up believing that homosexuality is rejected by God. I'll take a stand against religious leaders who encourage violence, hatred, and bigotry against gay men and lesbians.

True fulfillment as a human being comes when each of us is able to recognize the masculine and feminine within ourselves. . . . That's one of the enormous contributions the strong gay movement can make.

— JANE FONDA

Do you find that you often repress how you really think, feel, and wish to act and instead express the thoughts, feelings, and behaviors expected from you because of your gender? As a lesbian you may downplay the "nonfeminine" things that are a big part of your life (motorcycles, competitive sports, camping, leather bars) while you don the required feminine wardrobe and feign interest in sewing, cooking, and discussions about boyfriends and husbands. As a gay man you may downplay the "nonmasculine" things that are a big part of your life (cooking, taking care of your lover, decorating your home) while you participate in football pools, repress your emotions, and engage in bragging "straight-guy talk."

Yet your true fulfillment as a person—not just as a lesbian or gay man—depends upon your ability to freely express both your masculinity and your femininity. Today, spend your lunch hour browsing through your favorite magazines or newspapers or display pictures and posters in your office that reflect your interests. Or wear something out of the ordinary one day a week. Expression, not repression of your true self will make you much happier.

♦ Today I'll stop trying to show the world that I'm the "total woman" or the "total man," as defined by heterosexual standards. I'll do something that may be out of the ordinary for my gender, but that's right for me.

A child's world is fresh and new and beautiful, full of wonder and excitement. It is our misfortune that for most of us that clear-eyed vision, that true instinct for what is beautiful and awe-inspiring, is dimmed and even lost before we reach adulthood.

—RACHEL CARSON

When you were growing up, the difficulties you had to face in being different may have aged you beyond your young years. The family pressures you had to deal with, combined with inner worries, pain, and heartache caused by the rejection of friends and classmates may have resulted in a difficult childhood experience.

So when you look back on your childhood now, do you see that it was happy for you—happy because you could experience it with the joy and lightheartedness of a child? Or do you see yourself at the time as an adult who suffered in a child's body—unhappy, filled with remorse, dejection, or even suicidal depression?

Although you can't change the past or relive your childhood differently, what you can do in the present is allow yourself to feel childlike enjoyment in today's experiences. When you meet new people, try something new, or journey somewhere different, be filled with wonder and excitement. See such experiences as fresh, new, and beautiful—as if you were a child in an adult's body.

♦ Today I'll experience life with a much more playful, lighthearted attitude. I'll strive to see everything with a fresh outlook and expend more positive energy so I can transform myself into a happier human being.

A P R I L 14

If you do not find peace in yourself you will never find it anywhere else.

— PAULA A. BENDRY

Do you ever think, "If only I was settled down with the right person, had a job that really challenged me, was out to my friends and family, made more money, or lived in a different place, I wouldn't feel so restless and unhappy"? If you do, you may find yourself jumping from relationship to relationship, job to job, or apartment to apartment, certain that happiness is right around the corner somewhere.

Yet inner peace doesn't come from where you live, what you buy, or the person you make your companion. Inner peace doesn't emerge from such externals; rather, it's developed when you're willing to invest time, patience, and hard work into challenging, confronting, and resolving conflicts and issues within you.

Today, when you find yourself thinking that you'd be happier "If only . . ." take this as a sign that your inner peace is in turmoil and needs some attention. Think about things you can do that are self-loving and would bring you a feeling of inner peace. Get outside for some fresh air, tackle a project you've been putting off, settle down in a comfy chair with a cup of tea and a good book, luxuriate in a hot bath, listen to your favorite music, or watch an old movie on video. Make soothing your inner peace *your* responsibility.

♦ Today I'll keep in mind that there's no person, place, or thing that can substitute for the serenity I need to find and foster within myself.

'Tis pitiful the things by which we are rich or poor—a matter of coins, coats and carpets, a little more or less stone, wood or paint, the fashion of a cloak or hat. . . .

—RALPH WALDO EMERSON

Are you rich? That all depends on how you define the word. Maybe you think that a large bank account, a bulging wallet, a filled jewelry box, expensive clothes, fine furniture, a large home, or a fancy car make you rich.

But you can also view riches as intangibles—the things you can't see, touch, purchase, earn, or spend. By this definition, riches can be happiness, good health, a high sense of self-esteem, a loving circle of friends, a family that accepts your sexuality, the ability to feel and express love, a career that challenges you and makes you happy, an ability to appreciate nature, something or someone to get up for every morning, or being able to live as an out gay man or lesbian.

You need only read the gossip pages to learn that those who are rich in material goods are rarely happy and content in their lives. Yet every day you and others like you are rich in so many other ways.

Today, rather than focus solely on finances, take time to assess your "net worth" that comes not from what you have in your wallet, but what you have in your heart.

♦ Why spend all day focusing on taxes? Today I'll remember all the wonderful riches in my life that I don't have to declare to the Internal Revenue Service.

She will show us her shoulder, her bosom, her face; but what the heart's like, we must guess.

—EDWARD ROBERT BULWER-LYTTON

Do you express physical intimacy with other people in order to distance yourself from them rather than to connect with them? Engaging in casual sex instead of making love is one way to keep others at an arm's—and heart's—length. Leaving after having sex instead of spending the night sleeping together is one way to limit conversation, companionship, and closeness. Having a series of one-night stands or dating more than one person limits interactions and prevents anyone from getting to know you in a deeper way over time.

What is it that you're afraid of in letting another gay man or lesbian get close to you? Physical intimacy that's ruled by fear is a mixed message. On one hand, you're saying you want to be close to someone; yet, on the other hand, you're also saying, "But not too close." Fear encourages you to hold back rather than let go. Fear builds walls rather than bridges. Fear results in disconnection rather than connection.

Now imagine what being physically intimate with another gay man or lesbian would be like if you were able to let yourself go, if you could get close, if you could connect.

Today, identify one of the fears that makes you too afraid to give of yourself physically and emotionally. Then talk to a trusted friend about your fear and strive together to find a way to work through the fear.

◆ Today I'll take a truthful look at how I engage in physical intimacy with other gay men or lesbians. Then I'll explore the "whys" of my behaviors in order to uncover the truth behind my fears.

*People say, "Where's the mother? Is she dead? Which one of you
is the father?" We just say that our kids have two dads. It's kind of
fun for us. They have this frozen smile as the wheels begin to turn.*
— TIM FISHER

For many gay fathers and lesbian mothers, raising their children is sometimes not as difficult as dealing with societal
repercussions of being gay parents. There's no escaping the
glances of disapproval or curiosity that often follow gay parents and their families. There's little respite from the hostility
toward homosexual parenting. There's much ignorance that
needs to be confronted, such as the belief that homosexuals
make their children homosexual.

Yet youth workers like Edward Calderon-Melendez are
pleased to report that "homosexual parents raise children
more sensitive to issues of discrimination and oppression than
heterosexual parents."

Today, lend your support as a nonparent or parent to other
gay parents in your community. Offer baby-sitting or car-
pooling services. Speak openly and freely about what good
parents they are. Listen to their experiences or share some of
your own. And urge those in Congress to support gay fathers
and lesbian mothers through the same programs that benefit
heterosexual parents.

◆ Today I'll be supportive of how well gay parents are
raising their children in a homophobic, unsupportive society. Gay fathers and lesbian mothers who are teaching their
children to be well adjusted, happy, and to make a
contribution to society are terrific role models.

*My feeling is that the straight public still sees gays and lesbians
as victims. Right now we need a different perspective. Gay people
are surviving and living strong, positive lives.*

—John Scagliotti

Television producer John Scagliotti, who created *In the Life,* a
national show on gay and lesbian culture that aired on PBS, has
been disappointed that gays and lesbians are one of the few
minorities left that still struggle with positive visibility.

Lack of funding is one of the reasons why gay and lesbian
culture remains invisible to the public. Corporate underwrit-
ers, the traditional means of support for PBS broadcasts, have
shown little interest in backing gay programming. In fact,
much of the funding for *In the Life* was gathered from grants by
private foundations and a mailing list of three thousand sup-
porters. Getting on the air is also a problem—PBS never
made a full commitment to air *In the Life;* rather, it agreed to
place the show on satellite so its 320 affiliate stations could
broadcast it if and when they chose to do so.

Clearly it's up to *you* to ensure that positive and accurate
portraits of gay and lesbian life are made available to the public.
Support other gay and lesbian shows through a donation, write
letters to corporations urging their support of such programming, and lobby your PBS affiliate and cable networks to ensure
production and airing of gay and lesbian shows.

♦ Society's view of gay men and lesbians won't change if I
don't contribute to effecting such change. Today I'll support
the efforts others are making in producing gay-positive
media for the gay and straight communities.

I can't even THINK STRAIGHT.

——MOTTO ON A T-SHIRT

How many times have you heard straight friends or nonsupportive family members comment, "When are you going to come to your senses, stop all this foolishness, and settle down with a member of the opposite sex?" In the past you may have even tried to please these people by living the straight way of life—by dating members of the opposite sex they've fixed you up with, by becoming engaged to a longtime family friend, or even by getting married and raising a family.

But what good came out of such actions? While you may have made your friends or family members happy or relieved because you chose to live your life in the way they deemed acceptable, you were probably miserable. You may have had affairs with other gay people, and felt torn between living a lie and living your life in the way you wanted to.

But today you know that your sexuality is what's normal, natural, and right for you—and now there's no turning back! For once you decide to come out of the closet in a way that allows you truly to experience and express what has been in your heart for years—with self-acceptance and commitment—you know it becomes more and more difficult to pretend you're straight.

Today, why bother trying to think or act straight just to make others happy or more comfortable with your sexuality? Doing so may only raise false hopes or give the wrong impression—and make you miserable.

◆ Today I'll make certain that the messages I send out to the straight people I know continue to validate my sexuality. It's not fair to either them or me to participate in a lie.

Gentleness is not a quality exclusive to women.

—HELEN REDDY

Your options for how you respond to the gay men and lesbians in your life are vast. As a lesbian, you may choose to turn your back on gay men or treat them with anger or disapproval simply because they are men. As a gay man, you may choose to ignore lesbians, treat them with indifference, or criticize how they respond to you and your issues. While these are all options, they do little to build bridges between the sexes in the gay and lesbian community, and shut doors to useful and nurturing sources of support.

But there's another option available: rather than focus on the gender of others in the gay and lesbian community, look at each person *as an individual*. When you do, it won't matter whether you're looking at a gay man or lesbian; you'll be looking instead at a gay *person*. What you'll find is that he or she grew up and came out; faces the same discrimination, homophobia, and societal pressures as you do; loves, laughs, and lives in ways you can relate to.

Today, treat a gay man or lesbian with gentleness, kindness, and understanding for one important reason— because he or she is a member of your community who shares every day in your struggle always to follow where your heart leads you.

◆ Today, in spite of my personal feelings and prejudices, I can be warm, kind, and gentle in every personal exchange with a member of the opposite sex in the gay community.

If Ron did anything to leave behind for us, he made it OK for us to do the right thing. There's got to be members of this House who wondered up to this time whether supporting gay rights was right and proper. Ron showed it was right and proper.

—RALPH WRIGHT

In January 1993, Ron Squires, an openly gay member of the Vermont Legislature and campaigner for the state's gay-rights law, died from complications of AIDS. He was forty-one. Prior to his death, Democrat Squires was sworn in to his second term while he was in a hospital; House Speaker Ralph Wright attended the swearing-in after the House amended its rules to allow the hospital ceremony.

One of Squires's greatest accomplishments was working to win approval of a state civil rights law to protect homosexuals from discrimination on the basis of their sexual orientation. His efforts helped make Vermont the sixth state in the nation to extend such protections to gay men and lesbians.

Do you work hard in your life not only to protect your own rights, but also the rights of gay men and lesbians everywhere? Just because you're not a member of a governing body doesn't mean you can't assert that gay rights are "right and proper." Today, make future plans to attend a political march, participate in a protest or demonstration, or lobby a congressional representative.

◆ Today I won't sit back and count on someone else to fight for me and my rights as a gay man or lesbian. It's up to me to do what I feel is right and proper.

I believe this: When people do things that are mean, or, even unintentionally, that aren't good towards life and people—they're the ones that suffer more than anybody else.

—TOM CRUISE

The way you're treated by others is a reflection of their state of being. If they're at peace with themselves and feel good about who they are, then their response toward you can be loving, kind, and full of acceptance. But if they feel worthless and full of self-hate, then they can be mean-spirited, hurtful, angry, or even violent toward you.

Those people who live in a dungeon of self-despair often long to make others captive. They may choose to inflict their personal pain on you simply because you're a gay man or lesbian. They may fling epithets, fists, or objects at you; they may gang up on you; they may threaten or harm your home, business, children, or loved one; they may attempt to destroy everything you've worked hard for by revealing your sexuality or telling untruths about you.

But although the physical or psychological injury you might suffer at their hands may seem severe, it's often minor compared with the personal hell these people live in day after day. Today, remember that how other people treat you is often how they treat themselves—and even those they love.

◆ While I'll never forgive or condone gay bashing or hate crimes, I'll try to keep in mind how tormented and sick the individuals are who do such things, and how their behavior reflects their own feelings of self-hatred.

I was raised in a small town. All my life I have been told that being gay is wrong. Is it? It's what I feel inside. I have been out to three gay bars this month. The people act like sex-crazed wolves. I stand back and watch these people and ask myself if I am one myself. I don't know.

——A LETTER WRITER TO *OUT,* NAME WITHHELD, COVINGTON, KY

Every day, there are hundreds of gay men and lesbians who are imprisoned by insurmountable feelings of self-doubt, confusion, fear, anxiety, homophobia, paranoia, and depression about their sexuality. They hide behind closet doors kept firmly locked. They attend churches that tell them they will burn in hell for feeling such feelings. They struggle day after day to hide their sexuality in small hometowns and large cities, schools and summer camps, and heterosexual marriages. Their imprisonment is a life sentence of loneliness and despair, with no hope of a parole that would give them a taste of freedom of expression.

Today you can do things to reach out to these gay men and women in a positive way, to make them feel more accepting of their sexuality so they can come out. Provide copies of gay and lesbian publications to small-town libraries, high schools, or colleges. Volunteer on a gay and lesbian hotline. Or meet with other gay men and lesbians who feel the way you do and volunteer to speak at high schools or community organizations.

♦Today I'll be a positive resource of strength, self-acceptance, and self-love to a closeted gay man or lesbian who is questioning, "Why am I the way I am, and what can I do about it?"

. . . the healthy, the strong individual, is the one who asks
for help when he needs it whether he's got an abscess on his knee or
in his soul.

—RONA BARRETT

It's never right to shoulder your burdens alone. You have
around you access to other gay men and lesbians who share, in
so many ways, the difficulties in being gay—your grief in
losing a partner to AIDS or cancer, your pain in ending a
long-term relationship, your fears about coming out at work
or to your family of origin, your sense of invisibility, and so
on. You're also surrounded by gay men and lesbians who can
share in the celebrations of being gay—the excitement of
meeting someone new, the relief in coming out to accepting
coworkers and family members, the peace of commitment
ceremonies, the joy at the birth or adoption of a longed-for
child, the exhilaration of political gains and legal victories.

You and other gay men and lesbians can nurture and guide
each other's steps, for you all have the remedy for each
other's ills and the heart for one another's triumphs. But the
invitation to help must be extended. Today, ask your friends
or partner for help, or be there to respond to the calls for help
from others. Remember that you're not solo on this journey
through gay life, but traveling with many other men and
women like you.

◆ Today I'll remember that others may need my help, just as
much as I may need their help. One of the greatest gifts I can
give another gay man or lesbian is simply to be there when
I'm needed.

I think every work of art is an act of faith, or we wouldn't bother to do it. It is a message in a bottle, a shout in the dark. It's saying, "I'm here and I believe that you are somewhere. . . ."
— JEANETTE WINTERSON

One of the most celebrated openly lesbian writers is Jeanette Winterson, whose debut novel *Oranges Are Not the Only Fruit* won Britain's Whitbread prize for best first novel and has been translated into twelve languages. The author's television adaptation of the novel became the BBC's highest-rated miniseries ever, nabbing a BAFTA (an English Emmy) for the author and her collaborators.

What Winterson did with the enormous success of her book *Oranges* and the miniseries was break important ground in proving that lesbian and gay subjects could have a universal appeal. In fact, many credit the critical success Winterson received for her writing as well as acceptance of her lifestyle for such gay television programs as *Out on Tuesday* and the adaptation of David Leavitt's *The Lost Language of Cranes*.

Think back to the excitement and validation you may have felt when you first read a novel about a gay or lesbian relationship. "Finally," you might have sighed, "a book about me and how I feel." Today, "answer" the "message in a a bottle" that gay authors are sending by purchasing one of their books. In doing this, you're letting the authors and their publishers know you want and need such self-validating books.

♦Today I'll recognize the incredible level of creativity offered by talented gay men and lesbians. I'll visit an exhibit, gallery, or bookstore and take in their artwork, photography, and literature.

[Coming out was a] boulder being lifted off my back. But you have to be strong. You know that bad things will be said, and you have to anticipate the worst.

—MATT FLYNN

If you're involved in a confrontation, do you stubbornly hold your ground as you wait for the other person to make the first move toward verbal or physical action, or do you walk away? If you're on the receiving end of an insensitive, angry, or hurtful remark, do you immediately mount an attack or are you able to dismiss the remark as not even worth acknowledging?

While it's admirable to want to deal with conflicts as they occur and not to suppress your feelings, it's downright stupid to stand up to the hate-filled slurs flung at you because you're a gay man or lesbian. As difficult as it may be, the best way for you to deal with vicious verbal assaults or physical threats is to respond in a way that doesn't leave you vulnerable to continued assault or confrontation. This means you must take a deep breath, think, then act—not react—in a way that discourages and defuses conflict.

How do you find the strength to do this? Think about the strength it took finally to come to terms with your sexuality. Didn't you work for years to build up the emotional power needed to acknowledge what was in your heart? Today, use such emotional power and your pride as a gay man or lesbian to disengage from conflict.

◆ Today I'll remember that it takes two to perpetuate a conflict. Rather than stop and react to a verbal barrage or physical threat, I'll continue on my way.

> *The past is our cradle, not our prison. . . . The past is for*
> *inspiration, not imitation; for continuation, not repetition.*
> —ISRAEL ZANGWILL

Part of your process of healing and recovery from a dysfunctional childhood or addictions to drugs, alcohol, food, or sex often involves looking back to see where you've come from—what first brought you into a recovery program—so you can then look ahead to measure how far you've come since that time. Such reflection is like reading a history book; it can give you an objective view of what life was once like during a particular period of time so you can apply such history to your present way of life.

You can learn much from a past in which you were living as an unhealthy gay man or lesbian. While looking back may remind you of negative experiences and times you may prefer to forget, it can also offer you insights into past behaviors. Such insights can give you clues about your present behaviors, help you explain your mood swings, and provide you with an understanding of patterns of attraction to unhealthy people.

Today, use your past as a jumping-off point for improving your present way of living. Look at the negatives from the past and think of ways to develop them into positives. Identify your unhealthy patterns of behavior and choose not to imitate or perpetuate such behaviors. Use the past to inspire present recovery and healing.

◆ Today's motto for my recovery and healing is: Look back, then look ahead. I'll think of ways to use my personal history for positive present-day behaviors.

It's surprising that men can be victims, that not all men are perpetrators. Friends of partners where there's abuse going on think of it as two men fighting.

—GREG MERRILL

Naming the Violence, a 1986 book about violence in lesbian relationships, and *Men Who Beat the Men Who Love Them,* a 1991 book about gay male domestic violence, lists ways in which lesbians and gay men batter their partners. Included are assaults with firearms, knives, broken bottles, and lit cigarettes; beating and choking; forced sex; destroying property; abusing pets; humiliation and degradation; withholding of sexual intimacy; and threatened outing.

Activists in the field of gay and lesbian domestic violence say that awareness of the problem has caused confusion, silence, and lack of acceptance in the gay community, for it challenges the stereotypical domestic violence portrait of a violent man abusing a submissive woman. The trust lesbians and gay men have in being safe and protected with their partners is being shattered.

If you or anyone you know is in an abusive relationship, you must get help. Some organized services exist specifically for battered gay men or women, and a gay and lesbian hotline can tell you if one exists in your area. But always seek safety with understanding friends, obtain therapeutic and legal counseling, and terminate future interactions with an abusive partner.

♦ Today I won't remain silent about the abuse in my intimate relationship. I'll stop protecting my abuser, offering excuses for his or her behavior, and hiding what's being done to me. Today I will take the first step to free myself from this abusive relationship.

However much we guard against it, we tend to shape ourselves in the image others have of us.

—ERIC HOFFER

Your sense of how others see you and what they approve and disapprove of in your being a gay man or lesbian can be a compelling influence in your life. Sometimes this influence is strong enough to make you change, soften, or adapt your behaviors in order to make others feel more comfortable. You may be very cautious about the things you do and the words you say, selective about the clothes you wear, and hesitant about the causes you support lest you be perceived as "too gay."

Passively letting others exert their influence over you and how you behave as a gay man or lesbian gives them—not you—control over your life. When you let others control you, you're no longer living from your base of personal power; instead, you're letting their base impede your personal power.

While you can't control what others deem acceptable and comfortable for them, you can control what's acceptable and comfortable for you. Today, don't let any individual decide how gay you can be. Refuse to submit to the limitations presented by parents who accept you, but not your longtime companion; to the fears of a partner who wants to live with you and love you, as long as you remain closeted; and to friends who want to spend time with you but refuse to when you wear certain clothes or sport a particular haircut. Today, be who you, not others, want you to be.

◆ The image of myself that I present to the world is the one that's right for me. Today I'll accept that not everyone will approve of my presentation, and that's okay.

APRIL 30

*Awareness starts with our own bodies. I want women to be aware of
their bodies before they lose a breast to the knife, before their hair
falls out from radiation. For too long, lesbians have been the caretak-
ers of everybody else. It's time we took care of ourselves. . . .*

— JANE SEACREST

As a child, Jane Seacrest watched her aunt die of breast cancer.
Seacrest, an African-American lesbian, was diagnosed with
breast cancer at age forty-two—the same age her aunt had
been when she died. Jane elected to have a radical (complete)
mastectomy, chemotherapy, and radiation, but her prognosis
afterward was poor. Over 75 percent of women with late
diagnoses die within four years; in addition, breast cancer is
the leading cause of death for African-American women between the ages of forty-five and sixty-five.

Jane's story is not unusual. According to projections made
by the National Cancer Institute, one in three lesbians is likely
to have breast cancer in her lifetime. This is *three times* the
national average for *all* women.

No matter what your age, it's important for you as a lesbian to
begin risk reduction; urge your lesbian friends to follow the
breast-cancer risk-reducing program: get regular gynecological
care, including breast exams, and begin mammograms between
ages thirty-five and forty; do a regular breast self-examination;
reduce alcohol consumption; increase fiber in your diet (this rids
the digestive tract of estrogen excesses); and increase vitamin C
(this boosts your immune defenses).

◆ Today I'll give myself or someone I know a "wake-up call"
about lesbians being in the highest risk category for breast
cancer and emphasize the need for regular breast self-
examination to detect unusual lumps.

Have you learned lessons only of those who admired you, and were tender with you, and stood aside for you? Have you not learned great lessons from those who braced themselves against you, and disputed the passage with you?

—WALT WHITMAN

Wouldn't it be wonderful if being gay was an acceptable way of life! You could walk down the street holding hands with your lover, be out at the workplace, dance with another gay man or lesbian in any bar, never be the victim of discrimination or a hate crime because of your sexuality—even read "commitment" announcements in the newspaper!

If being gay was an acceptable way of life, you'd never have to struggle for anything. But while that might sound terrific, the learning and growing you've done thus far might never have happened had it not been for the energy, commitment, and determination you've had to expend in standing up for yourself and your rights. That's because any gains in your growth and learning are always a result of the amount of effort you put into getting what you want.

Today it's important to recognize that if you can't struggle for acceptance as a gay man or lesbian, then your motivation, determination, strength, and confidence as a gay man or lesbian can't grow. While some things in life will come easily, some won't. But the things you work on now will mean the most in the end.

♦ Today I won't be resentful of the energy I need to put into something I really want because I'm a gay man or lesbian. I'll do this so I can make things easier for me now and for other gay men and lesbians in the future.

*My brother is gay. He loves my kids and they love him, and he
likes to spend time with them, and I have no problem with that.
What I do have trouble with is letting the boys go to his apartment. I always orchestrate it so that doesn't happen. Now, all of
a sudden, my older boy is pushing me: Why can't we go there?*

——A FATHER OF TWO BOYS

When adults have ambivalent feelings about homosexuality,
it often becomes difficult for them to deal with their children's needs for honesty and information about the subject.
Parents may feel they're protecting their children by setting
limits in interactions with others they know are gay; in
reality, however, their lack of honesty often causes children
anxiety, confusion, and misunderstanding.

Children need open, honest, nonbiased information about
homosexuality by third grade, for that's when they begin to
hear the words "gay," "lesbian," "bisexual," and "homosexual"
from peers and start to notice their use in the media. If you're
a parent or a friend of someone who has a child, make sure
that child's questions about homosexuality are answered in
ways that counteract stereotypes and promote tolerance and
acceptance. If a child asks, "Why is Aunt Lisa a lesbian?" you
can say, "Nobody knows why some people are gay. It's part of
Aunt Lisa's life, just like she enjoys to swim and make quilts."

The key to communicating with children about homosexuality is to be matter-of-fact; in that way, children won't form
judgments or biases—unless *you* have.

◆ Because there's a homosexual relationship in my family,
it's important for me to communicate to the adults that the
kids should know that *all* members of my family are to be
treated with equality, respect, and dignity.

Dr. Walker had not intended to impersonate a man; it was simply a matter of convenience and comfort to wear men's clothing. We're doing the same thing now.

—SANDY KAPLAN

Dr. Mary Walker, a surgeon in the Union army, was well-known for what was considered to be an the oddity at the time: she wore men's clothing and high boots like President Lincoln's. Because she had been awarded a medal for her services during the Civil War and was held in high esteem, she had actually been given permission by Congress to wear men's clothes. Once she was arrested for appearing in public dressed as a man, but as soon as she reached the police station, she was recognized and released.

What type of clothing do you prefer to wear? As a gay man, you may love going out on a Saturday night dressed from head to toe in elegant women's clothing. You may enjoy shopping for women's clothing or modeling outfits for your friends. As a lesbian, you may love wearing a tux to parties in your community, like to shop for men's clothes or wear men's cologne, or feel comfortable lying around the house in men's athletic wear. In wearing clothing that feels right to you, you've made a conscious decision not to let gender identification dictate your fashion.

Today, spend money on and wear what feels right to you—not what the media says should feel right or should be worn because you're a man or a woman. Let your body feel the comfort of clothing that fits you and your way of life.

♦ Today I'll have fun with my wardrobe! I'll shop at a used-clothing store for styles in which I'll feel comfortable and fashionable.

M A Y 4

My mother was dead for five years before I knew that I had loved her very much.

—LILLIAN HELLMAN

When you were growing up, did you ever scream at your parents, "I hate you! I wish you were dead!" While you can recognize today that such statements were made by an immature child who didn't get his or her way, what you may not be so quick to recognize now is how much you may truly miss a dead parent or parents.

Even though, while alive, your parent may have rejected your way of life or made nasty comments about your being gay, weren't there things that your parent did or said that you miss today? Maybe your father taught you fly-fishing, got you hooked on stamp collecting, or worked hard every day to put food on the table and send you and your brothers and sisters to college. Maybe your mother was accepting of all your friends, taught you how to sew, or always greeted you at the front door with a smile and a hug. Maybe what a parent passed on to you was something that you long to hear again today — "You're special to us," "I'm proud of your job," or "I love you no matter who you love."

Take a moment to reflect on a memory of a parent that you cherish. Keep this memory in your thoughts today and let it bring a smile to your face and put warmth in your heart.

♦ Today I'll think of a parent I've lost and remember something I truly miss about him or her. I'm so glad that I can think of this person now with love and longing.

Love is mutually feeding each other, not one living on another like a ghoul.

—BESSIE HEAD

There's a joke in the gay and lesbian community about how to date: on the first date, you sleep with someone; on the second date, you put your possessions in a U-Haul and drive to that person's house; on the third date, you exchange commitment vows.

While many gay men and lesbians joke about this "instant relationship" process of dating, you know there's a lot of truth to it. Most gay men and lesbians don't date—they don't see more than one person before making a conscious decision about the one person they'd like to commit to. Rather, many gay men and lesbians either fool around without any intention of settling down or settle down with the first person they sleep with after a relationship ends.

Today, before committing to one person, strive to see more than one person for a while. By doing so, you'll learn who you are and what you want in a committed relationship; you'll also experience the strengths and shortcomings of others and how well you relate with them. What the time and patience required in the process of "seeing what's out there" can teach you is that love is generally slow to develop. However, love *will* result when you're able to make a conscious, considerate, and mutual decision to commit to someone else.

♦ I believe that real love is compromise, sharing and taking turns, and putting another's best interests first. If I can't find the person who understands love in the same way, then we're not right for each other.

I am a homosexual—all of my lovers have been men. Some of them think they are straight, but that's my problem.

—KENNETH ANGER

Picture this: You meet a fabulous person. You spend a lot of time together. You fall in love. Then, just when you think your feelings will be reciprocated, you hear these three little words: "I am confused." What follows the three words is often a bounce-all-over-the-place explanation about how the man or woman of your dreams hasn't yet come to terms with being gay.

Involvement with people who hide in straight marriages while they "dabble" in homosexuality or are homophobic themselves can make for unsettling and sometimes crisis-filled relationships. What you lose in your involvements with such people is a sense of security, continuity, and the development of trust. What you gain is a challenge that forces you to define what's acceptable and unacceptable for you in a relationship.

Today, examine why you may be intimate with someone who's confused about their way of life. Are you falling in love with the potential of what could happen if/when he or she comes out? Are you choosing to be with such a partner because his or her confusion puts a limit on the level of intimacy you can feel? Do you view such a relationship as a challenge? Or do you feel that's all you deserve?

♦ Today I'll explore my reasons for choosing to be with someone who's uncomfortable being gay. Then I need to ask myself: Is it right for me to stay with this person? Am I getting my needs met? Am I happy?

The fundamental problem most patients have is an inability to love themselves, having been unloved by others during some crucial part of their lives.

— BERNIE SIEGEL

When you were growing up, how were you treated when you were sick or injured? Were you told that you were weak if you "gave in" to a cold or flu? Did you feel pressure to perform in an athletic event or do well in some other activity despite a high fever or injury? Was the principle "No pain, no gain" hammered into your mind long after you had crossed your threshold of pain? Were you ignored while you were sick at home or visited infrequently or not at all when you were hospitalized?

The childhood messages you received when you were sick or recovering from an injury may be the same messages you give yourself today as you strive to regain your health from illnesses related to HIV or rehab from an injury. Feeling unacceptable, wrong, disgusting, imperfect, or inferior can impede your ability to heal yourself, for it's not only the body but also the mind that participates in the healing process.

The first step to healing and recovery is to learn to love and accept yourself the way you are, even if you're feverish, weak, plagued by bouts of diarrhea and vomiting, or unable to dress or care for yourself. Once you accept that the way you feel *is* the way you feel, you'll be able to relax your mind and muscles so healing can take place.

◆ Today I won't let the shame of my illness or the difficulties caused by an injury affect how I feel about myself as a person. I'll strive to be a self-loving, self-accepting, healing, recovering gay man or lesbian.

It is stitched together with the tears and sorrow of those who have lost their family, friends, colleagues and neighbors. . . . displayed with their hope, and their rage, in an effort to help everyone understand the effect AIDS has had on our lives.

—THE NAMES PROJECT FOUNDATION

Between 1980 and 1987, more than one thousand people living in San Francisco died of AIDS. Cleve Jones sought to find a way to make the public understand the lack of government response to what people were experiencing in losing brothers, sisters, children, parents, friends, and lovers. He gathered a small group of neighborhood residents in an empty Market Street storefront and began the first panels of the AIDS Memorial Quilt. Word of the project spread throughout the gay and lesbian communities in New York, Los Angeles, and San Francisco; later, participation in the quilt broadened to include members of the straight community, corporations who had lost employees to AIDS, and countries outside the United States. By 1992 over twenty thousand panels had been received by the Names Project Foundation.

How can you become involved in the AIDS Memorial Quilt? If you've lost someone to AIDS, think about designing a quilt panel. Make a financial contribution to help pay for the cost of maintaining the quilt. Organize a quilt display in your community to raise awareness or to serve as a memorial. Or become involved in staffing a local HIV/AIDS service-organization hotline.

◆ Today I'll be inspired by the impact of the AIDS Memorial Quilt and donate food, clothing, or money to an HIV/AIDS organization so those with the disease can pay their rent and utilities and buy food and medicine.

*No song or poem will bear my mother's name. Yet so many of
the stories that I write, that we all write, are my mother's stories.*
—ALICE WALKER

Mothers aren't perfect. Your mother had a mother who
taught her; her mother had a mother before her. So what your
mother may have passed down to you today might be flawed
from the dysfunction of a past generation or inconsistent
because of inconsistencies she lived through; on the other
hand, your mother may have passed down to you warmth,
support, nurturing, and love.

Where you are right now in your life is, in part, a result of
some of the things you've learned from your mother—
learning that may have been good and wise, bad and crazy,
accepting or unaccepting of you or your way of life.

What are some of the things you learned from your
mother? What's the most interesting thing she ever taught
you? The funniest? The most beneficial? The most educational? The thing that's stuck with you since you were young?
The learning she could have given you could be as simple as
knowing how to tie your shoes or bake bread, or as all-
encompassing as your ability to believe in yourself.

Today, think about the positive impact your mother has
had on your life. Then remember that everything you've ever
learned from her, she's given to you freely—from her heart.

◆ Today I won't forget to send my mother a card or a
present, to take her out to dinner, or to call her. Despite our
differences, I know that in a basic way, we do love one
another.

Look, I expect the same standards from you that I expect from everybody else in my administration. And if the legislators give you a hard time, let me know. I'll get them off your back.

—BILL CLINTON

Mike Rankin met Bill Clinton in 1978 when he applied for the position of Arkansas commissioner of mental health. After Rankin chatted informally with the Arkansas governor for over an hour, Clinton offered him the job. Rankin wrote about his experience, "I wanted to work with him. . . . This was clearly a politician whose concerns and values were similar to mine on most issues. But how did he feel about gay people? I might return to Arkansas to join a Clinton administration—but I wouldn't return to the closet for anyone. Bill Clinton included. The best way to find out was to ask."

How often have you wanted to come out of your work closet? What's probably kept you silent is your fear of losing your job, but you may also feel that you want to keep business business and your sexuality your own business.

Coming out at the workplace is a far different experience than coming out to family or friends. It involves a greater risk; loss of a friend or family member is one thing, while loss of a current job and/or future jobs has a financial and professional impact on your life.

Today, decide whether coming out at the workplace is right for you and your career.

♦ The issue for me in coming out at the workplace is: What impact will this have upon me in the future, at this job or at any other I might have? Today I'll be clear about my reasons for coming out of the work closet—or remaining inside.

Prejudices such as sexism and the deeply related homophobia, racism, and classism are not just personal problems, sets of peculiar and troubling beliefs. Exclusions and devaluations of whole groups of people on the scale and of the range, tenacity, and depth of racism and sexism and classism are systemic and shape the world within which we all struggle to live and find meaning.

—ELIZABETH KAMARCK MINNICK, FROM
TRANSFORMING KNOWLEDGE

Because you're a gay man or a lesbian, it may be easy to accept how other human beings are different—in the color of their skin; in their physical, mental, or emotional disabilities; in their religious beliefs or ethnic backgrounds; and so on. Such acceptance can stem from your ability to be tolerant. Tolerance is a concept you may have learned at an early age; you had to be tolerant of yourself so you could accept that you were different from others in your attraction to members of the same sex.

Yet not many people are tolerant. There's not a day that goes by where the media doesn't report on an act of violence aimed at those who were perceived by perpetrators as "different"—because they weren't white, they weren't born in America, or they weren't straight.

Today, don't stand for intolerance or prejudice directed at any minority group, not just gays and lesbians. Fight back against vandalism, assaults, and murders of those who are different by protesting against the legal system when it doesn't fairly punish the criminals.

◆ Today I'll follow the court cases of criminals who have made a member of a minority group a victim. I'll applaud fair punishment but protest—through phone calls, letters, and organized groups—an unjust verdict.

We must make safe sex a part of our consciousness. The use of a condom can help remove a lot of fears and allow us to once again enjoy the beauty and intimacy of our very special private moments.

—IAN FALCONER

You live in a period when there's no time to ponder the morals of sexual and social mores. Today, because of AIDS, one of your very basic needs of life—the desire to have sex—has brought on the potential of premature death.

If you're a gay man, you're in one of the highest risk groups for contracting the AIDS virus. If you're a lesbian, even though you're in one of the lowest risk groups, you can still be at high risk if you have sex with a man, a bisexual, a lesbian with AIDS, a hemophiliac, someone who has had major surgery, or a person with a history of drug use. In other words, no matter if you're a gay man or a lesbian and no matter who your partner is, you need to practice safe sex.

Always use a latex condom, dental dam, gloves, or finger cuffs for vaginal, anal, and oral sex. Don't use lambskin condoms because they have very small pores through which the virus can pass; don't use a store-bought plastic wrap because of the possibility of tearing. Avoid transmission of bodily fluids—blood, semen, urine, feces, saliva, and vaginal secretions. And, if you've had a history of multiple partners, get tested today.

◆ Today I'll remember that AIDS is a preventable disease. Its prevention relies upon me, my sexual partner, and our commitment to practicing safe sex.

I have lots of gay friends because there's a lot of homosexuality in the business. The worst thing that's going to happen is people are going to say I'm a lesbian. Who cares?

—CINDY CRAWFORD

Supermodel Cindy Crawford, angry over rumors that alleged she and husband Richard Gere were homosexual, chose to respond to the rumors. She not only expressed a nonhomophobic attitude about homosexuality in the entertainment industry, but also a positive attitude about being labeled a lesbian herself. Her summarizing question, "Who cares?" is often asked today by many others in the industry. But if she had posed such a question in the 1950s, she would have found a lot of people who cared; in fact, she and her husband probably wouldn't have been able to work another day in show business.

Homophobia in the entertainment industry has existed for as long as there have been homosexuals in the industry—in other words, since day one. You simply *knew* some entertainers were gay; you also had your own list of those you "suspected." But where in the past people in the industry didn't come out or even discuss homosexuality, now they do. And many of the people who are most vocal and supportive of gay men and lesbians are heterosexual entertainers.

Today, support the works of those men and women in the entertainment industry who are outspoken in fighting homophobia, supporting boycotts, raising awareness about antigay amendments, and promoting gay and lesbian rights.

◆ I'm indebted to those in the entertainment industry who, through their financial clout and powerful personalities, support my way of life. I'll thank them for the work they've done on my behalf by supporting their work.

I have never met anyone nowadays who admits to having a happy childhood.

—JESSAMYN WEST

No one emerges from the time spent on a childhood battle-field bombed by incest or sexual abuse, ripped apart by emotional abuse, or damaged by the effects of alcoholism and other addictions without scars. When you're a child, it's relatively easy to hide the scars. But as you move through adulthood, it can become harder and harder to ignore the tragic marks imprinted on your body, mind, and spirit.

The gay and lesbian population as a whole suffers greatly from the effects of emotional and sexual abuse and incest; in addition, a high percentage of gay men and lesbians have problems with drugs and alcohol because of the genetic pre-disposition presented by chemical addictions.

The process of healing and recovery from the effects of a dysfunctional childhood is threefold: emotional, physical, and spiritual. Therapy, self-help groups, reading literature, jour-nal writing, and even confronting sexual abusers or dysfunc-tional parents can open the doors in adulthood to a more positive emotional outlook, a greater trust in developing physical intimacy, and a faith that, over time, things *will* get better.

♦ While I'm powerless to change the past, I'm empowered to heal in the present. Today, with the help of a supportive friend or professional, I'll confront a memory from my past so I can recover from it in the present.

> *Sin is a queer thing. It isn't the breaking of divine commandments. It is the breaking of one's own integrity.*
> —D. H. LAWRENCE

You may know of heterosexuals who think of themselves as fine, upstanding, moral people. Perhaps they go to church every Sunday. Maybe they volunteer to help a scout troup. Perhaps they are devoted parents. Or maybe they have a Bible displayed prominently in their home.

But these same people can cheat on their spouses, pad their expense accounts, fudge on their taxes, slap their kids, fondle a trusting child, organize a group to pressure a black family to move out of the neighborhood, and speak out against homosexuality.

When others you know—straight or gay—profess to have a moral code and then repeatedly violate it through dishonesty, deception, immoral acts, and hatred, you eventually lose respect for them. When those same people lose the respect of others, they often end up losing respect for themselves.

Today, be honest about the way you live your life. If you're against adultery, then don't cheat on your partner. If you can't tolerate dishonesty, then be honest in all that you do. If you want to be treated kindly, then do unto others as you would want done to you. Sinning isn't always as blatant or severe as killing someone, committing grand larceny, or selling a country's secrets. Sometimes sinning is merely the breaking of your own integrity.

◆ Today I'll remember that if I don't have integrity, I have nothing. I'll be true to myself so that others can be true to me.

We are your doctors, lawyers, shopkeepers, bus drivers, waiters and florists. But best of all, we look, walk and talk like everyone else. There are many more of us in the closet than out, but it's becoming much easier to be open. . . .

—SIGNED "BOSTON," IN ANN LANDERS

The letter writer, who identified himself as a thirty-two-year-old chairman of a multimillion-dollar high-tech company, felt compelled to write Ann Landers after he attended his first meeting of the Greater Boston Business Council. When he walked into the ballroom of a hotel where the meeting was to take place, he "couldn't believe [his] eyes—more than 200 professional gay men and women. If I hadn't known where I was I would have sworn it was a meeting of the Chamber of Commerce."

Think about what would happen if, for one day, every gay man and lesbian in every profession could identify themselves—without fear of job loss or discrimination. Imagine walking down a city street and seeing bus drivers and cabbies, street cleaners and construction workers, shopkeepers and restaurant personnel, business and professional people, students and professors all wearing pink triangles and smiling. What a sense of unity could come from such a professional outing!

Today, remember that "we are everywhere." Anyone you meet, in any profession, could be a brother or sister!

◆ When another gay man or lesbian has the courage to identify himself or herself to me, then I won't hold back. Today I'll let my professional gay pride show when it's shown to me.

How many cares one loses when one decides not to be something but to be someone.

—Coco Chanel

There's a difference between being gay and being a gay man or a lesbian. When you identify yourself as gay, you're embodying the entire gay and lesbian community, their issues, their politics, their trends, and their activities; in other words, you're identifying with the externals—those things that define who you are as a member of the gay community. But when you identify yourself as a gay man or a lesbian, you're focusing on your issues, your politics, your interests, your activities, your thoughts and feelings; in other words, those things that identify who you are as an individual.

When you strive to be part of the gay and lesbian community, sometimes that means you must put the community's needs above your own or do things that make you feel, behave, or look like you fit in. So you may place a rainbow decal in the back window of your truck or dress in a fashion that's acceptable to a bar you frequent.

But when you strive to be yourself as a gay man or a lesbian, then you're able to put your needs above the community's or do things that make you feel more comfortable with yourself and your way of life. Today, you can be yourself as well as a member of the gay and lesbian community. It's up to you to decide when you'll be a something in the community and a somebody on your own.

♦ Have I been spending too much time trying to fit into the gay community? Today I'll focus some of my time and energy on making decisions and doing things that are right for me, as a gay individual.

Psychological injuries usually take longer than physical injuries to heal.

—Dr. Mark Bloch

You've probably seen an animal that's been abused. Even though it may have long since been removed from the person who abused it, no longer endures painful beatings, and is healed from injuries it received, it will still shy away from you. The hand that you extend to it in friendship and caring and your touch that caresses with gentleness and love are feared. Sometimes time and patience eventually "cure" the threat of abuse, but most often the animal will always react with fear and mistrust to sudden moves, new people, or changes in its environment. The abused animal often can't fully recover from its psychological injury. Such an injury leaves an invisible scar—one that extends across its heart and says, "Don't trust anyone."

After you've been abused in any way as a gay man or a lesbian—verbally, emotionally, or physically—you, too, are left with psychological scars. It can become harder for you to trust walking down the street at night in safety, to enjoy living alone, or to express and receive physical intimacy. When this happens, the whole world—every place you go and every person with whom you interact—can make you feel frightened and mistrustful.

Today, think of at least one person you can trust. Maybe it's a parent or sibling, a neighbor, or someone you've been friends with for years. Remember that when this trusted person extends a hand to you, it's always based on gentleness and love.

◆ Not everyone I meet is going to abuse me. Today I'll try to keep in mind that there are more wonderful, caring people in this world than there are abusive, hate-filled people.

To have no gay teens go through what Richard did would be the best memorial.

— CHRISTOPHER MUTHER

When Christopher Muther appeared before the Massachusetts Health and Human Services Subcommittee of the Governor's Commission on Gay and Lesbian Youth in 1992, he spoke of his friend Richard. Muther said Richard had committed suicide the previous year after suffering repeated taunts from high-school classmates. He was also beaten after he left a public library by two men who hid in his car. "They called him faggot," Muther said, adding that the assailants were never apprehended.

According to a 1989 report of the U.S. Department of Health and Human Services, 30 percent of teen suicides are gay and lesbian youth. The report also concluded that "homosexuals of both sexes are two to six times more likely to attempt suicide than are heterosexuals."

What can you do to help ease this problem? Urge your state governor to call for public hearings throughout your state so gay and lesbian youth, their friends, family members, and teachers have a forum in which to express their particular problems. Suggest that support systems for gay teenagers be established. And recommend to school committees and high-school principals that school curriculums be enhanced to teach tolerance for homosexuality.

◆ Today I'll remember what it felt like to have homosexual feelings when I was a teenager. I'll ask a teacher I know to reach out to a troubled gay teen so the young man or woman doesn't feel alienated.

. . . there was no intent to use [Beauty and the Beast] as a metaphor for AIDS. But you can't deny that Howard's illness had some influence on his work. Certainly when he wrote about a mob mentality ["The Mob Song"], you can't help but think that it's somehow about the way people react to people with HIV.

—BILL LAUCH

When the Disney animation factory fell on its face in the mid-1980s, the known-to-be conservative and heterosexual-family-oriented studio did a very surprising thing. They called upon the help of openly gay lyricist and screenwriter Howard Ashman. Ashman brought in his collaborator and composer Alan Menken, who worked with him on *Little Shop of Horrors*, to help resurrect the Disney magic in *The Little Mermaid*, *Beauty and the Beast*, and *Aladdin*. Ashman's lyrics earned him two "Best Song" Oscars, including the first Academy Award given posthumously to a person with AIDS.

Bill Lauch, Ashman's lover, has praised the wonderful way Disney treated Ashman; the studio was aware of Ashman's homosexuality, his disease, and his life partnership with Lauch. Right before he died, despite being very sick, Ashman was hard at work on three songs in *Aladdin*.

Disney didn't give up on Ashman because of AIDS. Today, don't give up on anyone you know who has AIDS. There's a whole world of wonderful things that are still left for them to do—things that you can share in, too.

♦ Today I'll remember that even though a friend's body is affected by AIDS, his or her mind is still active, alert, and creative. I'll encourage my friend to write poetry, sing songs, play the piano, take pictures, draw or paint—to be creative!

*If people in this community say, "Do you want to play?" they
mean "Do you want to do S/M?" This is the language of childhood, and in some ways, S/M is a grown-up version of playing
cowboys and Indians.*

—KAREN MENDELSOHN

Sexually, men have typically been described as being aggressive, promiscuous, and exclusively genitally focused;
women, on the other hand, have been known for having a
monogamous nature, a desire more for romance than sexual
pleasure, and a need for gentleness in sex.

Gay men and lesbians, however, have challenged such sexual
characterizations. As a gay man, you may not necessarily be
aggressive, you may desire commitment and monogamy, and
you may enjoy hugging and holding hands as much as having an
orgasm. As a lesbian, you may be very sexually active, rank your
sexual needs high above romance in importance, and enjoy
aggressively and freely exploring your sexuality.

S/M has become a big part of the gay and lesbian community;
it not only challenges boundaries in sexual expression, but also
heightens sexual awareness. S/M can be expressed between two
people in various ways, from fantasy role-playing to light spank-
ing to bondage to body piercing. But no matter how it's consen-
sually expressed between two or more people, "playing" is a gay
and lesbian way of saying, "I'm proud of my sexuality, I'm happy
to break out of expected sexual behaviors, and I'm not afraid to
see what turns me on."

◆ Today I'll accept all expressions of my sexuality; there are
no inappropriate or "wrong" ways to seek sexual pleasure
with another consenting adult.

My mom's pretty open about it. She has known for a really long time. And just recently my grandmother read one of the local newspaper articles about the controversy, and she called me up and said congratulations for standing up for my principles as an artist.

—LETITIA HOUSTON

When she was eighteen years old, Letitia Houston sparked a censorship controversy in Los Alamitos, California. As an art student, she had created a five-by-six-foot acrylic painting of two bare-breasted women embracing; she titled it *Loving Another Woman*. She refused to allow her painting, which was about to be exhibited, to be covered with a cloth or to change the name of the painting to *Loving Another Person*. Because of her adamant refusal to compromise her artistic integrity, the school administrators ended up backing down. Her work and title went on public display as the artist intended them.

Have you ever felt that you've compromised your gay integrity with another person, with your family, or with a larger group of people? Why couldn't you refuse to back down? Why did you do what others wanted you to do?

Today, think about how you'd change a past situation if it occurred in the present. What would you do or say this time that would keep you from compromising your gay integrity?

◆ I'm tired of always trying to make everyone else feel more comfortable with my sexuality. Today I'll stand up for myself in one situation or with one person so I can go to bed tonight filled with pride and dignity.

When health is absent, wisdom cannot reveal itself, art cannot manifest, strength cannot fight, wealth becomes useless, and intelligence cannot be applied.

—HEROPHILUS

Think of today as the first day in the process of rebuilding yourself into a healthier person. This can mean quitting smoking or drinking. It can mean resuming an exercise program you abandoned. You can start a diet to lose weight or stick to a diet that will lower your cholesterol and keep your heart healthy. Becoming healthier might mean paying more attention to the amount of sleep you've been getting or the relaxation or meditation time you've been missing. It can mean cutting back on your work time and allowing more time for socializing.

Whatever it is you feel you need to do today to become healthier, today is the time to do it. Even if you're physically weak from disease, illness, or injury, you can still work toward health by developing your spiritual and mental wellness. Join a meditation group for gay men or lesbians, attend a church that welcomes gay men and lesbians, read spiritual literature, listen to meditation tapes, or set aside quiet times during the day in which to talk with a higher power.

True health doesn't involve only outer appearances; it's also about your state of inner healthiness. Good nutrition, plenty of rest, a balance of exercise and relaxation, prayer and meditation time, and a balance between work hours and home hours are all needed for your best health.

♦ Today I'll look at my overall health and identify areas that need improvement. I'll structure my days and nights to include time to be more considerate of my mental, physical, and spiritual health.

I don't care how anyone identifies me as long as I can do my work.

—LILY TOMLIN

How much of an issue do you feel your homosexuality is to what you do for a living? When the Minnesota Senate elected an openly gay legislator as its president, gay men and lesbians were ecstatic that Senator Allan Spear became the nation's highest-ranking openly gay state lawmaker. But Spear's colleagues saw it differently. "It's a nonissue," Senate Majority Leader Roger Moe said. "Senator Spear was elected president of the Senate by virtue of the fact that he is one of the most respected members of the Senate. He is eminently fair."

Would the qualities you have as a worker in your profession be altered in any way by others knowing you're a gay man or a lesbian? Some might respond that your being out would have a positive impact on the gay and lesbian community, like the little girl who knows that there are female physicians, other gay men and lesbians might see you as a positive role model.

But do you feel you'd be a better worker if you were out? It shouldn't matter what the entire gay and lesbian community thinks or how others would benefit; what should matter is how you think and whether or not *you* would benefit.

Today, don't let others talk you into coming out in your profession if you don't feel it's necessary. Ultimately, you're the one who knows what's right for you.

◆ Does it matter whether I'm a lesbian or a gay man in my profession? Today I'll remember that who I am in my career is what is most important.

*. . . you don't get to choose how you're going to die, or
when. You can only decide how you're going to live. Now.*

—JOAN BAEZ

Have you ever asked yourself, "Why did I get sick? What is my
purpose in life now? What am I supposed to be doing now that
I know my time on earth is limited?"

You might first look for answers from other people. Your
life partner may tell you, "Love me as much as you can, for as
long as you can." Your family of origin might suggest that you
move home with them so they can take care of you. Your gay
men and lesbian friends might urge you to spend every day
fighting your disease. A legal counsel may advise you to begin
putting your affairs in order. A spiritual adviser might suggest
that you spend more time talking with and listening to your
higher power.

You might look for answers from others, yet only *you* have
been charged with the awesome responsibility to find out
what it is you need to do from this day on. The enormity of
such a responsibility can be scary, for you may fear that you
might make a wrong decision, waste too much precious time,
or head down an unfulfilling path.

But if you simply look to today and concern yourself with
how you want to live for the next twenty-four hours, then
you might feel less fearful. Give your attention to this day
only and make decisions that will make you feel happy,
healthy, and whole right now.

◆ Today I'll live by the motto "Just for today." So, just for
today, I'll live as well and as fully as I can.

Young children should be taught about the way the world is, and more important, that gay people should be treated with respect and fairness, and not discriminated against or harassed—that is, they should be treated as one more group in the rainbow of humanity, alongside whites, blacks, Hispanics, Asians and so forth.

—JOSEPHINE ROSS

One of the biggest questions being asked of educators today is: Should schools teach students about homosexuality and the lives and achievements of gays, and if so, when and how? There are those who advocate such teaching as a way of combating discrimination against homosexuals and of showing children the way the world really is. There are others who feel that such teaching sends a message of support for homosexuality that they don't agree with. In fact, E. L. Pattullo, former director of the Center for the Behavioral Sciences at Harvard University, comments: "[Some children] might succumb to the temptations of homosexuality in a social climate that was entirely even-handed in its treatment of the two orientations."

Josephine Ross, executive director of Gay and Lesbian Advocates and Defenders in Boston, feels that schools have an obligation to teach the truth: that there have been many gay people throughout history who have significantly contributed to the world today, from Alexander the Great to James Baldwin, and that educators have waited too long to respond to the reality of social structures.

♦ Today I'll urge parents and guardians in my neighborhood and those in the gay and lesbian community who have children to collaborate with educators in teaching the truth to children about the world they live in today.

> *Let your tears come. Let them water your soul.*
>
> —EILEEN MAYHEW

When you were growing up, did you try hard not to cry when you were sick, hurt, frustrated, anxious, fearful, or alone? Did you feel that suppressing tears was a sign of strength—that you were a "big girl" or a "big boy" when you let your feelings roll off your back rather than down your face?

Assuming dominance over your emotions may seem admirable when you're younger, but repression of your true feelings for years can have strange side effects as you get older. For example, in comical moments you may be the only person who's not laughing; in romantic moments you may giggle; in times of sadness you may act nonchalant and uncaring.

Being human means being in touch with your emotions. One of the strongest emotions you may experience as a gay man or lesbian is grief—grief about childhood losses and pain; grief over alienation from friends and family members because of your way of life; grief about the ending of a relationship; grief over the death of a dear friend; grief over exclusion or discrimination because of your sexuality; grief over the loss of a brother or sister to senseless gay bashing. When you try to stop tears of grief, you're suppressing a natural, normal cleansing that has the sole side effect of healing your sadness and pain.

Today, remember that tears are a necessary part of working through the past and accepting the present. So let yourself cry; afterward, you'll always feel more peaceful, clear-headed, and unburdened.

◆ It's not a sign of weakness to cry; in fact, to be able to express sadness without fear is a sign of courage. Today I'll be courageous so I can accept and express all of my emotions.

Constant togetherness is fine—but only for Siamese twins.
—VICTORIA BILLINGS

Fusion in gay and lesbian relationships can be self-destroying. Bonding tightly with one person with little or no time spent apart is a perfect set-up to a love or sex addiction. When you become addicted to a person and then temporarily or permanently part, you can end up as desperate and suffering as an addict without a fix.

When you were growing up, you may have spent hours fantasizing about how wonderful a future gay relationship would be. You may have placed so much hope in coming out and having the perfect relationship that once you met someone, you unconsciously smothered the other person and yourself in constant togetherness. You may have clung desperately to your partner, believing that time spent apart meant your partner didn't love or care for you or signaled the end of the relationship.

Today, think about a relationship in terms of flowers in a garden. Each flower has a separate set of roots, separate stems, leaves, and buds. Although the flowers may be the same variety, each is different in a subtle way. Similarly, you need to grow with a partner like two separate flowers sharing the same garden. Your roots may intertwine and your leaves touch, yet you can still grow and flourish separately from one another.

◆ Today I'll look ahead at the week and the weekend and decide what time I'd like to set aside to spend with a lover, what time I'd like to set aside to spend with friends or family members, and what time I'd like to set aside to spend just with myself.

When you have become willing to hide nothing, you will not only be willing to enter into communion but will also understand peace and joy.

—Anonymous

Do you keep secrets? Maybe you haven't told your partner about a painful childhood secret. Perhaps you've been seeing someone outside your relationship. Maybe you haven't told family members that you're gay. Perhaps you know something that you're not telling your best friend. Or perhaps you're keeping to yourself the results of a medical test.

Keeping secrets is synonymous with staying stuck. Your secrets burden you and stifle your true feelings, your ability to communicate openly and honestly, your growth as a human being, and your potential for growth in your interactions with others.

The choice to shield your inner self from others is most often based on uncertainty about the outcome, the fear that if and when you do share a secret, you'll be betrayed, rejected, abandoned, or lose something or someone dear to you. But the gifts of total honesty and openness are greater closeness, deeper intimacy, and the development of trust. These are gifts that make possible a level of friendship that dispels self-doubts, a level of family interactions that can bolster self-esteem, and a level of loving that can earn self-respect and self-love. While releasing a secret takes strength, today take that risk. Through release comes relief from the incredible burden of holding on to a secret.

◆ I may be tempted to keep a secret today. But today I'll remember that allowing another to really know me by sharing a secret means that together we'll have greater opportunities for growth and happiness.

This womb is my womb/ It is not your womb/ And there is no womb/ For Randell Terry. . . .

> —SUNG TO THE TUNE OF "THIS LAND IS YOUR LAND"
> BY CHURCH LADIES FOR CHOICE

The Church Ladies for Choice is a fifteen-member, New York–based gay male performance activist group that takes their role as "the USO for women's-health activism" quite seriously. The Ladies have appeared in front of abortion clinics in Manhattan, Queens, Brooklyn, Buffalo, and Dobbs Ferry, N.Y., as well as at related demonstrations at the 1992 Democratic National Convention and in Washington, D.C. Although some in the gay and lesbian community, as well as in the straight community, have criticized the ladies as mocking serious female health issues, member Lady Harmony Moore says, "As men, we wait for the women who lead this movement to tell us what to do."

For gay men to spend their time and energy in supporting women's health rights at clinic defenses, marches, rallies, and benefits shows that there's an interest in supporting a cause that's not only outside their own community, but also in no way directly affects them as gay men. It also suggests that there can be similar support in the lesbian community.

Today, think about a men's or women's issue you could support that doesn't directly affect your community or yourself as a gay man or lesbian. Offer your time and energy as an individual, or organize group support within your community.

♦ I can create the hope of a better world today for men or women by promoting an interest in an issue that affects them. Today I'll offer protection, advice, creative energy, or emotional support to members of the opposite sex.

> *And it really humbled me to see this old man, possibly old*
> *enough to be my grandfather, cry just because he had met me.*
> —SERGEANT LEONARD P. MATLOVICH

When Sergeant Leonard P. Matlovich was discharged from
the air force in 1978 after disclosing his homosexuality, he
became a powerful role model for homosexuals who had
served before him in the military and those who continued to
serve—as well as those who would join—after his coming
out. Matlovich's exemplary service record as well as his
engaging demeanor captured the fancy of the media, who
closely followed his legal battle with the military. His picture,
which graced the cover of *Time* magazine, had the words I AM
A HOMOSEXUAL printed across his chest. Matlovich battled with
the military for five years; in the end, he accepted $160,000
and a retroactive promotion to the rank of captain. When he
later died of complications related to AIDS, he was buried in
the Congressional Cemetery.

Today an estimated 200,000 gay men and lesbians serve in
the United States armed forces, quietly doing a professional
job that puts their country's peace and freedom first. This
Memorial Day, think of those who have chosen a career in the
military—one that takes away their personal freedom to be
who they are so they can help you live with the freedom to be
who you want to be.

♦ Today I'll attend my community's Memorial Day parade,
read a local honor roll with the names of deceased service
men and women, place my country's flag on the grave of a
war hero, or write or call a friend in the military.

JUNE 1

You know, I grew up expecting to fall in love, to mate for life and to raise a family. Just because it was a man I fell in love with doesn't mean I have to change that.

—TIM FISHER

When Tim Fisher turned thirty several years ago, his "biological clock" began to sound loudly. So he and his lover ran an ad in the local paper that read: "Long-term gay couple want to be dads. If you have any interest in or knowledge of adoption or surrogacy, please contact us." A woman contacted them and, after being artificially inseminated with Fisher's sperm, gave birth to Katherine Anne Fisher Davenport. A different surrogate mother later gave birth to the couple's second child, Cameron Frederic Fisher Davenport.

Gay and lesbian parenting can be seen as evidence of maturation within the gay and lesbian community— maturation that comes from the desire of more and more gay men and lesbians to have fewer short-term affairs and more long-term, family-style relationships. Same-sex parenting may also be a result of the impact AIDS has made on the gay and lesbian way of life. Or it can be seen as a reflection of a broader achievement of the gay rights movement: that of self-acceptance.

Think about how you— within the evolving gay and lesbian community—have accepted parenting for yourself or for others in your community. Today, you may be able to recognize yourself as legitimate not only as a gay person, but also a gay parent.

♦ Today I'll recognize and applaud the many gay men and lesbians in the past and in the present who are claiming their birthright to be parents and to form families.

JUNE 2

We hate others when we hate ourselves. We are tolerant towards others when we tolerate ourselves. We forgive others when we forgive ourselves. It is not love of self but hatred of self which is at the root of the troubles that afflict our world.

—ERIC HOFFER

Do you ever tell yourself, "I'll feel much better about myself when . . . I lose twenty pounds, meet someone nice, change my job, come out to my family, get out of my relationship, begin exercising, feel more comfortable with my sexuality?"

Setting such conditions implies that you're not a good person yet or that you'll only be a good person once you meet certain criteria. But is that the way you approach loving other people, by setting conditions that need to be met before you allow yourself to feel love for them?

Unconditional love is accepting everything about yourself or someone else without any reservations, conditions, or criteria. While this may be easier to do with someone else, you can learn how to love yourself unconditionally. One way to do so is to stand in front of a full-length mirror, with or without clothing, and look at your face and body. Some parts you may like to look at; some you may not. But stay focused. Fight the urge to look away. Then say aloud, "Whatever my defects or imperfections, I accept myself and love myself for who I am in the present moment." Say this over and over again for two minutes every morning and every night for a week; over time, you'll begin to love yourself just the way you are.

◆ Today I'll treat myself as I would treat someone with whom I was madly in love. I'll pay attention to how I feel and to the thoughts I'm thinking, and I'll do special things to make me feel good.

I'm glad that gay people are so free with their words, and they're not hiding. . . . If I were gay, I wouldn't want to have to hold it in.

—MARKY MARK

Noncommunication is one of the most unhealthy forms of communication. It can be based on anger—for example, using the defiant "silent treatment" as a weapon or form of punishment with an intimate partner. Or it can be used to protect someone—for example, refusing to reveal the secret of your sexuality to your parents to keep from hurting them or causing them unhappiness.

But noncommunication is neither a protector nor a healthy outlet for anger. In reality, noncommunication prevents you from relating to other people by preventing the act of talking about feelings that's so critical to communication. Noncommunication consciously excludes one person's input from decision making, processing, or sharing; as a result, relationships with a noncommunicator are often based upon tension, resentment, and built-up frustrations.

How can you learn to be more open and forthcoming? Since communicating with others means telling them, through words, who you are and how you feel, you need to eliminate negative thoughts that prevent you from speaking. Don't think, "I shouldn't be feeling this way," or "My parents may be hurt by what I have to say." Think instead, "I accept the feelings I have and will verbalize them so others can get to know me."

◆ Today I'll keep in mind that the goal for healthy communication is to be aware of what I'm feeling and to share this feeling with others.

J U N E 4

We need to discuss these issues before we're sick. But, realisti-
cally speaking, it's when someone gets sick that it really creates
what I call "the teachable moment," the prime opportunity to
share feelings and attitudes about death.

—JOAN McGIVER GIBSON

Do you talk about death? While you may not like to talk about
death at all, concerns such as AIDS, cancer, and aging in a
long-term relationship have made dying an issue that affects
you, your partner, and your friends in the gay and lesbian
community. Right now, the opportunity to talk about death is
greater than ever before.

If you're exploring the scenario of your own death or the
death of a loved one, you need to discuss health-care alternatives, living wills and durable power of attorney, and the
goals of medical treatment. For example, what kind of life-
sustaining care do you want if you're unable to make or
express such decisions? What will be the goals of your medical
treatment: relief from pain, prolonging life, or remaining
independent? Would you prefer to die at home or in a hospital?

Today, start to explore such options as a living will or a
durable power of attorney for health care. Appoint an attorney to help you work on a will that would recognize the
people who have been important to you in life. If you take
care of such business while you're alive, it can ease your pain
and suffering at the end.

♦ Today I'll keep in mind that while I don't have to decide
on every last clinical procedure in the event of my illness, I
can begin to talk about my views on health care that are
important to me.

*If you removed all of the homosexuals and homosexual influ-
ence from what is generally regarded as American culture, you
would be pretty much left with* Let's Make a Deal.
—FRAN LEBOWITZ

Think for a moment what the required reading for a college
literature course would look like without the literature created by gay men and lesbians. Think about what the fashion
industry would be like without the influence of gay male and
lesbian designers. Think about all the gay men and lesbians in
the creative arts—theater, music, painting, sculpture,
dance—and then consider the impact gay men and lesbians
have had in the sciences, politics, inventions and explora-
tions, sports, medicine, and history. How would each of
these fields be affected if the influence of gay men and lesbians
had never been felt?

Those gay men and lesbians who have struggled against
public outcry and discrimination because of their sexuality
and then gone on to achieve success and recognition in their
areas of expertise are sources of inspiration for all gay men
and lesbians. Without such role models, you might feel that
there was no greatness in being gay.

You, too, can have an impact on the world of American
culture. Today, support a gay and lesbian history project,
urge a school in your community to include gay men and
lesbians throughout history in its curriculum, or begin your
own collection at home of works by gay men and lesbians.

♦ Today I'll educate myself about gay culture. I'll focus on
an area in the creative arts, history and invention, or the
sciences and explore the impact gay men and lesbians have
made in it.

JUNE 6

I feel we have picked each other from the crowd as fellow-travelers,
for neither of us is to the other's personality the end-all and the be-all.

— JOANNA FIELD

It's not by mere chance that you gravitate toward certain gay men and lesbians who become your friends during particular times in your life. When you were younger, you may have hung out with a crowd that partied heavily on weekends, closed down bars, and did some pretty wild and crazy things together. When you were at college or graduate school, you may have become close with your suite mates or a study group. When you left home to live on your own, you may have become friends with housemates or coworkers.

As you think about the people who are your friends today, you may discover that some you've known since you were young while some you've only known for a short time. That's because over time, as you matured and your interests changed, you probably made friends with those you met while pursuing activities that interested you—camping, softball, traveling, playing bridge, discussing books, or organizing a neighborhood potluck.

Each of the friends in your life—including the ones who are no longer your friends—have played an important role in helping you become who you are today. That's because every day you're on a journey in your life, and much of what you have to learn is from those you have gathered around you. Each of your friends is a valuable teacher.

◆ Today I won't discount the value of any friend in my life, no matter how long I've known this person or what kinds of experiences we've shared together. My journey with *any* friend will always be a process of enlightenment.

The younger generation is not as intimidated as earlier generations were in acknowledging who they are. Every school is going to have to deal with this. The question is whether this will be a productive or a painful process.

— KEVIN JENNINGS

A recent report by the National Gay and Lesbian Task Force found that 45 percent of gay males and 25 percent of lesbians nationally had been victims of verbal or physical assaults in high school. The cruelty that gay and lesbian students suffer can be so severe that it forces many to drop out of school; for those who stay in school, the constant jeers of classmates can create the kind of stress that affects academic work and batters self-esteem.

But there are things you can do to help foster greater tolerance for young gay men and lesbians in schools. Target your city's high school, the high school attended by a young gay man or lesbian you know, or a high school that has received press for being intolerant. Supply the school with positive literature on the gay and lesbian community. Speak to the school's principal about sensitivity training for school staff. Offer to provide an informative lecture at a student-parent night or parent-teacher meeting.

Then focus your efforts outside the school. Write letters to the city's newspapers about the need to infuse school curricula with gay and lesbian issues. And inform city politicians that you, as a citizen, will not support their reelection if they continue to allow gay students to be harassed.

◆ Today I'll show how strongly I feel about the protection of gay and lesbian youth from harassment by providing support for those students individually, within their community, and within the school system.

It's really a lot less complicated than we usually think. Life is playfulness. Children know this. That's why they spend so much of their time playing. They are aware of wonder. Adults often need help remembering how to play. We need to play so that we can rediscover the magic all around us.

—FLORA COLAO

Have you felt overwhelmed lately by personal hardships? Perhaps coming to terms with your sexuality has been a difficult process for you. Maybe you've lost a life partner to AIDS or are yourself battling the disease. Perhaps you've been verbally, physically, or sexually assaulted by a loved one or by a homophobic member of society. Maybe life just seems a bit complicated today, with bills to pay, obligations you dread, or the lonely ache of being single.

This is the time to call upon the child within you—the child who has always been able to work through times of difficulty. As a child growing up in a dysfunctional home, you could lie on a field of soft grass on a summer's afternoon, look up at the sky, and see all sorts of wonderful shapes in the clouds. Or you could deal with the first stirrings of a sexuality you knew would alienate you from others by picking a black-eyed Susan and plucking the petals off, one at a time, to determine whether that special person might someday love you.

Today, find the opportunities within your difficulties by asking your inner child, "As hard as today's lesson may be, what can I learn from it?"

◆ Today I'll be thankful for the child within me—a spirit who can help me look at my world through eyes of innocence, wonder, and playfulness. How can I apply each of these visions to something in my life that has me down?

One of the ways in which homophobia is expressed is in the idea that being gay is a sort of wilful perversion or chosen lifestyle, something that you're doing almost to flout the norms of society, rather than as a response to your own nature.

—SIMON LEVAY

When you've come out to friends, family members, or others, have you ever received such responses as: "You're only doing this to get back at us," "If you really don't want to marry me, you can just say so," or "You were always a rebel—someone who wanted to walk against the wind." The belief that you've chosen to be a gay man or a lesbian to make a statement, to retaliate, or for some other reason can lead others to believe that being gay is a temporary condition—just a phase you're going through.

That's why coming out to others should be done in a way that leaves no doubt in anyone's mind that your sexuality is a permanent part of your nature. So never come out when you're in a heated argument or feeling pressured to "confess." Don't try to soften the reality of your way of life to spare someone hurt by suggesting that things might change over time. And don't come out at the same time that you're also introducing your life partner; there's simply too much to process at one time. Keep coming out simple, make your reasons for coming out honest, and show that coming out is not only what you want, but also what makes you happy.

♦ Today I'll remember that how I come out to others will show how I feel about my sexuality. Do I want them to see that I'm ashamed or that I'm proud?

When I'm watching a performance, I want to feel anger, I want to have tears, and I want to laugh uproariously. . . . And we do it. We do it every night.

—DONALD MONTWILL

When Valencia Rose, a cabaret at the edge of San Francisco's Mission district, opened in 1982, it showcased something new and completely different: gay and lesbian comedy and talent. Today, Josie's Cabaret and Juice Joint, Valencia Rose's daughter club in the heart of the Castro district, has helped launch the careers of scores of gay and lesbian performers. The growing alternative performance circuit has signaled the emergence of more and more gay, lesbian, and bisexual comics, who are putting together "out" performances that satirize the gay and lesbian community. People such as 1960s burlesque performer Michael Greer, along with Charles Pierce and Wayland Flowers, and mid-to-late 1970s talent like Robin Tyler, Lynn Lavner, Kate Clinton, and Karen Ripley have paved the way for countless young, out comedians today.

As a gay man or lesbian, you need to be able to laugh at the absurdities and conventions of your way of life. And who knows them better than other gay men and lesbians? As performer Marga Gomez once defined the gay-humor ethic: "You can't make fun of any group you don't belong to." Today, support humor in the gay and lesbian community by purchasing gay and lesbian greeting cards and comics and attending shows by gay and lesbian performers.

♦ Today I'll reject straight comedians who make gay men and lesbians the butt of their jokes. Instead, I'll support "out" performers who can laugh at gay men and lesbians because that's who *they* are.

We tend to think of the erotic as an easy, tantalizing sexual arousal. I speak of the erotic as the deepest life force, a force which moves us toward living in a fundamental way.

—AUDRE LORDE

Writer Audre Lorde, who died of breast cancer after a fourteen-year battle, was one of the gay and lesbian community's most fervent spokeswomen. She often called herself "a black lesbian feminist warrior poet"; her commitment, in her life and her work, was for people to recognize and understand their differences. In fact, she was insistent that people realize the differences race and sexuality make.

In what ways are you different from others? Begin with your sexuality and the fact that you're a gay man or a lesbian. Next consider your race, nationality, religious beliefs, educational background, and politics. Then explore your abilities and interests—perhaps you're a lesbian who's into body building or a gay man who's very good with children. Continue by examining your personal goals and dreams of the future; consider also your sexual fantasies and the types of lovemaking you enjoy.

After you've identified all the ways in which you're different from those in the straight community as well as in the gay and lesbian community, string those differences together to create one broad statement that describes you, just as Audre Lorde did. Then, like Audre Lorde, be "unapologetic and strong" about your differences.

♦ Just because I'm the same as everyone else under my skin doesn't mean that I'm just like everyone else. Today I can celebrate my differences and continue to be courageous in recognizing such differences.

Our ordinary mind always tries to persuade us that we are nothing but acorns and that our greatest happiness will be to become bigger, fatter, shinier acorns; but that is of interest only to pigs. Our faith gives us knowledge of something much better: that we can become oak trees.

—E. F. SCHUMACHER

You may struggle at times with a sense of worthlessness and helplessness created by negative feelings about your sexuality. Sometimes this sense of not being as good as everyone else or feeling powerless to change who you are can lead you into self-destructive behaviors—drinking, taking drugs, overeating, etc. Sometimes it can be accompanied by self-pity— "I'm no good because I'm gay." You might believe that if you could live up to what others expect of you or be who others want you to be, it might be easier to accept yourself. So you might think, "If I met a lover my friends liked, maybe I'd be happy," or "If I don't tell my parents I'm gay, maybe they'll love me."

The truth is, however, that only you have the power to transform such feelings. Instead of feeling like an acorn lying helplessly on the ground, waiting to be eaten by a pig, empower yourself. Plant yourself firmly in the ground and say, "I can protect myself from my feelings of worthlessness and powerlessness. I am who I am, no matter what others think or how they feel about me. Today, it's up to me to feel better about me."

◆ Today I'll choose to grow from my lack of acceptance rather than hope that somehow, some way, someday, I'll feel better about me. The time to feel better is *now*.

With knowing comes responsibility;
With responsibility comes choice;
With choice comes the future.

— ANONYMOUS

Once you know you're gay, you have a responsibility to address that fact. You're not only obligated to do this in order to create a positive, fulfilling life for yourself, but also because, at some point in the future, family members and friends will need to know who you are and what's going on in your life.

But are you avoiding taking such responsibility today through a variety of ruses? Perhaps you're continuing to maintain the extra room in your house or apartment as your "roommate's" bedroom. Maybe you keep your gay and lesbian literature hidden. Perhaps you respond to questions about your sexuality by making up stories or changing the subject. Maybe you avoid hanging around with gay men or lesbians who are more out than you are so you're not "guilty by association." Or you may even be telling yourself, "Sure, I have sex with men/women, *but I'm not gay!*"

Maybe you're not taking responsibility for your sexuality because you don't accept it. Maybe it frightens you. Maybe you don't believe you can handle living as a gay man or lesbian.

But, just for today, try to deal with being gay. For the next twenty-four hours, allow yourself to be gay. It may be easier to be gay in the present than think what it means for the future.

♦ Today I'll strive to know myself in a way that opens doors rather than closes them. Let me feel what it's like to simply be me right now; I'll deal with tomorrow when tomorrow comes.

It doesn't matter who my father was; it matters who I remember he was.

—ANNE SEXTON

The childhood memories you have of your father may be filled with joy, sorrow, happiness, or pain. The child within you may still be yearning to form a connection with him—a connection in which he accepts you and your way of life as well as shares in your joys and growth. You may feel cheated out of such a relationship with him while you were growing up because of his lack of acceptance of who you are, his dysfunctional behavior, his estrangement from you through divorce or remarriage, or his death.

A loving, healthy, accepting father is a great blessing. You may not have had such a blessing while you were growing up. But instead of thinking about your father with anger, frustration, bitterness, or disappointment, you need to believe today that your father has always been there as much as he could be. When you were growing up, he had to deal with his own imperfections and challenges at the same time as he was trying to be your father; today he may have the same issues to deal with as well as new ones.

This Father's Day, try to look back and remember at least three good things about your connection with your father when you were growing up. By looking at the good, you'll be able to see that there have always been some positive ways you connected with your father.

◆ Today I need to see my father as another human being who's sharing my path in life. Can I see the good in him and the positive ways in which we have connected from time to time?

J U N E 1 5

*"I'm gay," Philip Benjamin blurts out to his parents. "I just
didn't think it was fair for you not to know such an important part
of my life."*

*His mother responds, "Keeping certain secrets secret is impor-
tant to the general balance of life."*

—DAVID LEAVITT

Which secrets do you feel are necessary to keep? Perhaps
there's something you know about a best friend's lover that's
best not told. Maybe an opinion you have about the unflatter-
ing clothing or appearance of others is best not shared. Perhaps your job requires keeping government, military, or new
product secrets. Maybe a skeleton in your family's closet is
best left where it is.

David Leavitt's book *The Lost Language of Cranes* deals with
the emotional impact on a family who keeps secrets and then
reveals them. When Philip Benjamin tells his mother and
father about the secret of his sexuality, his father must then
deal with his own secret homosexuality. To the mother who's
trying to hold her failing marriage together, her son's revelation is a disruption to the already fragile family balance she's
trying to maintain.

While you may feel that some secrets need to be kept—those
that maintain national security or trade secrets or those that
don't inflict unnecessary hurt—some need to be revealed: those
that build walls or maintain silences between loved ones or
deceive them. Today, reveal a secret in order to help someone
better understand who you are or get to know you better.

◆ Why do I choose to hold on to a secret? Today I'll divulge
a secret to someone I trust so I can remove the power this
secret has over me, my life, my interactions with this person.

Friendship improves happiness, and abates misery, by doubling our joy, and dividing our grief.

—JOSEPH ADDISON

Sometimes you may equate loneliness with being gay. If you're living in a small, rural location, you may feel as if you're the only gay man or lesbian within a hundred-mile vicinity. If you're living at home, you may have to deal with isolating restrictions and limitations. If you're living in a city, you may find that a lively nightlife spent in crowds of people only makes you feel lonelier. Even if you're in a relationship, you may feel content with your partner but ache to interact with others outside your relationship.

There's no question that you feel better and your life becomes much richer when you have friends who share your joys and troubles. But you're not going to meet and make friends unless you're first willing to admit that you're lonely and want to do something about it. Those gay men and lesbians who have overcome loneliness have done so when they made a real effort to reach out to others, no matter where they were living or whether they were single or in a relationship.

Breaking isolation means participating in activities that involve being around people. Today, join a gay or lesbian book discussion group, an athletic team, or a social or professional group in your community. Put out your hand, and you'll soon find you're holding another.

◆ Today I know that loneliness is avoidable and treatable—as long as I'm willing to do something about it. It's only when I reach out to others that I can allow them to reach out to me as well.

Free will is not the liberty to do whatever one likes, but the power of doing whatever one sees ought to be done, even in the very face of otherwise overwhelming impulse.

—GEORGE MACDONALD

There are certain things you can't do because you're a gay man or a lesbian. Depending on the laws in your state, you may or may not be entitled to fair housing or employment regardless of your sexuality. Depending on the policies in your place of employment, you and your life partner may or may not be covered by health care or family leave. Depending on safety concerns where you live, you may or may not feel comfortable walking down the street holding hands with your lover or displaying political stickers on your vehicle.

Free will doesn't mean that you can do anything you please, regardless of legal, moral, or safety issues. Rather, free will means doing things like making changes that will benefit not only you as a gay man or lesbian, but also the entire gay and lesbian community. With free will, you have the choice to put your time and energy into helping overturn court decisions against gays, organizing successful boycotts, enlightening the public about issues that affect gay men and lesbians, writing government officials to urge passage of legislation to benefit gay men and lesbians, and working hard to protect the freedom of all gay men and lesbians.

◆ Today I'll use free will to make changes or improvements in areas that restrict my freedom to live as a gay man or lesbian. Rather than fight existing legal or moral boundaries, I'll seek ways to broaden them.

JUNE 18

Nothing happens that God doesn't have a reason for. . . . He tries to reach down and shake us out of our ignorance. I know He made me crippled for a reason. He wants me to learn something. It may be patience or it may be forbearance or it may be how to dress without standing up. He doesn't tell you what it is, you just have to learn it.
— RUTH IN *MARVIN'S ROOM* BY SCOTT MCPHERSON

When playwright Scott McPherson died in 1993 from AIDS-related complications at the age of thirty-four, he left behind the smiles and sorrows of his life, as captured in two important plays. His first play, *'Til the Fat Lady Sings,* was based on the death of his twenty-one-year-old brother, Bret, who was killed in a motorcycle accident. *Marvin's Room,* which completed a run of 214 performances Off-Broadway and won six awards, was written while his lover, Daniel Sotomayer, was dying of AIDS. Funny, motivated, clear-thinking, articulate, and positive were some of the adjectives used to describe McPherson, who learned how to endure the sorrows in his young life and live with AIDS.

Today, as you or others you know live with AIDS, think of the adjectives that would best describe who you are and they are. Do the adjectives lean more toward the positive than the negative?

Today, you can hold death at a standstill by learning and growing from what God has given you. Fight hard and keep your spirits up. Do this for yourself, and for those who care about you.

♦ I know that I'm not the only one who's fighting the battle with AIDS. I'll try to limit my self-centered depression and self-pity and work hard instead to see the positive, enjoyable, and humorous things in my life today.

It's thrilling to know that there are people out there who would happily kill me because of my sexual orientation. I am delighted that the government discriminates against me at tax time and I can't file jointly. I'm ecstatic that I'm barred from serving my country in time of war. I'm overjoyed that all major religions reject my lifestyle. I love it that I could lose my job if the truth were known. Best of all, it's great to be viewed as an outcast by one's own family. This is what it means to be gay.

—"LEXINGTON, KY," IN A LETTER TO ANN LANDERS

What does it mean to you to be a gay man or lesbian in your country today? Are you more focused on the drawbacks to living a gay way of life, or are you able to see benefits to being gay?

Some people would look back to the 1940s, '50s, or '60s and say, "Look at how far we've come as gay men and lesbians! There are more bars, meeting places, and social and political organizations. There are PRIDE marches, openly gay men and lesbians in visible positions of power."

Others might say, "But look at how violence against gay men and lesbians has risen, how gays are portrayed in the media, how difficult it is for young people to come out, and how far there is still left to go in attaining gay civil rights."

Today, in a journal or discussion with other gay men and lesbians, respond to the views expressed by the letter writer from Kentucky. In what ways do you agree or disagree with what the writer had to say?

♦ "This is what it means to be gay . . ." is how I'll begin exploring my own views about being a gay man or lesbian today.

The most important reason to address the issue [of homosexuality] with children is that 10 percent of them are or will be gay. They need to know that being gay or lesbian is a part of who some people are. The kids know that I'm gay. But they also know lots of other things about me.

—NANCY ALACH

The Cambridge (Massachusetts) Friends School, a well-respected Quaker elementary school, has asked parents of the children who attend the school to sign a statement that reads, in part: "Our children live in a world where racism, sexism, classism, heterosexism, and other forms of discrimination exist; as a community of faith, we are challenged to empower them to change that world."

Part of changing the world involves doing what after-school director Nancy Alach has done—she has shown students, teachers, school administrators, and parents that she's not only an "out lesbian teacher," but other things as well.

You, too, are not only a gay man or a lesbian, but also a lover, a friend, a son or daughter, a sister or brother, a niece or nephew, a cousin, a grandson or granddaughter; you may also be a father or mother and an aunt or uncle. Additionally, you're defined by your profession, the things you like to do, the country in which you were born, your ethnic heritage, your religious beliefs, and your political alignment.

Today, don't think of yourself just in terms of being a gay man or a lesbian, but all "the people" you are.

◆ Life is made up of diversity. Today I'll display such diversity by showing how many different parts of me I embrace on a daily basis.

JUNE 21

When you feel you can communicate only with other entities in physical bodies, you have cut yourself off from a powerful source of inner guidance.

——BARTHOLOMEW

When was the last time you were emotionally and spiritually close to another person—not through sex, but through some other experience? Perhaps you snuggled with a loved one while watching a favorite video, talked for hours while lying in bed together, took a bath in a warm, candelit bathroom, prayed together, or attended church.

While having sex can leave you feeling peaceful, relaxed, and serene, so can spending quality emotional and spiritual time with someone. Quality time can involve sharing your thoughts and feelings and then listening to the thoughts and feelings of another, providing a comforting hug or holding each other close throughout the night, listening to a soothing meditation tape together, or taking turns reading aloud from a daily meditation book.

Although it's your sexual preference that determines your sexuality, it's your heart, your head, and your spirit that actually express and show love for another gay man or lesbian. Today, think about ways you and your partner can balance your expression of sexual passion with experiences that allow for emotional and spiritual passion. Set aside time this week in which you can be together to talk freely and openly or explore ways you can meditate or worship together as a couple.

◆ With an open mind and an open heart, my partner and I can learn more about each other than what physically turns us on. Today I'll discover my partner's emotional and spiritual turn-ons, and I'll let my partner know mine.

The pink triangle, like the Christian cross, was founded on "man's inhumanity to man," and they both have transcended themselves to become images of love.

—RON MEYERS

The pink triangle was created by Adolf Hitler, who marked homosexuals for especially cruel treatment in Nazi concentration camps during World War II. In only fifty years since that time, the pink triangle has evolved from a feared symbol of one of the world's most horrifying atrocities against human beings to a symbol of gay and lesbian pride.

Sometimes it may be difficult to understand what gay pride really is and how it can manifest itself in your life. When you have to live each day with homophobia, read in newspapers and magazines about the atrocities still being committed against gay men and lesbians, experience discrimination on the job, see in your parents' eyes pain and confusion, and keep much of your life hidden from the public eye, it can be difficult to feel pride as a gay man or lesbian.

Yet it's pride that can help you transcend such difficulties and make you feel important, worthwhile, respected, and accepted. Today, don't let the negative responses, unfair practices, violent and abusive behaviors, and lack of acceptance influence how you feel about yourself and your sexuality. Let what makes you happy and what feels right to you also make you proud. Feel the symbolic meaning of the pink triangle in your heart.

♦ Today I'll view the pink triangle no longer as a symbol of elimination of gay men and lesbians, but of proud assimilation of gay men and lesbians into society.

JUNE 23

I thought I was the only abused child in the world, just as I thought I was the only lesbian in the world. Discovering that there were others who'd gone through similar experiences was one of the things that helped to save my life.

—DOROTHY ALLISON

Most of Dorothy Allison's book *Bastard Out of Carolina* is based on her experiences growing up in Greenville, South Carolina. Like the novel's young protagonist, she was born to a fifteen-year-old unwed mother. And Allison, too, was the victim of a sexually abusive stepfather. But it wasn't until she went to a consciousness-raising group after completing college and heard another woman talk about the physical abuse she had endured as a young girl that Allison felt she could begin to deal with her past.

You, too, may have had a dysfunctional childhood in which you felt you were the only one who ever had to endure the effects of incest, abuse, alcoholism, divorce, adoption, chronic illness, and the death of a sibling or parent. But today, as an adult, you have a multitude of options available for you to deal with the past. Twelve-step and other support groups, self-help literature, workshops, treatment and recovery centers, individual- and group-therapy options, and guided meditation audio cassettes can all be used today to help you confront the pain and hurt of the past. In so doing, you can learn how finally to put the past to rest.

◆ To deal with some of the darkest conflicts of my past is one way to enlighten my life in the present. Today I'll use one tool of healing and recovery to help me confront difficult childhood memories.

JUNE 24

I will not let this nightmare stop me. Since I have been incarcerated, I have learned to not let a dream be destroyed by a fall. . . . I want to work with people who have problems. There are so many things that can be prevented if we take the time to find out what goes on in the minds of people, to hear their cry for help.
—DEBRA DENISE REID

When Debra Denise Reid told her lover, Jacqueline Gary, that she was leaving her on August 12, 1989, Gary did what she had always done when she didn't approve of something Reid did or said: she began to physically abuse her. But that night, Reid grabbed a kitchen knife and stabbed her lesbian lover to death.

Today Reid is serving nine to fourteen years at MCI-Lancaster, Massachusetts, minimum-security prison for manslaughter. Even though psychologists and specialists have diagnosed her as a classic battered woman, no legally acceptable data has yet been produced that shows that her actions, as a lesbian, can be considered in the same way as those of a victim of male-female battering.

Reid is just one of many gay people who are incarcerated and must struggle within a system that further alienates them because of their sexuality. While in prison, many gay men and lesbians endure further abuse and are cut off from the support of the gay and lesbian community.

Today, reach out to an incarcerated brother and sister. Become a pen pal or provide back issues of gay publications to a prison facility.

◆ I won't let gay men and lesbians behind bars feel they're forgotten by their community. I'll become a support to at least one prisoner and provide him or her with news about the gay and lesbian community.

JUNE 25

Whatever course you decide upon, there is always someone to tell you you are wrong. There are always difficulties arising which tempt you to believe that your critics are right. To map out a course of action and follow it to an end requires . . . courage.
—RALPH WALDO EMERSON

When you were in your first gay relationship, you might have wanted to shout your happiness from the rooftops. You might have felt as if you had finally found what you were looking for—something that made you feel "right," something that made you feel as if you finally fit in. But then, when you came out to a close friend or family member and shared your happiness, you might have been deflated with comments such as, "You're in for a long, hard road," "Why would you ever want to choose such a difficult way of life?" or "I'm sure you'll come to your senses after you see how tough being gay is."

But now, years later, you're still gay. While being a gay man or lesbian hasn't always been easy, you haven't deviated from your heart's desire. What has made you so committed to being a gay man or a lesbian when you must often face, on a daily basis, criticism, discrimination, harassment, abuse, or rejection?

Perhaps it's because being a gay man or lesbian makes you feel like you belong. Like a hand that fits into a glove, a sock that fits into a shoe, or a ring that slips onto a finger, living life as a gay person has become the *only way* you know how to live.

◆ Today I'll be grateful for the courage it took for me to be gay, even though it's never been totally easy. I know now that I belong with other gay men and lesbians, and I never want to lose that desire.

JUNE 26

The gay parade is a jubilant expression of pride. Its primary function is to make the enigmatic notion of community a tangible force that cannot be ignored.

—NICOLE EISENMAN

If you took apart the gay PRIDE parade bit by bit, separating it into all the different floats and organizations that march in it, what you'd find are numerous bars and social groups, representatives from different professions, cross dressers and drag queens, butches and femmes, country-western dancers as well as those who love a funky beat, straight parents of gay men and lesbians as well as gay and lesbian parents, children, gay youth, religious organizations, a large contingent of those who are clean and sober, motorcyclists and leather and S/M factions, physically challenged gay men and women, those who are politically conscious, representatives from health services, activist groups, and city gays as well as suburban gays.

The proponents of the parade are enormously varied and the motivations to march are infinitely diverse. But for one day out of 365, gay and lesbian ideologies crisscross. Consensus is established in the challenge the parade presents to those who are gay as well as to those who are straight. And this challenge is: "Gay men and lesbians are here. We are valid. We are real. *Deal with us.*"

This year, go to a gay PRIDE march in a nearby city or travel to one in another state. Be part of the celebration of gay men and lesbians who see value in themselves and their way of life.

◆ Today I'll remember the real importance of the gay PRIDE parade: it promotes unity while it allows me to publicly proclaim my value and pride as a gay man or lesbian.

JUNE 27

Acceptance is the activity of love.

—SAMUEL KIRSHMER

You may find it hard to accept your own physical condition—what you look like on the outside or how you feel on the inside. Perhaps you're not pleased with your present weight and long to look slimmer. Maybe you're unhappy with the fact that you haven't exercised in a long time and wish you could get back into shape. Perhaps a nagging injury has prevented you from enjoying activities you used to participate in—hiking, camping, playing sports, running. Or maybe your body is fighting a disease such as AIDS or cancer and leaving you thin, weak, and undernourished.

You have two choices. You can rationalize your present condition so you don't have to do anything about it. You can say, "I'm not even going to bother going on a diet—it'll never work," "I don't have time to exercise," "I can't do anything because of my bad back," or "Fighting my disease is a losing battle."

Or you can choose to accept your present physical condition. Acceptance isn't resignation; you can accept any aspect of yourself without being resigned to it. But acceptance makes change possible. By first accepting your weight, your muscle tone, your injury, or your disease, you can get beyond the point of resistance to a gentler place—a place of acceptance and letting go. Then, once you accept how you look or feel, you can do something about it.

◆ Today I'll tell myself, "Whatever my physical condition, it's totally okay." I'll then explore different options for getting into better physical shape.

JUNE 28

Three weeks before Neil Armstrong landed on the moon and made world history, gays and lesbians were rewriting American history. The Stonewall riots—the gay world stood up as one.
—STEVEN TURK

On June 28, 1969, police raided the Stonewall Inn in Greenwich Village and beat, hosed down, and arrested many of its occupants. In response, gay men, lesbians, and transsexuals fought back in a riot that continued for three nights. Within months of the Stonewall riots, gay direct-action groups formed around the country, with the express purpose of protecting the rights and freedoms of gay men and lesbians everywhere. The first anniversary of Stonewall was commemorated with public demonstrations in several cities. In New York, more than two thousand people joined in a march on Christopher Street Liberation Day—the highlight of Gay Pride Week.

Since 1969, commemorating Stonewall has become an international tradition. For, as a result of the riots, one of the most historically important gay statements was made: gay men and lesbians have a voice and rights guaranteed by the United States Constitution, and *they will be heard!*

Today, celebrate the anniversary of Stonewall with other gay men and lesbians. Together, remember that out of the injustice, the anger, and the pain of the riots came the beginning of unity within the gay and lesbian community.

◆ Today I'll remember that Stonewall has given me new rights and freedoms. Let me never forget the courage and determination of a small group of my brothers and sisters to fight for my right to live openly as a gay man or lesbian.

> *To express unafraid and unashamed what one really thinks and*
> *feels is one of the greatest consolations of life.*
>
> —THEODOR REIK

Before you came out, you may have felt that no matter where you were or who you were with, you were different because you were attracted to members of the same sex. You may have been convinced that you were the only one in your neighborhood, your school, your town, your state—even in the whole world—who had such feelings. As a result, you may have believed that the only way you could get through the rest of your life was to keep quiet about your sexuality.

But when you became willing to break out of your self-imposed silence and tell someone about the feelings you were holding inside, you probably discovered that you were mistaken about being the only one. By risking open communication, you found—to your enormous relief—that there were others who felt exactly as you did.

Today you can share at even deeper levels of communication. Instead of relating to others only those things that feel safe and comfortable, you can now take greater risks and open up more to those who care for you and accept you for who you are. Don't be afraid to talk about a long-hidden feeling to a lover, friend, or family member. Risking open communication will allow you to connect with others in a way that enables you to see how you're similar— not different.

♦ Although I know I'm unique as an individual, in the final analysis I'm not really that different from other people. To prove that, today I'll share openly and honestly with someone else.

J UNE 30

During the parade, I feel such pride. What happens when I'm alone?

Does drinking or using drugs make you feel like you're part of a crowd rather than apart from it? Is it rare that you're at a bar or party or out with a group of people without a drink in your hand or a drug in your system? Do you determine whether you're having a good time by the "buzz" you have on?

Although you may have tried to stop drinking or using drugs in the past, on your own, you may have failed. What may have stopped you were the feelings you suddenly had to confront—feelings of intense emotional pain amplified by the pangs of withdrawal. So you may have rushed to soak your feelings in alcohol or drugged them so you once again could be "functional" around others and not fall apart.

The only way you can stop anesthetizing your feelings and learn to deal with them is first to reach a point where you say that drinking and drugging is no longer an option. You have to admit that you're powerless over alcohol and drugs and then enlist the help of others to keep you clean and sober.

When you do, you'll have to face some pretty painful emotions—fear, anxiety, loneliness, and depression. But this time you'll be able to use the support of a self-help group and trust in your higher power that the painful feelings will pass.

◆ Today, when I go through a rough time, I'll admit that I can't soothe it with a drink or a drug. Instead, I'll trust that if I hang on to sobriety one minute at a time, serenity will return.

I think people are in the closet because they're fearful of reactions. You don't want to be on top of a roof and need the support of a firefighter and he doesn't give it to you because you're gay.

—SHARON BRETZ

In 1972 the city of San Francisco ruled that its fire departments could not discriminate on the basis of sexual orientation. The city's firefighters, who had and still have their own paramilitary-style culture, obeyed the ordinance but didn't embrace it. Those who resisted the change have, for the most part, "won." Today there are 1,508 firefighters in uniform in the city; only one is openly gay, Lieutenant Anne Young. Lieutenant Young feels her Oceanview Station House 33 is unusual; almost everyone has been in the department for less than five years; her captain knows she's a lesbian and doesn't have a problem with it.

No one can predict what your life on the job would be like if you revealed your sexuality to supervisors and coworkers. You might receive the support of others; you might be harassed. Even if your job requires you to be dependent on others, such as in firefighting, in a police department, on a construction site, or in a hospital emergency room, that doesn't mean you should hide who you are.

Today, rather than remain quiet and closeted through fear, become open through trust. Showing that you accept yourself can help coworkers accept you.

♦ Coming out can affect coworkers with whom I interact as a "team member." Today I'll be careful and cautious—but not necessarily closeted.

I am more involved in unlearning than learning. I'm having to unlearn all the garbage that people have laid on me.

——LEO BUSCAGLIA

What are some of the messages you received while growing up about homosexuals and homosexuality? That homosexuals were abnormal, sick, immoral, sinful people? That homosexuality was an abomination that sentenced people to a lifetime of unhappiness? Such messages may have actually turned into beliefs as you grew older, particularly if you attended church regularly or were close to your family of origin. Rather than believe that such messages were wrong, you may have carried them with you into adulthood, where they surfaced in your relationships with other gay men or lesbians.

But you can start today to unlearn some of the messages you learned in the past. Imagine that you're a teacher who's in charge of the lesson plan of your life. Will you perpetuate the horrible, image-reducing messages about your sexuality from the past, or will you apply what you've learned today from the positive, nurturing, self-accepting gay men and lesbians you know? Today, be totally honest as you work from your lesson plan. Believe what's truly in your heart and what's real in your life. Believe in the *reality* of being gay rather than an unreality.

◆I don't have to believe anything today unless it's something I can use to ensure my own healthy growth and a positive self-image as a gay man or lesbian.

Walk on a rainbow trail; walk on a trail of song, and about you will be beauty. There is a way out of every dark mist, over a rainbow trail.

—NAVAJO SONG

How often do you get out and appreciate nature with other gay men or lesbians? Too often you may interact with gay people within the confines of support groups, political organizations, workshops, or networking functions. Or you may find it too hard to be with others and enjoy the beauty of a summer's day or night when your total concentration is taken up by your own troubles, stresses, conflicts, or dark moods.

Yet there's much growth, healing and recovery, peace and relaxation, and reconnecting that can occur when you're experiencing the mood-enhancing benefits of being outdoors with others. Breathing deeply of the fresh, warm summer air, hiking by a refreshing, babbling brook, picnicking at the summit of a mountain that overlooks a breathtaking valley, or camping in the lush pine-scented woods of a national forest can be shared with other gay men and lesbians.

Today, contact a gay and lesbian camping, hiking, bicycling, or other outdoor group and find out when their next function is. Or use gay and lesbian travel guidebooks to discover campgrounds, bed-and-breakfast inns, beaches, and resorts that cater to a gay clientele. The best way out of any dark time in your life is to face and feel the sunshine.

◆ Today I'll begin a folder in which I'll collect travel brochures, campground information, literature about day trips in my area, and calendar pages from a gay newspaper so I can begin exploring the great outdoors with others.

JULY 4

It's time we did something to assert ourselves. After all, we do comprise 10% of the population.

—ALLEN GINSBERG

After inspecting the damage after the Stonewall riots in 1969, Allen Ginsberg expressed his support of the uprising; to him, it signaled the beginning of a more vocal assertion of gay and lesbian freedom.

This Independence Day, think about the ways in which you express and assert your freedom as a gay man or a lesbian. You have the freedom of choice—you can choose to live a heterosexual way of life if you want, or you can choose to express your sexuality through a gay way of life. You have the freedom to write and read gay and lesbian literature, to listen and dance to gay and lesbian music, to enjoy and act in gay and lesbian theater, to view gay and lesbian films. You can subscribe to gay and lesbian publications and have them delivered to your door. You can start your own business and cater just to gay and lesbian clients if you want. You can attend gay-only support groups. You can play team sports and enter road races with gay men and lesbians. You can be a parent. You can pick and choose who knows you're a gay man or a lesbian.

But most of all, you have the freedom to love yourself, to love others like you, and to love even those who don't approve of you.

◆ Today I'll appreciate all the freedoms I have as a gay man or a lesbian. Even if the world doesn't totally embrace my sexuality, no one can take away my basic freedoms of life, liberty, and the pursuit of happiness.

Casual sex is the junk food of the heart.
—LAUREN WRIGHT DOUGLAS, FROM *A TIGER'S HEART*

When you're hungry and want something quick and easy, you might pick up the phone and place a take-out order, get in your car and drive to the nearest fast-food restaurant, or pop a frozen entrée into the microwave. In a matter of minutes, you can satisfy your hunger cravings.

Do you do the same types of things when you have sexual cravings? If you're horny, you might pick up the phone, dial a 900 number, and get off through the help of a faceless voice. You might get in your car and drive to the nearest hot spot for a pickup. Or you might go to bed with someone you've just met. In doing such things, your sexual cravings can be satisfied in a matter of minutes, hours, or in one night.

But just how satisfying is either junk food or "junk sex"? While junk food's quick, it's also nutritionally unsound and often unfulfilling. A diet that consists of only junk food will leave you feeling low on energy and fill you with empty calories. The same is true of casual sex. While the point of having sex—to get off, to fend off loneliness, or to feel like someone wants you—is satisfied, often what you're left with is an unfulfilled, lonely feeling.

Today think about the limits posed by casual sex, then consider the benefits of greater sexual intimacy. Like a finely prepared meal with fresh foods, extended intimacy with another person often can be more enjoyable and longer-lasting.

♦ Today I'll physically share myself with another person in ways that are more meaningful than casual sex. I'll strive to be patient, open, and giving as I feel and express intimacy.

JULY 6

We can easily forgive a child who is afraid of the dark; the real tragedy of life is when adults are afraid of the light.

—PLATO

Do you do things that help you escape from the difficulties you face in being a gay man or a lesbian—difficulties presented by society's homophobia, your family's rejection, or your own inability to accept who you are? Using drugs, alcohol, sex, or food may not actually enable you to escape the real world, but they may serve as buffers against such difficulties by altering your consciousness and deadening your feelings.

Why do you need to eat, drink, use drugs, or have sex to make life easier or more bearable? What is it that you're so afraid of that sometimes prevents you from being able to go through a day, a week, or a weekend without a chemical or other substance as a crutch?

Facing the reality of your sexuality is one of the major challenges that you—and every other gay man and lesbian—have to deal with in your way of life. Facing the challenge requires that you're able to see, feel, and think clearly within that reality. Today, strive to face reality head-on. Take a long, hard look at whether you use substances to help you handle your internal conflicts. Then ask yourself: "How can I get through a difficult time without needing a drink, a drug, sex, or food?"

♦ The initial test of my willingness to face reality without a crutch may be the hardest. But today I know that once I begin to do so, it'll become easier and I'll become stronger over time.

That raises the question of why they attack gays and lesbians. The answer seems to be that gays and lesbians are the most maligned group the perpetrators can find. They think they can get away with it because they believe that no one really cares if gays and lesbians are attacked.

—GARY DAVID COMSTOCK

July 7 is a day set aside to remember Charlie Howard, a young man who was killed in an unprovoked homophobic attack in 1984. On that Saturday night Jimmy Baines, who was fifteen, and two of his teenage friends went out to drink and look for gay men to harass. Before the night was over, they had beaten Howard and thrown him off a bridge into a stream, where he died. Baines and his accomplices were quickly apprehended. Because they were juveniles, they were sentenced to two-year terms at the Maine Youth Center.

After his release in 1986, Baines went to work for a businessman who encouraged him to speak publicly about the crime to deter would-be gay bashers. The Portland (Maine) Police Department Hate Crimes Task Force chose Baines to speak about gay bashing at a police convention.

Although Baines seems to have turned his life around, Gary David Comstock, who wrote *Violence Against Lesbians and Gay Men,* says that Baines fit the "profile" of a typical gay basher: "a middle-class teenage boy with average grades." He adds, "In the right situation, good kids can get involved in this activity, often purely out of boredom."

◆ Today I'll honor Charlie Howard's memory. I'll write letters to judges in cities where hate crimes have been reported to urge them to impose the strongest possible sentences on perpetrators.

Fear of death keeps us from living, not from dying.
—PAUL C. ROUD

What's the thing you fear the most in facing your own death? Some people fear feeling pain, others fear being alone. Some people fear the unknown, others fear not being close enough to God. Some people fear for the ones they leave behind, others fear for the dreams they'll never realize. Some people fear having to account for their sins, others fear not having sinned enough.

Yet, when was the last time you read an account of a near-death experience or a spiritual book on death that spoke of dying in fear-based terms? Poets, religious teachers, spiritual guides, and people who have almost died all agree: death can be an enlightening, rewarding, breathtaking experience.

Today, think about death as a risk that you're going to take. Certainly facing it is scary and unsettling; any risk is because you often don't know what to expect. But then visualize something wonderful happening from the experience. Perhaps you can see or talk with someone you lost years ago. Maybe your weakened body regains its strength and you're able to run again. Perhaps you find relief for the pain that tears at your insides. Or maybe you can explode into a new dimension—an uncharted territory where you become a brave explorer in a new world.

♦I need to remember that when I'm not afraid to die, I won't be afraid to live. Instead of holding back, today I'll live my life fully so I can experience my death fully.

My parents have no problem with my being a lesbian, because my parents are lesbians.

—JENNIFER DIMARCO

Do you feel cheated out of a "normal" childhood because your parents couldn't love, accept, and support you for the child you really were? You might think: "If I had dated members of the opposite sex like my sister did, shown an interest in activities that were supposed to be important to members of my own sex, like my brother did, or if I hadn't told other family members about my sexuality, maybe my parents would have loved me as they did my other siblings."

But chances are if you talk to your siblings and ask if they felt loved, accepted, and supported while growing up, they might remember things they did that disappointed or angered their parents or made them feel as if they always fell short of what was expected of them. So you may be wrong to blame your sexuality for certain things you didn't get from your parents as a child.

It's a rare set of parents who can love, accept, and support you as you're growing up *no matter what*. Most parents want their children never to make mistakes, feel pain or sadness, or be deprived of experiences and opportunities. Even the healthiest parents can have expectations of their children that are difficult to attain.

Today you need to realize that your parents brought you up in their own way. They may not have been perfect, but they did the best they could.

◆ Today I'll remind myself that there are no sets of perfect parents in this world. Even gay children with gay parents may feel that their parents sometimes let them down. *No one's perfect!*

In the moment of creation you were given incredible gifts; and one of the most important is the gift of sexuality.
—MARY MARGARET MOORE

Do you know what it's like to use sex? Maybe you've slept with others not because you loved or even liked them, but because you wanted an orgasm. Perhaps you and your lover engage in lovemaking after an argument rather than talk about the conflict. Maybe you manipulate or control others by withholding physical contact.

Or you may be able to recall feeling, at one time or another in your life, ashamed about your sexual feelings for members of your own sex, about your body, or about your sexual history. You may have felt—and may still feel—that sex is dirty or "bad" because of your homosexuality.

But your sexuality is a special gift. It's a pleasurable, joyous way to connect with another human being. It's a mysterious wonder of physical responses. It's a physically and emotionally healing act. And it's a healthy, normal, natural activity for gay men and lesbians.

Today it's time to reject the ideas that sex is a useful tool or something that's fundamentally bad because of your sexuality. Reclaim your sexual life by joyously experiencing lovemaking with another man or woman. Delight in the passion and the intensity of something you were given as a gift of your creation.

◆ Today I'll focus not only on my emotional and spiritual well-being, but also on my physical well-being. I'll see myself as a sexual person who's willing to accept and express my sexuality.

*Nor is it an objection to say that we must understand a prayer
if it is to have its true effect. That simply is not the case. Who
understands the wisdom of a flower? Yet we can take pleasure in it.*
—RUDOLPH STEINER

One of the things that most baffles scientists is the cause of
homosexuality. While there are many theories, there's not
yet any rational, logical explanation or existing proof that
explains what makes someone gay.

In a way, prayers are like your sexuality. While there's no
rational, logical explanation or existing proof that determines
why they work, they do. For many people, prayers have
provided answers to their most perplexing questions, guidance when they're lost, enlightenment during times of confusion, and spiritual support to ease the pain of loss and
loneliness.

Spiritual awakenings through prayer usually happen when
you're willing to surrender understanding. Giving up intel-
lectual efforts to try to figure out the purpose and meaning of
prayer lets prayer work. You simply don't need to know *why*
in order to benefit from prayer.

Today, let prayers work in your life. Use a childhood
prayer to get you through a difficult time, "talk" to a higher
power about something that's troubling you, or "listen" to a
spiritual guide through meditation. It doesn't matter what
prayer you say or how you say it—the act of praying *will*
bring results.

◆ Today I'll pray for something that matters to me—
guidance, forgiveness, strength, courage, support—or for
the health and welfare of someone dear to me.

Even though I have been openly gay, I can't say that I was really that active in the gay community. If I went on a gay pride march once a year, I'd done my duty, so to speak.

—SIMON LEVAY

When Simon LeVay was twenty-five years old, he dropped out of medical school and entered a neurobiology Ph.D. program in Germany. It was there that he met Richard Percy, his life partner. Together they returned to America, settling in Boston. Percy worked mainly as a doctor of internal medicine, while LeVay was a faculty member at Harvard Medical School. Their relationship lasted twenty-one years, until Percy's death from AIDS-related complications in 1990. It was then that LeVay, who had cared for his lover throughout his four-year illness, turned his energy to the gay and lesbian community. "Something like that wakes you up," LeVay commented, "makes you think about what is important to you and what isn't."

Would you like to restructure your life in a way that would allow you to give more time and energy to the gay and lesbian community—to the many gay men and lesbians who work long hours putting together gay and lesbian newspapers and magazines, organizing marches and demonstrations, opening businesses that benefit the community, and keeping an interest in your rights and freedoms alive in your state government?

♦ Today I won't wait for a major change in my life to motivate me to give something back to the gay and lesbian community. I'll seek out an organization, group, or program that interests me and set aside a few hours a week to make myself available as a volunteer.

Love is patient and kind; love is not jealous or boastful; it is not arrogant or rude. Love does not insist on its own way; it is not irritable or resentful; it does not rejoice in wrong but rejoices in the right. Love bears all things, believes all things, hopes all things, endures all things.

—I CORINTHIANS 13:4–7

Because of a dysfunctional childhood background or a series of relationships with emotionally unstable or unhealthy partners, you may have a skewed vision or definition of what love is. You may believe love is hurtful and unkind, unforgiving and angry, manipulative and controlling, rejecting and abusive, short-lived and based on lust. Your fear of love hurting you in some way may have even caused you to run from love for so long that today you don't know how to let love back into your life.

To reexperience love, you first need to relax around someone. Let down your guard a bit so you can begin to trust him or her. Then be patient. Let the time that you spend together evolve from a few hours to several hours and then, eventually, to weekends. Try to not draw back from compliments, kindnesses, and expressions of caring. By allowing yourself slowly to open up, you can gradually begin to feel trust and understanding developing. Over time, such positive expressions of caring can help your interaction blossom into a loving relationship.

◆ Today I'll begin to let love into my life by being willing to take small risks. I won't draw back automatically when someone reaches out to help me or reject positive, safe, reassuring expressions of love.

I think macho is the core of the American problem, which is why the gay movement is so important. America must accept that macho is not healthy.

——JERRY RUBIN

Remember the images of the Old West, where cowboys would down a slug of whiskey and then bite a bullet as a deep wound or injury was treated without the benefit of painkillers or anesthesia? "Yeah, that's the way I'll be from now on," you might have said the first time you got burned in a gay relationship. "No one and nothing's ever going to hurt me or get through to me again. No matter what happens in my life, I'll just 'bite the bullet.' "

So you may have embarked upon a journey to project the ultimate in macho male gayness or macha lesbian butchness. Dressing in leather, adorning your body with tattoos or piercings, riding a motorcycle, choosing to work as a heavy laborer, lifting weights to swell muscle size, exuding an attitude of toughness, and living by the philosophy of "love 'em and leave 'em" may have helped you achieve a tough-guy role for the purpose of self-protection. But how happy are you this way?

Even though you may claim you're really a pussycat inside or as cuddly as a teddy bear, you need to show that side to others. Living behind a stone wall or wearing impenetrable masks isn't healthy. But being real is. And that means letting your true self—not some fictional character—be seen by others.

♦ It's okay to fantasize about being a tough guy, as long as I can separate the fantasy from the reality. Today I'll let others see the real me—a sensitive, caring gay man or a gentle, kind lesbian.

Later. I'm still young. I'll think of spiritual things when I'm older. On my deathbed.

—GARRISON KEILLOR

Too often you may think that being more spiritual is for the aged, the sick, or the dying. You may feel that since you're young and healthy today and have your whole life before you, there's no time now to stop and think about developing a relationship with a higher power. "I'm fine today," you may say. "But I'll think about meditation, church, or my beliefs in the hereafter later—when I really need to."

But open your eyes and look around you. The time to establish contact with a spiritual belief or entity is *now,* for all around you your friends are dying young as AIDS and cancer ravage the gay and lesbian community. Your time to reach out to a higher power is not when your body is riddled with disease or run down over time. Now is the time to ask for spiritual direction, to seek spiritual knowledge, and to become open to receiving divine guidance.

From the minute you come into this world until you take your last breath, there's a power greater than yourself watching over you. This power guides you, strengthens you, and helps you grow without your even acknowledging it is there. Today, reestablish contact with this power. Set aside half an hour every day to strengthen this contact so it's there when you need it.

♦ If I open myself up now to developing my spirituality and contacting my higher power, I'll have a valuable door opened to my spiritual growth. I'll make time today and every day to communicate in some way with my higher power.

What, after all, is a halo? It's only one more thing to keep clean.

—CHRISTOPHER FRY

Do you ever criticize yourself for not being the perfect partner, the perfect roommate, the perfect child or parent, the perfect employee, or the perfectly politically correct gay man or lesbian? Continually striving for perfection can place incredible demands upon yourself, for you may feel as if you have to do everything right. But what is right? And is there a right way to do something and a wrong way?

The perfectionist in you may spend every moment of every day trying to be perfect in your relationship, your family interactions, your career, your purchases, your home, your cooking, your clothes—even the way you live your life as a gay man or lesbian. But the truth of the matter is, there is no perfection. There is no right way or wrong way of doing anything. There's only your way. Sometimes you may be unhappy with the way you do things, but that doesn't mean you've done them wrong, just as being happy with the way you do things doesn't mean you've done them perfectly.

Today, if you choose to try wearing a halo of perfection, understand that it can be tarnished, tipped to one side, or misplaced every once in a while. That's because there's really no way even to wear a halo perfectly!

♦Today I'll remember that I'm not a perfect angel. I'll accept that working every day to attain my halo and wings is an imperfect, ever-changing, lifelong process.

When I got to my new workplace, I walked through the doors as "the gay bomber." [But] a lot of people surprised me: Every single one of my friends is very supportive. I'm not an "avowed homosexual activist." I just want to be back in the cockpit.

—TRACY THORNE

Tracy Thorne is a grounded naval flight officer stationed at Virginia Beach, Virginia, who's waiting for final judgment on his court challenge to a discharge from the military because of his sexuality. Until a legal decision is made, he reports to work at "a petty little desk job" while he yearns to be flying a plane.

Having to suspend or give up dreams of things you'd like to have or do because of your sexuality can be frustrating. You may have been shut out of a profession you love because of your openness as a gay man or lesbian, refused necessary services because of AIDS, had the front door to your family home slammed in your face after revealing your sexuality, been denied a mortgage because of your refusal to exclude your life partner's name from the application, or been legally barred from marrying the one you love. In the face of such barriers, you may find it hard to hold on to your dream and to believe that someday you'll get what you want.

Today, don't let anything or anyone prevent you from believing in your dreams. Tell yourself, "It doesn't matter how long it'll take before I get what I want. What's most important is that I never give up my dreams."

◆ Do I have any dreams I think might never come true because of time or circumstances? Today I won't be discouraged from believing that any dream can't come true. I'll keep my dreams alive by keeping hope in my heart.

JULY 18

Do not take life too seriously. You will never get out of it alive.
—ELBERT HUBBARD

Is there a balance in your life between living life as a gay man or lesbian and living life simply as a person? Sometimes, when you first come out or after you've gotten your first taste of involvement in the gay and lesbian community, you may have a tendency to take yourself and your way of life too seriously. So you may immerse yourself in activities involving only the gay and lesbian community—going to bars, attending gay-only twelve-step meetings, or participating in workshops for gay men or lesbians. You may read only gay or lesbian literature. You may interact only with gay men or lesbians. You may support only those businesses that are sensitive to gay or lesbian issues. You may display gay political bumper stickers on your vehicle or wear buttons on your clothing. You may take your sexuality so seriously that you can't imagine doing anything or interacting with anyone outside the community.

Today remind yourself of the motto "Life is a garment to be worn loosely." Nothing should be so important or dominate your thinking so obsessively that you have to devote twenty-four hours a day, seven days a week, in its pursuit. If you devote most of your time and energy to being a member of the gay and lesbian community rather than a member of society, tell yourself, "Keep it all in perspective. Learn to be more carefree and to experience everything and everyone life has to offer."

◆ To revise an old saying, "Don't sweat the gay stuff." Today I'll begin to live a more balanced life that has me enjoying the gay stuff as well as lots of other stuff.

A man needs self-acceptance or he can't live with himself; he needs self-criticism or others can't live with him.

—JAMES A. PIKE

Believing that coming out will take care of all of your problems is like thinking that a new coat of paint will strengthen the rotting wood on your home. While you may feel better about yourself by letting out the secret of your sexuality, doing so won't make everything better about you. You may have character faults, behavioral difficulties, and shortcomings that haven't been resolved or won't disappear simply because you've identified yourself as a gay man or lesbian.

Accepting your sexuality is like taking one small step in the overall journey toward self-acceptance. But there are many others. To find them, you need to make an honest assessment of yourself and discover those things about you that you may need or like to change.

Today, think about creating a character list. On this list, record your character faults or weaknesses as well as your strengths and positive points. Be sure to concentrate as keenly on your assets as you do on your drawbacks. Then step back from your list and review it. Look at the pluses and minuses. Then strive to balance the two by using your strengths to conquer your weaknesses.

♦ Today I'll make sure that my character list contains just as many positive points as shortcomings so I can see both sides. Then I'll use my assets in ways that help me to feel better about myself.

Could Hamlet *have been written by a committee, or the "Mona Lisa" painted by a club? Could the New Testament have been composed as a conference report? Creative ideas do not spring from groups. They spring from individuals.*

—A. WHITNEY GRISWOLD

Imagine being shipwrecked on a deserted island or surviving a plane crash in a remote location. You might think your survival would be much easier if you had others to help you build signal fires, hunt for food, construct shelters, and care for the injured. But wouldn't you also be able to survive equally well on your own, without being slowed down by the injuries of others, dividing meager food supplies several ways, or having to reach a group consensus on major decisions?

The input, support, and companionship you receive from others can be helpful, particularly when you're dealing with issues that affect you as a gay man or lesbian. There's certainly a strength that can be found in numbers as well as in shared ways of life. But there's also a strength that can come from you as an individual—an inner strength that defines who you are and makes your thoughts, feelings, and actions different from others.

What qualities do you recognize within yourself that make you feel strong as a gay man or lesbian? Today, spend less time gravitating to the strength of groups and recognize instead your inner strengths.

♦ Today I'll make my inner strengths even stronger by looking to myself first for answers and solutions to the conflicts and complexities in my life.

> *Be glad you can suffer, be glad you can feel. . . . How can you tell if you're feeling good unless you've felt bad, so you have something to compare it with?*
>
> —THOMAS TRYON

How many times have you come home at the end of a work day ranting and raving about how difficult it is to deal with straight coworkers? How many holidays have caused you unhappiness because of your need to remain in the closet to family members? In how many ways has the pain and suffering of other gay men and lesbians affected you?

You may wonder how you can ever feel good about your way of life when you have to endure such difficulties day after day or holiday after holiday. One way to do so is to change your way of thinking. You can apply the old saying "Opposites attract" to those times of frustration, stress, unhappiness, and pain. What that means is that you can balance the bad feeling with a good one by telling yourself you wouldn't know how to smile if you didn't know how to frown; you wouldn't know how to cry if you didn't know how to laugh; you wouldn't know how to suffer if you didn't already know what it felt like to be well.

Bring balance into your emotional responses rather than just always feeling the bad. Recognize today that there may be a coworker you've come out to who accepts you, there have been holiday times you've shared with your life partner that have been enjoyable, and there are many wonderful, inspiring stories about gay men and lesbians.

◆ Today I'll remember that knowing how things feel—both the good and the bad—will help bring greater awareness into my life. I can be grateful today for *all* the feelings I experience.

Sometimes you have to look hard at a person and remember that he is doing the best he can. He's just trying to find his way. That's all.

—ERNEST THOMPSON

Certainly those who are HIV positive, afflicted with AIDS, or battling cancer are acquainted with the concept of living in the present. Sometimes it's all they can do to get through each day one hour at a time or even one minute at a time. Ryan White, who died of AIDS-related complications in 1992, was asked whether he planned for the future; he replied, "Oh yes, I plan for the future. I plan go to college. But I really just live one day at a time."

You may not be so capable of being present-focused in your interactions with someone close to you who is ill. You may wonder, "Why isn't this person doing more? Why aren't they worrying about next week, next month, or next year? Why aren't they making plans for the future right now?"

One positive thing that AIDS can teach every gay man and lesbian is how to live one day at a time. When you live for tomorrow or in some future time, you're not living in the present moment. When you get so busy that all you can think about is what you'd like to do when you're no longer busy, then you miss the chance to be here right now—to experience the happiness and experiences in this minute.

Today, strive to live in the present moment. Live and enjoy your plans for the future today. It's the best way to live.

◆ Today I'll remember that I only have to live this day. Nothing more is asked of me. So I'll experience today as it should be experienced, one second at a time.

I care not so much what I am in the opinion of others as what I am in my own; I would be rich of myself, and not by borrowing.
—MICHEL EQUEM DE MONTAIGNE

Are you guilty of self-inflicted suffering—feeling bad about who you are as a gay man or lesbian because of how others perceive or react to you? Maybe you feel horrible about who you are because of your parents' unhappy response when you revealed your sexuality. Perhaps you have a low self-image because of the negative pressures put on you by other family members to change your way of life. Maybe you feel ashamed at your straight friends' hesitancy to be around you after you told them you were gay. Or perhaps you've taken on a distorted, degraded view of yourself because of society's homophobic opinions about gays and lesbians.

What does it take to get yourself out of the harsh, judgmental rut you keep pushing yourself into? First, in order to make any change, you have to be truly fed up with your self-inflicted suffering. Ask yourself, "When is *enough enough?*" Then you need to make conscious and repeated efforts to reverse the low self-image you're carrying around. You might find it helpful, when you become aware that you're automatically attacking yourself, to stop in midsentence or midthought and say out loud, "No, that's just not true." Or you might like to enlist the help of a supportive gay friend who can periodically point out to you your good qualities.

◆ Today I'll give myself a break! I won't let a distorted self-image make me feel bad about myself. I care a great deal about myself and want to show that to others.

JULY 24

When we were doing it, [my character] was supposed to be very, very drunk. I said, "Why does she have to be very, very drunk?" I mean, if you're going to bed with a woman . . . and she looks like Catherine Deneuve, and she's as charming as Catherine Deneuve, why make [my character] drunk?"

—SUSAN SARANDON, ABOUT *THE HUNGER*

The morning after the first time you got drunk, do you remember telling yourself that you'd never drink again? But over the next several years you may have repeated the same routine countless times—getting drunk and then swearing off alcohol the next morning.

Now when you wake up after a night of drinking, do you find it difficult to remember things you did the night before? Perhaps your friends call to tell you unbelievable stories about things you did. Your lover may refuse to speak to you. Your house or apartment may look as if someone trashed it. But perhaps the most telling sign that you're unaware of drunken behaviors from a previous night may be waking up next to a stranger and not remembering his or her name or whether or not you had safe sex.

There's a big difference between being a social drinker and having a problem with alcohol. A social drinker doesn't *need* alcohol in order to have a good time. And sexual intimacy that's coupled with alcohol is a warning sign that you need to take a look at your drinking patterns.

♦ Today I'll take a long, hard look at the role alcohol plays in my life. Is it hard for me to imagine going without a drink? Is sex and sobriety together a frightening concept? I'll seek out the advice of a recovering alcoholic who can help me deal with issues involving alcohol.

To know what you prefer instead of humbly saying amen to what the world tells you you ought to prefer, is to have kept your soul alive.

—R. L. STEVENSON

You are not like anyone else in this world. You are not like any other gay man or lesbian; all you share with them is your way of life. You are not like your friends; even if you dressed, walked, talked, and acted like them, you would still not be them. You are not like your siblings, even if you're a twin; all you share with them is being a member of the same family. You are not like any other member of your profession, your support groups, your neighbors, or your class. No one is just like you.

You're an independent human being—emotionally, physically, and spiritually. The paths that you've chosen to walk in your life, although they may cross the paths of others from time to time, are still your own special paths. No one will walk them, experience them, or grow from them exactly in the way you will.

That's why it's important for you to be true to yourself and your individuality even when you share important life details with others. Self-growth as an individual as well as a gay man or lesbian is about standing on your own two feet and making your own decisions. Today, revel in your independence from others. Be your own person.

◆ Today I'll celebrate my own separate thoughts, feelings, and actions. I'll keep myself physically and emotionally alive through my independence.

Whenever I'm with my mother, I feel as though I have to spend the whole time avoiding land mines.

—AMY TAN

Do you feel as if you have to prepare for battle in order to visit your parents? You may imagine slipping into body armor that will protect you from low blows about your haircut or your tattoo, the people you hang around with, or the way you live your life. Maybe there's a bullet-proof vest you visualize putting on that will shield your heart from barbs fired at you about your life partner or about how your sexuality is breaking the heart of some beloved family member. Perhaps there are tiny plugs you imagine inserting into your ears that will help mute the harsh judgments and criticisms about who you are and how you're letting everyone down by being gay.

Armed in such a fashion, you may arrive at your parents' home tense, anxious, and on the alert. You may be so trigger-happy that you immediately become angry and defensive without even paying attention to a point being made. Or you may deeply entrench yourself in a protective foxhole and not respond to your parents at all.

But have you ever thought of approaching one or both of your parents not ready to do battle, but ready to stop fighting? Today think about ways you could behave with them that would create less conflict and tension and encourage a "cease-fire." Then, next time you get together, imagine holding up a white flag and surrendering so you won't engage in any more battles.

◆ It's up to me to change how I act when I'm around my parents. Today I'll choose to approach them or spend time with them as a friend, not a foe.

Any lie will find believers as long as you tell it with force.
—ROUBEN MAMOULIAN, FROM *QUEEN CHRISTINA*

Do you put on the mask of heterosexuality at different times in your life? It's a mask designed to fool others into thinking that you're straight, that you're married, or that you're interested in eventually settling down and raising a family with a member of the opposite sex. It's a mask that reassures your employer that you don't have a husband or wife because your career is all-important, that conveys to your parents that you're happy being single, and that convinces your friends you're interested in hearing all about their weekends with their spouses.

While wearing a mask might make you feel uncomfortable from time to time, it may be something that's difficult to remove because of the protection it offers. Without it, you might feel naked, exposed, vulnerable. Without it, you might have to reveal the reality of your way of life.

Today, summon the courage to drop the mask so an important person in your life can see who you really are. To do so, believe in yourself enough to trust that sometimes your naked vulnerability is okay. And take reassurance from the fact that *every* gay man and lesbian has, at one time or another, worn the mask of heterosexuality because they, too, have been vulnerable and afraid.

◆Can I be courageous enough to drop my mask of deception and risk showing myself as I really am? Today I'll consider whether to hold on or drop my mask around someone special.

Perhaps her most lasting legacy is having lived as an open homosexual while competing. Other gay superstars duck questions, solicit a conspiracy of silence, make marriages of convenience. Navratilova has told the blunt truth to everyone, from biographers to Barbara Walters—not for sensation but to promote understanding and advance causes. . . .

—WILLIAM A. HENRY III

Both on and off the tennis court, superstar Martina Navratilova has assured herself of a place in gay and lesbian history. Her standing as the all-time greatest player in her sport is beyond challenge. She has played and won more singles matches than any other tennis athlete, male or female. She has captured more titles and earned more prize money—$18.3 million by 1992. She has transformed sports for women by taking on the training disciplines of men. And through it all, she has lived as an open homosexual and let her controversial private life become part of her public spectacle.

She has never denied or suppressed the truth about her sexuality, even though it has cost her corporate endorsements and nontennis public appearances. "People in this country don't know what to think about gays," she has said. "I just hope we turn the energy away from prejudice to something positive. . . . I hope my career and name mean that I can be involved on some level, making a difference."

♦ Today I'll make a difference in the causes that are important to me as a gay man or lesbian. I won't be afraid to immerse myself in political controversy, fighting antigay legislation, or protesting against discrimination.

We've all got one, don't we, tucked away somewhere in a fold of our brain, a torn and frayed-around-the-edges picture of the ideal family. Admit it. Whether it's the Cleavers, the Bradys, or the Huxtables, visions of a functional group different from our own family dance in our heads. It's part of the American Dream.
— ELISABETH NONAS

Do you ever wonder why your family of origin couldn't have been more like the families portrayed on television shows? When you were a child, maybe you couldn't see the qualities your family was lacking; now, as an adult, maybe you can look at how healthy and unhealthy families are different.

To distinguish between healthy and unhealthy families, keep one word in mind: CARING. Each letter in CARING stands for a quality that healthy families have. The first is Communication, accomplished by a listening-sharing, open and honest give-and-take process. The next is Acceptance, where family members are seen and accepted for who they are, without attempts to change them. Then there's Reality, or the ability to see the family as it really is, without lies, secrets, or family myths. Next, Individuality involves your sense of being a whole person within your family. Needs help you develop this sense of self so you can identify and seek out what you want as an individual. Finally, Growth that occurs from within as well as outside the family helps you to mature and grow apart from it while you're still a part of the family.

♦ Today I'll think about how my family of origin's lack of acceptance of my way of life is related to the lack of CARING in my childhood home. In what ways can I ensure that CARING exists in my own family today or in my relationships with others?

Her kitchen had been taken over by a Real Woman. If this is what happened after a one-night stand what would a relationship be like?
—ROSE BEECHAM, FROM *INTRODUCING AMANDA VALENTINE*

Too often you may jump into a relationship with another gay man or lesbian long before you've gotten to know each other. A few hours at a party, one night of passion, or a weekend away from home spent in the company of someone new can make you excited and raise your expectations to think that you've finally met the love of your life.

Looking forward so earnestly to falling in love can sometimes mean that instead of seeing a potential lover for who he or she really is, you create in your mind the type of person you'd like him or her to be. Or you may confuse love with infatuation or lust. Or you may start a new relationship in order to avoid working through the ending of a previous one.

But healthy relationships are not formed from a chance encounter, a glance across a crowded dance floor, or orgasmic delight. Healthy relationships are patiently built over time as you slowly begin to get to know someone, to trust, to honestly and openly share who you are, to grow separately as well as together, and to enjoy common interests as well as work toward common goals.

Today, don't expect that you're going to meet the "right" person, fall in love, and be together for years. Understand and experience the other person *first;* make and take the time to let things grow.

◆ When I'm learning about love without even realizing it, that's probably when I'm building and strengthening a healthy relationship. Today I'll simply let love happen rather than try to make it happen.

JULY 31

We come into this world crying while all around us are smiling. May we so live that we go out of this world smiling while everybody around us is weeping.

—PERSIAN PROVERB

How much do you think you matter to other people—to your life partner, your friends, coworkers, roommates, and family members? Has your life touched the lives of others in some small way, perhaps by things you've done or said, experiences you've shared, smiles you've exchanged, love you've given and received, or ways you've grown together?

There are many lives you've touched since the day you were born; there are many lives you still touch in a day, a week, month, or year. Each of these lives was meant to intercept yours at some point. You were meant to exist together for a reason, no matter how much or how little time you've shared. Even though the time you may have left is drawing to a close and is much shorter than you'd like it to be, it doesn't mean that your life matters any less to those who have experienced some part of it with you.

You *do* matter to those around you. Birth as well as death herald the entrance and the exit of a life filled with meaning and purpose. You were meant to be here now, not only for yourself but also for the many lives around you. Your life has been important and worthwhile to all the people you know. Don't ever forget that.

♦ Help me see today that my life matters. Today I'll believe that just as others have touched me, so have I touched the lives of others.

Although the act of nurturing another's spiritual growth has the effect of nurturing one's own, a major characteristic of genuine love is that the distinction between oneself and the other is always maintained and preserved.

—Dr. M. Scott Peck

When you were growing up, did you ever hear the motto "The family that prays together stays together"? What it was saying was that if your family attended church as one, that made your family spiritually healthy. When you came out to your parents or family members, were you ever told, "You wouldn't choose to be that way if you loved us"? What they were saying was that your love for them was based on who you were, not how you honestly felt about them. When some God-fearing straight people discovered you were gay, were you hit by condemnations such as, "God doesn't love homosexuals. You're going to burn in hell for who you are"? What they were telling you was that you were spiritually unacceptable to their idea of God.

None of these statements is spiritually nurturing or loving; rather, they're statements based upon personal beliefs that reject. Today, rely upon your spiritual core to strengthen you when you need to interact with others who preach from a pulpit of hatred or hostility. It's up to you to preach the true gospel of love, understanding, and forgiveness.

♦ Today let me give honest evidence of my spiritual love for others by showing everyone encouragement and acceptance—even those who must struggle to come to terms with the fact that my sexuality fits my spirituality.

> *They intoxicate themselves with work so they won't see how they really are.*
>
> —ALDOUS HUXLEY

Can you relate to this story about a female basketball coach who's also a lesbian? She's so closeted that no one who works with her at the university knows that she lived with a lover for nearly twenty years—a lover who recently lost her battle against cancer. All anyone knows is what they see: a hard-working, dedicated, highly motivated coach who puts the team and school first. Every day the coach arrives early at her office to tackle piles of paperwork. Then she works out at the gym, returns to her desk to eat lunch alone, and spends the afternoon talking team strategy and schedules with her assistants. Her early-evening hours are spent at team practices or traveling to games. Late at night, she returns to her empty house with a briefcase full of work, heats a frozen dinner in the microwave, and settles down to do more work.

Because she uses work to hide herself and her sexuality, she's never been able to process the ending of her long-term relationship, to create a supportive gay and lesbian network, to feel comfortable with her sexuality, or to make friends and allies on campus.

Today, examine your work habits to determine whether you're a work addict who uses work to escape from who you are. Ask yourself: "Do I engage in abusive work or healthy work?"

♦ Although work abuse can draw recognition, success, and great rewards, it can destroy my connection with others and myself. Today I'll cut back on my work time so I can spend more time connecting with and strengthening my life as a gay man or lesbian.

Camping is a good way to meet people: you share a tent with someone and get to know them! If you can't put up with someone who hasn't showered for two or three days, then you know you don't want to be with them.

— JOE PEREZ, PRESIDENT OF HOG (HOUSTON OUTDOORS GROUP)

It's not always easy to meet other gay men and lesbians with whom you can share support, friendship, or love. Most gay men and lesbians cram bars on weekends in the hope of making new acquaintances or meeting a new lover. Some use twelve-step support groups to form friendships with those who have similar backgrounds or behaviors. Others comb the personal ads in gay and lesbian publications to locate a friend, a date, or a potential life partner.

Another way to get together with people in a less formal, less forced way is to combine socializing with an outdoor activity such as biking, hiking, running, team sports, or camping. Instead of focusing on getting to know someone and having them get to know you, you get to enjoy the activity you're sharing. And in the process of enjoying the activity and experiencing "the great outdoors," you may make a new friend or lover.

Today, take out a personal ad in a gay or lesbian publication so you can make contact with others with whom you might share common outdoor interests. Or join a gay or lesbian outdoors group that already draws hikers, bikers, campers, or softball players together.

◆ It's important to me that I share a love of the outdoors with others. Today I'll seek alternatives to the bar scene and personal ads by bonding with other gay men and lesbians through outdoor activities.

Success is to be measured not so much by the position that one has reached in life as by the obstacles which [were] overcome while trying to succeed.

—BOOKER T. WASHINGTON

When hurdlers race, they look ahead to see each hurdle that must be leaped. High jumpers visually measure the height of the bar they have to clear. Businesspeople look at corporate charts to see their current positions and the positions they must pass in order to attain their goals. Students are well aware of the number of credits and course requirements needed for a degree.

But not all of the obstacles in life are so easy to see. As a gay man or a lesbian, you've had to overcome tremendous obstacles to get to where you are today. In the past, you may have had to clear such hurdles as a low self-image, loneliness, isolation, ridicule, gay bashing, violence, threats, or countless other blocks to your growth as you discovered the path that led to your way of life.

There are still obstacles you have to work through today—invisibility on the job, family acceptance, rejection, discrimination, deciding when and who to come out to, and so on. But every time you leap over one of those hurdles, you've achieved a great success. Today, be satisfied when you do so; overcoming just one obstacle means there's one less hurdle that stands in your way.

♦ Today I'll continually review my day and look for my small successes. I know I can overcome some of the obstacles in my life as a gay man or a lesbian through persistence, patience, and perseverance.

AUGUST 5

I don't fully understand, I tell him. You've survived boot camp. You've faced the Saudi Arabian desert. You've shown repeated physical bravery. Why does it scare you to serve next to a gay man?
——BARRY YEOMAN

Barry Yeoman, associate editor of *The Independent,* a weekly news magazine in Durham, North Carolina, was sent on assignment to Jacksonville, North Carolina, home of U.S. Marine Corps' Camp Lejeune. The incident that drew him to the city was the January 30, 1993, beating of a gay man by three Camp Lejeune marines. According to some witnesses, the marines were shouting, "Fag, you should die!" as they fractured the victim's skull.

Yeoman sat in the Lucky Lady Night Club in Jacksonville and talked to Corporal Corey Lafreniere about homosexuals. Lafreniere said he hated homosexuals. He said he wanted to kill them. "It wouldn't bother me a bit," he said, then mused, "[when] you hate somebody so bad . . ."

Hate crimes are rarely based on actual feelings of hatred; rather, they're often based on fear, discomfort, nervousness, and lack of knowledge. So the best way to combat hate crimes is not by legislation but by education. Today, take part in educating America about gay men and lesbians to end hate crimes. Let your gay viewpoint be heard on talk-radio shows and read in letters to newspaper and magazine editors.

♦ Today I'll keep in mind that most people who say they hate homosexuals have never met anyone gay. Because the only knowledge they have of gays is through stereotypes or wild imaginings, it's up to me to help show them the truth.

This kind of work is pretty compelling. I get to work every day with lesbians, who are the most extraordinary people. But things have been so fast and furious this year, it's taken its toll. Sometimes I come home and just sit in front of the TV for hours, watching whatever just to chill out.

—DONNA RED WING

Since Donna Red Wing arrived in Portland, Oregon, she has worked tirelessly as executive director of Portland's Lesbian Community Project as well as laid the foundation of broad-based organizing that made the defeat of antigay Measure 9 possible. As one of the nation's leading lesbian activists, she has often spent hours on the road, delivering speech after speech, organizing and handling presentations, and attending rallies and fund-raising dinners. "I'm blessed with extraordinary energy," Red Wing has said. "I don't roll out of bed—I shoot out of bed."

Yet life as a "giver" in the gay and lesbian community can take its toll. Whether you work as an activist, in a health clinic, for a women's shelter, on a gay newspaper, as a fund-raiser, or for a political candidate, long hours for little or no pay and sometimes insignificant impact can take its toll on you.

Today, take time out from giving to the gay and lesbian community and do something you'd like to do. Make a cup of freshly ground coffee, take the dog for a long walk, listen to your favorite music, or spend quality time with a loved one.

◆ While I enjoy giving to my brothers and sisters in the community, sometimes I just need to chill out. Today I'll set aside time to do something I want to do—not for the community, but for me.

Watching this year's Olympics, I saw women athletes with impractically long hair and nails, neither of which are easy to maintain when training many hours a day. . . . I've heard interviews in which female athletes quickly bring up the fact that they have a boyfriend or husband when the reporter has not asked any questions about their personal lives.

—DONNA LOPIANO

Have you ever done something to disguise yourself from being perceived as a gay man or a lesbian? As a gay man you might go to a ball game with the guys from work, wear a wedding band, or display a picture of a "wife" on your desk. As a lesbian you might wear skirts or dresses, put on makeup, grow your hair long, or talk about a boyfriend.

Living in such fear of discovery by coworkers, friends, family members—even total strangers—may affect your relationships with other gay men and lesbians. You may impose restrictions on the behavior, style of dress, interests, or topics of conversation of your life partner or gay friends. While such impositions may be appropriate for you, they can be insulting or even degrading to others.

The next time you want to impose gay-limiting restrictions on yourself or others ask, "What is it I'm so afraid of?" Awareness of your fears can be a first step toward conquering them.

◆ What am I gaining by keeping myself in the closet? Today I'll be honest with myself about the benefits of such a disguise by asking, "What's more important—image or individuality?"

*I just called up a girl this afternoon, and I got a real brush-off,
boy! I figured I was past the point of being hurt, but that
hurt. . . . I—I had enough pain.*
                                    —PADDY CHAYEFSKY, FROM *MARTY*

When you get dumped by that special man or woman with
whom you thought you'd spend the rest of your life, it's easy
to think how great it would be never to get involved with
anyone again. The thought of never having to reexperience
the intense physical and emotional pain of such a loss can be
exhilarating. Then, you might think, all will be well in your
life; once the potential for hurt is removed, anything might be
possible.

Yet hurt is part of the cycle of growth and learning. You had
to skin your knees a few times in order finally to learn how to
ride a bicycle. You may have had to miss a longed-for event in
order to learn how much it meant to you. You may have had
to grieve over the loss of someone dear in order to learn how
much love you felt for that person.

Today you need to accept that there are no assurances that
you'll never be hurt again. You, like every other gay man and
lesbian, will lose a relationship at one time or another and will
feel emotional and physical pain. But you can be sure that
you'll always be able to ease your pain—through the support
of friends, through faith that you'll get through the dark time,
and through trust that time *will* heal all wounds.

◆ Today I won't live with a wall around me, trying to protect
myself from ever feeling hurt again. Escaping into a never-
never land by shutting myself off from people only prevents
me from feeling love, caring, and warmth.

Humor is an affirmation of dignity, a declaration of man's superiority to all that befalls him.

—ROMAIN GARY

With any long illness such as AIDS or cancer, there are hardly any fun times; rather, there are many tense and tearful moments. But humor can play a big part in helping you or others you know who are suffering take their minds off their distress and ease their pain.

Humor can instantly take you away, even if only for a few moments, from your troubles and make them easier to bear. Humor can give you a breather—a minivacation that can allow you to regain your strength and pull your resources together so you can get through another day, another hour, another minute. When you can find humor in your discomfort and tragedies, you can begin to see the bigger picture and move forward instead of backward; you can embrace life again and heal some of your pain and sadness.

Today, tell a friend or loved one, "Hey, let's stop being so down in the dumps. I'm still here. *We're* still here. So let's find something to laugh at together." While shared laughter won't change the unchangeable or alter the course of a disease, it can help you feel better. Like the spoonful of sugar in the Disney film *Mary Poppins,* sharing a joke, a funny story, a humorous memory, or a silly song can make taking your medicine so much easier.

♦ Humor can minimize my suffering or the suffering of others by giving us power in what is a powerless situation. While the situation I or others may be in today isn't humorous, there are certainly laughs we can find and share together.

As an ex-drill instructor, she has to know something about discipline. I like a little discipline in all my relationships, if you know what I mean.

—Joan Jett Blakk

Do you and your sexual partner(s) like different things? Do you find that at the beginning of a sexual relationship, there's very little talking or verbal exploration of what the other person likes and what he or she is willing to do? Do you find that when you become monogamous with one person, gradually your sex life becomes established in a way that makes lovemaking very predictable?

You may tend to ignore the fact that exploring different sexual interests and fantasies can spark a change in lovemaking that can make your sex life work much better. If you're willing to make your sex life work in ways that are fulfilling as well as exciting to both you and your partner, then you need to make your desires known so you can work on them together.

In the process of such sexual communication, what you may discover is that you don't enjoy the "typical" ways of making love. As a lesbian, you might dislike oral sex but crave bondage, vaginal or anal penetration, or group sex. As a gay man, you might prefer a dildo, being blindfolded, or having more gentle, passionate sex. Through talking about and then experimenting with the things that give you both pleasure, you're learning to both be on the same team. And that means you both win!

♦ Today I'll be as specific as possible when I communicate with my partner about the different way(s) I'd like to be made love to. When my partner discusses what he or she wants, I'll respond by saying, "I'm so glad we're talking about this."

It's no wonder we know how to dress: We've spent centuries in closets.

—ISAAC MIZRAHI

Openly gay fashion designer Isaac Mizrahi believes that gay men and lesbians should express pride in their sexuality through their style of dress. Because of this, some of the hottest "lesbo" and "homo" couture can be found today in corporate headquarters, workout facilities, softball diamonds, gay resorts, and the bars. Whether preparing for bed, bath, or beyond, gay men and lesbians are often on the cutting edge of fashion, daring to be different not only in the clothes they wear, but also in their accessories, how they style their hair, and how they show off their bodies in their clothing.

Even if you work in a profession that encourages being conservative and discourages free expression in the way you dress, you can still avoid suppression of your creative gay fashion sense. What you wear *under* your clothes is your personal choice, as well as what you wear outside work. You may have your own favorite gaywear or dykewear fashion for workout sessions at the gym, hanging out at the beach, and dancing at the club.

Remember that there's no magazine that determines what's in and what's not for gay fashion, so you have the freedom to wear whatever's right for you. When it feels good on you and makes you feel good *about* you, then you know you're making the "right" fashion statement.

◆ Today I'll use colors, fabrics, and accessories to show off my pride in my sexuality and in my body. I don't have to follow any fashion rules or mimic what others in my crowd are wearing.

When the first person I knew died, I could not throw his Rolodex
card away. So I saved it. I now have a rubber band around 341 cards.
— DAVID GEFFEN

When someone you love dies, it may be hard to honor his or her death in conventional ways. The fact that he or she was gay may not be known to family members. Likewise, the fact that you had an intimate relationship with the deceased may either not be known or may be rejected by family members who have assumed control of the body, the burial, and the bereavement.

How would you like to commemorate the death of a loved one? You might create a panel for the AIDS quilt, write a poem, gather friends together for a private memorial service, or compile a scrapbook of memories you've shared together. Or you may prefer to become more active in the gay and lesbian community, to write letters to congressional members to urge passage of gay-related issues, or choose to be more open about your sexuality.

When Joseph P. Milano, USN, died with 240 others during the 1983 suicide car-bombing in Lebanon, he left behind his lover, a marine who was stationed in Okinawa at the time. Don learned about the news only after he had read a week-old newspaper account and then impersonated a chaplain to learn the names of the dead. "That was devastating," he says. "There was no one with whom I could share my grief." Today Don proudly displays a Silence = Death poster and a rainbow flag in his apartment.

♦ When a loved one dies and I have to invent a story or lie so I can openly grieve or be given funeral leave, then it's time for me to look for at least one way I can honestly and openly commemorate my loved one's death.

I think we should be tying up whole cities. We should cripple this country. We should throw bombs. We should set fires. We should stop traffic. We should surround the White House.

—LARRY KRAMER

What do you believe are effective means of activism in the gay and lesbian community? Larry Kramer—writer, founder of ACT UP, and cofounder of Gay Men's Health Crisis in New York City—responded to the AIDS crisis in 1987 with the above statement. In 1992 he said, "I have no idea what to do or where we go from here. I have tried every trick I can think of and made every suggestion my brain and my imagination can spit out. Whatever it is we are trying to get—a cure for AIDS, equality, a place at the table of life—we are failing miserably."

Many activists feel that their time and energy is often wasted because there's no one in any position of power that truly cares about gay and lesbian issues. Even openly gay elected officials, advocacy groups in Washington, and political organizations around the country are demoralized, exhausted, and bureaucratized beyond effectiveness.

The only way you can make a difference in the gay and lesbian community is to unite with others. Empowerment begins with numbers, not individuals. Today, let go of any separatist tendencies you may have—excluding men/women, people of color, those with AIDS, etc.—and unite with them so you can fight with them.

♦ Today I'll keep in mind that the gay and lesbian community cannot effectively march forward if we are all marching in different directions. I'll join with my brothers and sisters so we can be united, not divided.

Women spoke to me about how exalted they felt after seeing something on the screen that represented a truth in their lives. I was high for about three days after that.

——HELEN SHAVER

Actress Helen Shaver was seen in the popular lesbian movie *Desert Hearts* in 1986. The movie prodded lesbian visibility to move two steps forward by being released in mainstream movie houses. But since that time, few lesbian movies have gathered as much praise and interest in the lesbian community. *Fried Green Tomatoes,* with its all-star cast and Hollywood backing, was a wonderful production and a great story. Yet it dishonored Fannie Flagg's original novel and moved the lesbian community two steps backward by carefully avoiding anything more than a hint of the "L" word.

Gay men have also had little to rave about in the theaters as resoundingly as they did with *Longtime Companion.* Bit parts for homosexuals in mainstream movies such as *Single White Female* or *JFK* have done little to move gay men forward in visibility or to challenge some of the tired stereotypes of homosexuals.

It's up to you to demand of Hollywood that the good books or plays that probe universal themes with gay men and lesbians as main characters be produced for mainstream cinema. Think of engrossing stories of women who are lesbian and men who are gay, then send copies of the books or mention them in letters to motion-picture studios. Someday, someone just might pay attention.

◆ I'm not helping good gay and lesbian stories get on the screen by complaining just to my community. Today I'll voice my opinion to those in positions to make changes. That's the only way my voice can truly be heard.

I was to give a child security and tenderness, but didn't feel I received enough of this myself.

—Liv Ullmann

Low self-esteem, self-destructive behavior, and trouble with intimacy are not always caused by same-sex attractions. Rather, psychotherapist Rik Isensee believes they stem "from the most part from the intense oppression experienced while growing up in a dysfunctional family within a homophobic society."

If your parents abused you as a child or were dysfunctional themselves, you may not have felt that it was safe while you were growing up to have or express your feelings. So whatever you felt at the time—fear, anxiety, depression, blame, doubt, guilt—were internalized and "put on hold" to be dealt with at another time. Add to these internalized feelings your own confused and sometimes frightening feelings about your attraction to members of your own sex, and you may have grown up feeling very insecure and quite traumatized.

In order for a child to heal from traumatic events or to release suppressed feelings, an understanding, nurturing, and gentle adult is often essential. Today you can heal that child within you. The emotional support you can receive from twelve-step recovery groups or therapy can connect you with gentle, understanding, and nurturing adults who can help soothe the pain of the past.

◆ Rather than try to escape from my feelings, today I'll take steps to learn how to tolerate them. To help work through the hurt, fear, anger, and sadness, I'll enlist the help of a supportive recovery group.

The majority of us lead quiet, unheralded lives as we pass through this world. There will most likely be no ticker-tape parades for us, no monuments created in our honor. But that does not lessen our possible impact, for there are scores of people waiting for someone just like us to come along. . . .

—LEO BUSCAGLIA

Have you ever thought about the first person who brought you out, the first gay man or lesbian you admired, or the first person—gay or straight—who accepted your revelation that you were gay? What impact did that person have on your life as a gay man or lesbian? What positive messages or experiences did he or she leave with you?

Today you can pass on to others the positive messages or experiences of your past. There are many men and women of all ages and from all backgrounds who are questioning their sexuality or wondering if there's anything wrong with them because they love someone of the same sex. These people may appreciate your understanding, guidance, knowledge, and nurturing as they struggle to seek the way of life that's right for them.

You may even enable someone to have a happier life because of the time you took to share from your voice of strength, hope, and experience. Today, don't underestimate the power of a touch, a smile, a hug, or a listening ear. Each of these things has the potential to turn someone's life around.

♦ Is there a small act of caring I can extend to someone who I know is having a rough time dealing with his or her sexuality? Today I'll offer my hand in friendship, my shoulder in support, and my heart in love.

*The more you learn to love and accept yourself, the more you will
realize that you are doing exactly what you need to do to provide
yourself with experiences to grow into higher consciousness.*

—KEN KEYES

Have you ever applied the slogan "Live and let live" to being a
gay man or lesbian? The familiar slogan from twelve-step
recovery programs can actually be used in your daily life to
help you develop self-acceptance.

First, concentrate on the beginning word of the slogan—
"live." This tells you to enjoy your life fully the way you want
to live it, regardless of how other people are living their lives.
When you focus on how you're going to live, rather than on
how you think you *should* live as a gay man or lesbian or on
how others—straight or gay—would *like* you to live, your
life can become fulfilling in many ways.

However, it's all but impossible to move forward in life if you
continually allow yourself to be upset or offended by the actions,
attitudes, or behaviors of others. This can bring you to an understanding of the words "let live." These words mean that you need
to accept your powerlessness over others. Every person in your
life needs to live as he or she chooses, free from your criticism,
judgment, contempt, or resentment.

Today, meet the challenge presented by the "Live and let
live" philosophy. Concentrate on learning to love and accept
yourself as you would love and accept others—and as you
wish them to love and accept you.

◆ When I concentrate on my own life, I'm less likely to
scrutinize the way others live or to shift the focus from me.
Today I'll acknowledge the right of every person—
including myself—to live as he or she chooses.

There has been very little support within my community for people my age. I wish that there could have been an older gay or lesbian person there for me when I was coming out who could have helped to take the fear away. . . . A lot of the time I was having sex, what I really wanted was love, to be cared for, to belong.

—DAVID KAMENS

David Kamens began going to gay bars at fourteen years of age and having unprotected casual sex with older men. At sixteen he got sick and was diagnosed with AIDS. "Although I had a very supportive family," he says, "I didn't have support anywhere in my life for being gay." Today he is trying to make a difference in the lives of other kids who are gay and lesbian by delivering lectures at their schools and by working with teens in youth-oriented organizations.

Do you realize how much gay teens need your support? Think of the struggles you may have had in coming out, the pressures that may have been placed upon you, the isolation you may have felt as you grappled with your sexual identity, the harassment or abuse you may have had to absorb from those who were homophobic.

You *can* make a difference in the life of a young gay man or lesbian. Help a gay youth feel less isolated and alone today by volunteering in a teen organization, speaking at a high school about safe sex, providing a listening ear to ease their fears, or offering a kind and gentle hand of support and friendship.

♦ I need to support gay and lesbian kids in order to provide them with a sense of unity, community, and validity for their sexuality. Today I won't wait for a gay youth to reach out to me; I'll take the first step.

When I hear somebody sigh, "Life is hard," I am always tempted to ask, "Compared to what?"

— SYDNEY J. HARRIS

It used to be that you could pick up any gay or lesbian periodical and read details of horrible hate crimes or gay bashings; today you can read such things in the local newspaper or hear about them on the evening news. Unfortunately, on any given day, you can trust that somewhere in the world, in your country, in your state, in your city, or even in your neighborhood, a gay man or a lesbian is the victim of verbal, physical, or sexual abuse.

Certainly there are many experiences in your life as a gay man or a lesbian that are hate-filled and cruel, unfair and inhumane, indecent and based on ignorance. You've been conditioned from years of struggle and fears for the loss of your freedoms to believe that horrendous acts against gay men and lesbians are the norm.

But some very wonderful things happen in the gay and lesbian community, too—relationships that last for decades, court cases that uphold the rights of a gay man or a lesbian, PRIDE marches, openly gay people in positions of visibility and power, children born or adopted into loving gay and lesbian households. There's much good in your way of life that you can see, if you let yourself.

Today, get off your "life is difficult" soapbox and hear the humor, see the smiles, and feel the love and caring in your community. Although life may be difficult at times, it can also be quite fulfilling.

◆ I need to feel that my way of life has good, positive things in it. What event can I look forward to today? Who can I spend time with who will make me feel good?

The person I am now is far more sophisticated, far more aware, conscious, and mature, and the externals are less defensive. . . . I'm not saying that now I'm sorted out, have a baby, have therapy, everything's perfect. But with age and time and experience, things just pass.

— ANNIE LENNOX

Growing up in the gay and lesbian community is a process of realizing not only who you are, but also how you're changing through the passage of time and your experiences. When you were younger, you may have gone through periods of uncertainty, doubt, and confusion about your sexuality or way of life. You may have asked yourself: "Is this way of life right for me? How out do I want to be? Can I find a life partner with whom I can be happy? How do I deal with conflicts my way of life may create within my family or in my interactions with others?"

Every gay man or lesbian knows what it's like to go through such periods of questioning and uncertainty. But getting through such times can bring you closer to certainty—to times when you have more answers than questions, you're more accepting and comfortable with who you are, and you're capable of making decisions that are right for you.

Today, keep in mind that periods of uncertainty will always come up. However, they can be processed more quickly and easily when you rely upon your maturity and listen to your voice of experience.

◆ If today takes me through a period of uncertainty in my growth as a gay man or a lesbian, now is the perfect time to rely upon what I've learned in the past to provide me with answers.

I have enjoyed the happiness of the world; I have lived and loved.

—FRIEDRICH VON SCHILLER

Do you focus compulsively or without interruption on one or more areas of your life except the one that matters the most—living? Maybe you devote all your time and energy to working on difficulties in your relationship. Perhaps you focus much of your attention on coming to terms with your sexuality or childhood issues. Maybe you're working twenty-four hours a day, seven days a week on your program of recovery from an addiction to drugs, alcohol, food, or sex. Perhaps you've become immersed in programs, publications, or protests on behalf of issues that affect you and the gay and lesbian community.

But aren't you missing the whole point of being alive? Your existence was not meant to be one- or even two-dimensional, nor were you chosen to be the expert in one or two particular areas. It was never intended that your days and nights be spent with blinders on, focusing only on certain people, places, or things in your life. To the contrary, life was designed to be a continuous unfolding of glorious and multidimensional possibilities—myriad places to go, people to see, things to do, and wonders to experience.

Today, make your first order of business to live. Discover, develop, and enjoy every area of your life by concentrating on the whole experience of living.

◆ Today I'll bring more meaning into my life by keeping all areas of my life in balance. I can fully enjoy the rewards of everything I do if I can do a little bit of everything.

I believe my sexuality is a gift from God. For any institution to encourage that a person lie, or that a person cannot say or be who they are, I am deeply troubled by the decision.

—REVEREND JANE SPAHR

Lesbian minister Reverend Jane Spahr's selection as pastor of the Downtown United Presbyterian Church in Rochester, New York, was barred by the General Assembly Permanent Judicial Commission of the Presbyterian Church (USA) late in 1992. To explain its ruling, Reverend Ronald Sallade, who led the opposition to Spahr's appointment, said: "We did not do this as an anti-gay kind of thing. The Presbyterian church's policy has been very clear, that unrepentant homosexual practice is a sin."

It may be very difficult to feel comfortable expressing your religious beliefs when you're a gay man or a lesbian. You may find that you act openly and honestly to the outside world most of the time, but during your time of worship, you hide who you are so you can worship at the church you choose. Or you may seek to exercise your religious freedom in a church that allows gay men and lesbians to join in worship and spiritual healing. Yet no matter what you do, it may be hard for you to come to terms with the double standard that you are loved and accepted by your religion as long as you don't reveal who you really are.

If you want to progress spiritually, you can't allow yourself to be deceptive about who you are. Your higher power has no double standards in offering you love and acceptance.

◆ Today I'll take a look at the spiritual principles I want to live by in my life. I won't disguise who I am so I can exercise my religious freedoms.

I told several heterosexual friends, most of whom responded with excessive melodrama. The subtext was the same: "I'm upset because you're going to die." This is not a message you want to hear while you're trying to maintain a positive attitude.

—RANDY SHILTS

When Randy Shilts—reporter, author, and one of the most prominent gay men in the nation—announced in early 1993 that he had AIDS but was not willing to talk about it further, his disclosure renewed discussion about the intrusiveness of an AIDS diagnosis, particularly for the famous or semifamous. Shilts's decision to keep his diagnosis private was consistent with his dedication to being a person who was writing the stories, not the focus of the stories.

Shilts's disclosure has also opened up discussion on the topic of trust on many levels in both the gay and lesbian communities. In other words, how open should you be with others, what topics or issues ought to be discussed, and how willing are you to have your "dirty laundry" aired if information told in confidence escapes from your circle of friends and provides grist for the gossip mills in the close-knit gay and lesbian communities?

Before you consider sharing private information with another today, consider the trustworthiness of that person. Then ask yourself: "Will it be a problem for me if this information gets out to others?"

♦ When I need to share an issue today that's close to my heart or very private, I'll be conscious of the person I'll be using as my resource. I'll choose someone who can be a source of strength and not a spokesperson to others.

Never bend your head, always hold it high. Look the world straight in the face.

— HELEN KELLER

One of the most difficult challenges you may have to deal with as a gay man or a lesbian is coming out to someone who matters to you. To talk face-to-face with this person and be open, honest, and vulnerable can be excruciatingly uncomfortable. Because of this, you may try hard to sidestep such conversations. But when they're unavoidable, you may resort to any number of "escape techniques" to keep from making eye contact—lighting or smoking a cigarette, sipping on a drink, eating a meal, playing with a paper clip, watching people walk by, or staring at the person's forehead. Doing such things may make you feel less exposed or lessen the intensity of your fear and discomfort, but they will also prevent you from connecting with the person to whom you're speaking.

Today, make a conscious decision to stop "hiding" from a person to whom you'd like to reveal your sexuality. Let the expression "The eyes are the windows to the soul" guide you in letting someone see deeply into who you are as you also see deeply into who he or she is. When you stop trying to "hide," you'll find that your self-consciousness, fear, and discomfort gradually diminish. What slowly takes their place is trust, pride, self-respect, and self-worth.

◆ Today I'll treasure one of my most valued freedoms: to reveal, easily and fearlessly, who I am when I talk with others—and to look them squarely in the eye when I do so.

I came to understand that it was all right to do things for people as long as I did it for the sake of doing it . . . the value being more in the act than in the result.

—JOANNA FIELD

How much do you give of yourself to other gay men or lesbians? You may have heard the sentiment "It's better to give than to receive." Yet you may find it difficult to give to others—an ex-lover who may have hurt you but who now may be going through a difficult time, a life partner who seems to be able to take more than give, a group that's become disorganized or whose members have conflicts with one another, a friend who's suffering with AIDS-related illnesses, an insensitive roommate, or a friend who's having a hard time letting go of a relationship. It may be hard for you to let go of the expectation of getting something in return as you care for someone who's ill, run an errand for a friend, give a back rub, or extend an invitation to someone who's alone.

To give unselfishly of yourself exposes your feelings, shows you care, and demands nothing of another. Sometimes this may fill you with resentment; other times you may be afraid to be so open. Yet if you can look beyond your fears and release your resentments, there can be a great reward in giving. Knowing that you had the courage to risk giving to someone opens the door to the home of your heart; it not only touches others in its goodness, but can also touch you.

◆ Today I'll make time to give to others. I'll risk giving to someone close to me, whether that giving involves an actual gift or simply an act of giving of myself.

> *Eve [in* All About Eve*] is a fascinating character—
> ambitious, scheming, very strong. One might say she's a rather
> masculine kind of woman—if one equates drive with masculinity.*
> —Anne Baxter

Once, when a daughter came out to her father, she was greeted by his sad expression. "It makes me very unhappy that you're going to be one of them," he said.

"One of them?" the daughter repeated.

"Yes." The father sighed. "One of those women who looks and acts like a man."

"But, look at me," the daughter protested. "Just because I'm gay doesn't mean I'm going to look or act like other lesbians or your idea of them. I'm going to be me."

If you don't fit into the stereotypical image of what a gay man or lesbian is supposed to look and act like, you may find that those you come out to have a hard time taking your sexuality seriously. "But you couldn't possibly be gay," might be their response. "You're so masculine/feminine."

One of the joys of being a gay man or a lesbian is that you don't have to be, act, or behave in any given way. As a gay man, you can play a game of racquetball at the gym and then later go out to a club dressed in drag; as a lesbian, you can be outfitted in a stunning designer skirt suit at work, then change into sweats to tinker on your motorcycle at night.

Today, embrace both your masculine and feminine sides. They are what makes you *you*.

◆ Am I a "typical" gay man or lesbian? Today I'll nurture both my masculine and feminine qualities; they're important parts that contribute to who I am and how I act as a whole person.

You telling me God love you, and you ain't never done nothing for Him? I mean, not go to church, sing in a choir, feed the preacher and all that? . . . if God love me, I don't have to do all that. There's lots of other things I can do that I speck God likes. . . . I can lay back and just admire stuff. Be happy.

—ALICE WALKER, FROM *THE COLOR PURPLE*

When you were growing up, you may have learned that homosexuals were "bad people"—sinners who went to hell when they died. You may have learned the story of Adam and Eve and been told that it was normal and natural for men and women to be together. So you may have suppressed your sexual desires and gone to church so you could get "good marks" from the great power in the heavens.

Today you might still believe that a God or a higher power is watching over you, judging your way of life. You might still practice the religion of your childhood because you think that's what you should do. You might be selective about the things you feel you can do as a gay man or a lesbian so you can still remain in "good favor" with the Almighty One.

Yet a belief in any power greater than yourself isn't based on what you can give or what you do. Rather, all that's necessary for a belief is that you have trust and faith in some power greater than yourself. There are no rules or regulations that tell you how to pray or when to pray or what things you have to do to get the approval of this power. All you are asked to do is to believe.

♦ Rather than seek to be what I think my higher power wants me to be, I'll simply be myself. Today I'll come to believe in a power greater than myself and trust in this power.

The responsibility of tolerance lies with those who have the wider vision.

— GEORGE ELIOT

You, perhaps more than others, are more familiar with tolerance. You may be only too aware of how necessary it is to treat people equally regardless of their color, sex, religious beliefs, or way of life. As a gay man or lesbian, you may be so sensitive to the intolerance of others that you weep at films showing the race riots of the 1960s in the South, at photos of gay men or lesbians who have been brutally murdered or beaten because of their sexuality, at news reports of children who have been abused, or at stories about women who have been raped or murdered.

Yet the majority of the population tends to think of tolerance mainly in terms of job equality, equal opportunity, open housing, and so on. How can you help others go beyond this "democratic" concept of tolerance to one in which they learn to recognize and respect the opinions, practices, and right to life for everyone?

Today your goal can be to live in the fullest partnership, peace, and fellowship with all men and women—gay or straight. Living without criticism, judgment, and fighting everything or everyone is one way to exhibit a concept of tolerance that has a deeper significance. By widening your vision, you can increase the capacity for others to see the world the way you do: a world filled with serenity, respect, and fellowship with all peoples.

◆ Redefining tolerance isn't something that can be achieved quickly or absolutely. But if I exhibit true tolerance today, I may be able to increase the vision of one person so he or she can begin to look at the world differently.

Mostly I just sleep. Or go out and walk around. I end up asking myself, "What am I going to do? Who am I going to be with? Am I really loved? Am I not?" I don't know. I get really emotional because I want to be with the family. But my mother doesn't want that.

—DANNY FERGUSON

In California there are programs designed for "queer youth," such as Gay and Lesbian Adolescent Social Services (GLASS), and there are a number of lesbian and gay youth groups around the country. However, gay youth are generally ignored by the adult gay and lesbian community as a whole.

With little education in the school systems, a lack of positive adult lesbian and gay role models to counteract the impression made by negative gay and lesbian images, few places where below-legal-age gay and lesbian youth can meet and socialize, and little or no AIDS prevention or safe-sex discussion on the teen and preteen level, lesbian and gay youth are pretty much alone as they come to terms with their sexuality.

Today, consider ways your community could benefit *all* members. Creating space for youth in the adult community may be as simple as opening a bar one night to allow teens to meet, dance, and drink nonalcoholic beverages, or as ambitious as beginning some type of lesbian and gay big brother/big sister program for gay youth. Rather than require each gay youth to come out alone, invest your energy into helping a young person come out to a community of support.

◆ Today I'll remember that I, too, was once a gay youth. I'll help eliminate the isolation that may be felt by lesbian or gay youth by creating for them a physical space in the community or an emotional space in my heart.

. . . they've been going through this for years and they've been really taking care of their own. You have to give the gay and lesbian community a lot of credit for that. The rest of us have a lot to learn from that.

—MAGIC JOHNSON

When soldiers march together and one falters or falls to the ground, the others don't step around or over the fallen body. Rather, they reach down and pull up the body together so the unit can continue to march as one.

As devastating as the AIDS epidemic has been on the gay and lesbian community, the community has often responded as one. There have been many fallen soldiers that have needed to be picked up and carried; others have had to be buried. But the community has, as one, taken care of the sick, the dying, and the dead in ways that can only be viewed as admirable. Remarkably, instead of the marching unit becoming weaker or smaller, the community has been strengthened by the epidemic, and the numbers who march with the community have increased.

Today, continue your march in the battle against AIDS. Participate in walks, runs, and other special events that benefit AIDS. Volunteer as an AIDS buddy to a member of the community who needs you. Donate money for medicine for those who can't afford it. And be there for your loved ones when they need a strong arm to cling to when their steps falter.

♦ Just because I'm HIV negative doesn't mean I'm safe from the effects AIDS has had upon my community. Today I'll join hands with those who are HIV positive or who have AIDS and let them know that they're never alone.

Know yourself. Don't accept your dog's admiration as conclusive evidence that you are wonderful.

—ANN LANDERS

Do you view your pet as the "perfect partner"—a companion who doesn't make demands, have expectations, judge you, criticize you, cheat on you, mistreat you, ignore you, or let you know you're just not good enough? If so, you might choose to spend more time caring for your pet or accumulating pets and less time with people.

While interacting with your animals may feel safe and secure, there's not much risk taking you can do or self-awareness you can develop when you're with them that can help with your individual growth. That certain sameness that happens in taking care of animals may seem sane compared with some of your interactions with others; however, it can lull you into a routine that does little to encourage changes you need to make in your behaviors or to provide you with personal challenges.

Yet you can get such things in your interactions with other gay men or lesbians. Whether you're in a support group, a social organization, a friendship, dating situation, or an intimate relationship, that "certain sameness" is often lacking. It's usually replaced by conflicts, connections, communication, doubts, risks, uncertainties, fears, joys, laughter, tears, and all sorts of other unexpected pleasures and displeasures that can contribute to your overall growth as an individual.

◆ Today I'll keep in mind that my pet isn't a life partner who can meet all my needs, wants, and desires. I'll seek to create a balance between connecting with my pet and connecting with humans so I can enjoy both.

SEPTEMBER 1

Your profession is not who you are, it is only a costume.

—ANONYMOUS

There are people who, when they retire from their jobs, suffer great hopelessness, lethargy, depression—even death. Because they identified for so long and often so loyally with a company or a career, they may have neglected to nurture other interests. As a result, being out of work can feel like a personal loss or "death" to them. With their work "costume" gone, they may not know how else to identify themselves.

Do you feel a similar need to wear a gay or lesbian "costume"? Perhaps you wear T-shirts with slogans, plaster bumper stickers or pink triangles on your car, read only gay and lesbian literature, socialize only with gay men or lesbians, or focus your life predominantly on issues that affect the gay or lesbian community.

But if such things define you, give you a sense of direction, or bring greater meaning to your life, then you're using them to create your identity. Ask yourself today how you'd feel if an external—such as gay-identified clothing you wear—were taken from you. Would you feel naked and without purpose?

Today, start nurturing what's beneath your gay or lesbian "costume." Develop your own interests outside the community, focus on your spiritual growth, or experiment with changes you can make in yourself. Doing such things can help you put away the "costume" so you can strengthen your identity.

♦ Am I content with just being myself, without living day in and day out behind a gay identity? Today I'll let go of the need always to belong to the community and belong instead just to myself.

We should be careful to get out of an experience only the wisdom that is in it—and stay there, lest we be like the cat that sits down on a hot stove-lid. She will never sit down on a hot stove-lid again . . . but also, she will never sit down on a cold one any more.

—MARK TWAIN

Every gay man or lesbian can recount a difficult experience he or she has gone through in becoming more open about his or her way of life. There are horror stories about sons or daughters being disowned after revealing their sexuality to their parents. There are tales of friends who freak out when they hear their best friend is gay. There are painful relationship breakups, gay bashings, losses of a life partner, and so on.

One bad situation with one person doesn't mean that everyone else will behave in the same way. If you believe all your friends will freak out when you come out to them, you may not come out to any of them. If you believe every family member will react as your parents did, you may remain estranged from your entire family. If you don't believe you can trust another lover, you won't.

But there isn't any growth in this kind of thinking. Today, take a risk so you can see those who are your friends, those family members who love you, and those lovers you can love and trust.

◆ If I get rejected by someone, that doesn't mean no one can be trusted. It means I need to take another risk or two to find those who can truly be there for me.

Are gay people happy? Actually, some of us are, despite the fact that we live in a society that calls us "sick," "depraved" and "evil." With those labels it's not easy to maintain self-esteem. If straight people have a problem with my being gay, that's their hang-up, not mine. . . . People who are sure of their own sexuality are willing to live and let live.

—A LETTER SIGNED "CHICAGO," TO ANN LANDERS

Can you say "I like myself" and really mean it? To say that statement and mean it, you have to like *everything* about yourself: your good qualities as well as your bad, your appearance, the way you interact with others, the way you express yourself, your sexuality, and the way you live your life. Liking yourself should never be contingent upon how others feel about you—whether they approve of you or your way of life or whether they even like you. Liking yourself comes from how you feel inside about who you are, not from the approval of others.

You already know firsthand that not everyone is going to like you; add to this the fact that not a whole lot of people will like your being a gay man or a lesbian. But today, don't let such things influence how you feel about yourself. You don't deserve any low opinion you may have of yourself. Instead, think of at least five qualities about yourself you like. Then say, "I like me," and really mean it.

◆ While I may live my life in ways that aren't necessarily embraced by others, that doesn't mean I can't embrace them myself. Today I'll like who I am on the inside and not let others on the outside influence how I feel about myself.

Nature has been for me, for as long as I can remember, a source of solace, inspiration, adventure, and delight; a home, a teacher, a companion.

—LORRAINE ANDERSON

How often do you take time to notice the wonders of the natural world—the rainbow after a rainstorm, the birds frolicking around your bird feeder, or the silvery brilliance of a full moon? How often do you go out of your way to discover a new path through the woods at your favorite campground or a less traveled route to work? How often do you allow time in your schedule to quietly connect with nature in some small way—by getting up early to sit in a city park and watch the sunrise as the city slowly awakens or by peering up at a star-filled night sky?

The mad rush of day-to-day living, combined with working for gay community causes and socializing with friends and loved ones on nights and weekends, can distance you from the joys and wonders of nature. It's easy to forget that there's a natural world around you teeming with wonders when you're jammed into a smoky bar or trying to be heard over the interruptions of others at a heated gay rights committee meeting.

Today, reolve to get out of the bars and agitated meeting rooms and into the outdoors. Make picnic plans with friends, tune up your bicycle for a weekend ride, or make reservations to get out of the city for a short time.

♦ Today I'll pay attention to the natural wonders of the world. By taking time and opening my senses, I'll break my indoor routine and notice a whole new world around me.

While we have the gift of life, it seems to me the only tragedy is to allow part of us to die—whether it is our spirit, our creativity or our glorious uniqueness.

—GILDA RADNER

When Gilda Radner lost her life to cancer, it was not her medical battles or the various healing techniques she tried and detailed in her books that were most remembered by gay men and lesbians. Rather, it was her ability to make others laugh through the memorable characters she created on *Saturday Night Live:* Judy Miller, Roseanne Roseannadanna, Emily Latella, and many others. While Gilda Radner's courage to battle her cancer gave gay men and lesbians with AIDS or cancer the courage to battle their own diseases, her real gift was her ability to continue to live her life as a comedienne, not to be overwhelmed by illness, not let a part of herself give up and die.

Today, don't give up any part of yourself as you struggle to heal. Don't stop talking about who you are and how you feel, for silence equals death. Don't stop feeling about those you care for in your life, for numbness equals death. Don't stop dreaming your dreams, for dreamlessness equals death. Don't stop creating through drawing, writing, cooking, painting, gardening, or redecorating, for not creating equals death. And don't stop thinking about tomorrow, for hopelessness equals death.

◆ Today I'll push aside negative thoughts and the numbing dullness of depression and live my life to the fullest. If today is to be my last day, let me go knowing that I truly lived it.

A lot of people in England still find it difficult to believe lesbians do anything. Except perhaps knit together.

—DAME MAGGIE SMITH

"So what do you two do together?" is a question often posed by those who seem to be more curious about what you do in bed and how you do it than about who you are. How to respond to such crude sexual curiosity can best be summarized by actress-satirist Sandra Bernhard. When she posed intimately and provocatively with both men and women in *Playboy* magazine, she shrugged off speculation about her own sexual preferences by saying, "If people are that interested in my sexuality, it must mean they all want to have sex with me."

It's nobody's business what you do—or don't do—in bed with your lover. Nor is it anybody's business what you and your lover do in the general day-to-day workings of your relationship—who takes out the trash, who pays the bills, who's the "real" mother/father of your child, and so on.

Homo-curiosity expressed by hetero-curious people seeks to define you in ways that make you and your behaviors the same as those of every gay man or lesbian. But that's like determining who a person of color or a Native American person is, based on interactions with or information provided by one person from either group.

Today, when asked by anyone what you "do" as a gay person, respond with the question, "What do you do as a straight person?"

♦ Today I won't confuse the curiosity expressed by others about my way of life and how I live it with true concern about who I am as a gay man or a lesbian.

At every step the child should be allowed to meet the real experiences of life; the thorns should never be plucked from the roses.

—ELLEN KEY

Reality is not always pleasant, particularly for children of gay parents. More often than not, once the reality of having two mothers or two fathers is known to classmates, such reality can become the basis for painful lessons, as children are subjected to ridicule, harassment, isolation, exclusion, or even physical abuse. Accepting that there will be that pain is part of the process of your child's growth; shielding your child from the experiences of such pain is rarely beneficial, for it can directly hinder his or her ability to handle future pain.

Accepting pain as part of any child's growth is an important component in your growth as a parent. Opportunities for your child's growth will come about in many forms—from laughter and happiness to friendships to fun and play to sadness and heartache to questioning and processing. Letting your child absorb from every experience—the good as well as the bad—can help strengthen your child's character, facilitate the maturing process, and prepare your child for whatever lies ahead in life.

Today, accept that you can't hide your child from pain. You can only do what any parent should do: be there to help your child grow from the pain, whenever it appears.

◆ Today will offer my child both pleasure and pain. I need to let my son or daughter experience both in order to become a stronger person to deal with tomorrow.

There must be lesbians back there. I didn't know any at the time except my lover. I was real isolated in Ohio.

—BARBRA KAY

It's a rare person indeed who never feels lonely, but often gay men or lesbians feel loneliness more acutely than the population as a whole. Growing up can be a very lonely process when you're dealing with your sexuality. Add to that the experience of growing up in a rural community where little or no opportunities exist for interacting with other gay men or lesbians, and you may end up feeling as if you're the only gay man or lesbian in the world. So it's not unusual to grow up thinking, "What's wrong with me?" or being in a hurry to leave your small, isolated community.

But if you're still living in a rural location, you may feel from time to time that you're cut off from the gay and lesbian community. Even subscribing to gay and lesbian publications, traveling hours every few weeks to the nearest city's gay bar, or making friends with another gay person in your town can leave you feeling isolated and alone—a stranger in a strange land.

In order to achieve a balance and enjoy where you live as well as your way of life, extend a hand to the gay and lesbian population. Offer your home as a stopping-off point to gay men or lesbians traveling across country. Write articles for gay and lesbian newspapers. Or create a letter writing network that can unite other gay men and lesbians who live in rural communities.

♦ Today I'll pay attention to my feelings of isolation and open myself up to finding "cures." I'll be able to see and hear others around me when I can discover ways to connect with them.

I got called on the carpet by Walt Disney about it. It was toward the end of my contract, and he told me I was in trouble. He advised that I'd better start liking girls and fast."

—TOMMY KIRK

Child actor Tommy Kirk, who starred in such Disney films as *The Shaggy Dog* and *The Swiss Family Robinson,* has had an experience far different from that of the few openly gay people working for the Disney studios today. Yet if, in Disney's movie credits, every individual who was gay was noted, the management at Disney's studios might feel the same way Walt Disney did decades ago. For even though times are different from the days when Tommy Kirk's name was up in lights, in many ways gay men and lesbians—as well as the organizations they work for—feel more comfortable staying in the dark.

No one knows the reactions of straight people to an individual's gayness better than a gay man or lesbian coworker. "Do you honestly think the reaction to my coming out to one of them would be favorable?" is the usual formulation. "You don't have to work with them day in and day out to know. When it comes to us, believe me, their minds are filled with ignorance, stereotypes, and sleaze!"

Today, don't feel pressured to reveal your sexuality in any situation you feel isn't best served by such a revelation. After all, you're the one who has to feel—and deal with—the aftereffects.

◆ Today I'll come out only when I feel secure, when I feel that nothing can happen to me as a result of such a revelation.

For years I wanted to be older, and now I am.

—MARGARET ATWOOD, FROM *CAT'S EYE*

In some countries or cultures, the elderly are revered more than any other people. They are sought out for their opinions, wisdom, or mature advice. They are treated at all times with courtesy and respect. They are thought to be blessed with psychic, magical, or spiritual powers. Younger household members will even live in cramped quarters just so the older ones can have more space and attention.

In the gay and lesbian communities, however, many of the older members are not treated as kindly and respectfully. Some younger gays become impatient with older members who can't keep up with their pace or the times. Others view older gay men or lesbians as stepping-stones to use on the way to something bigger or better. Still others pay no attention to the wisdom or advice offered by those they view as being incapable of understanding how times and issues have changed for the gay men and lesbians of today.

Yet most older gay men and lesbians have had to face far greater challenges and to clear far more difficult hurdles than most young people will ever have to deal with in their lifetimes. Today, go out of your way to include an older gay man or lesbian in your plans. Consider how lucky you are to have him or her in the community—and in your life.

♦ Today I'll be compassionate and patient with older gay men or lesbians. The positive gains I'm able to enjoy right now in the gay community may have happened because of their past struggles.

Gays and lesbians know quite a lot about dignity. It's something that from a very early age we're told we can't possibly possess. We're sick, disgusting, and immoral, and if we insist on pursuing our so-called lifestyle, we should do it in utter silence and virtual invisibility. Overcoming such notions is a long and difficult process.

—DAVID EHRENSTEIN

What does the word "dignity" mean to you? For some gay men and lesbians it means facing pain, humiliation, discrimination, defeat, or embarrassment with their heads held high. For others it means having a strong sense of self-esteem and pride in who they are. Still others believe that dignity is the ability to give to themselves and to their community—and still have something positive to bestow upon those who criticize or condemn them.

But for all gay men and lesbians, dignity is something that rarely comes easily. It's something you may work hard to achieve and adamantly refuse to give up once you have it. It's an empowerment that comes from the head as well as the heart, an affirmative statement that says, "No matter what happens to me, I'm secure in myself and my way of life." It's not living a lie, refusing to return to the closet for anyone, sticking up for a brother or sister in the community, and working hard to ensure that everyone—gay or straight, black or white, young or old, rich or poor, sick or well—is treated respectfully, fairly, and graciously.

◆ In what ways do I display my dignity? Today I'll let my words, actions, and behaviors proclaim the dignity I feel for myself and my way of life.

Though people with disabilities have become more vocal in recent years, we still constitute a very small minority. Yet the Beautiful People—the slender, fair, and perfect ones—form a minority that may be even smaller.

—MARSHA SAXTON AND FLORENCE HOWE

Are you a gay person who has a disability? Do you have a friend or a partner who is physically impaired? Or is your awareness of gay men and lesbians with disabilities limited to seeing the local chapter of the Rainbow Alliance march in the PRIDE parade?

Most physically impaired gay men and lesbians feel as though they're the forgotten minority within the minority. While large or important events in the community are often wheelchair accessible and signed for the hearing impaired, the day-to-day needs of physically challenged gay people are not addressed.

The gay deaf have organized themselves in the United States and Canada under the umbrella of the Rainbow Alliance of the Deaf. Their address is P.O. Box 14182, Washington, D.C. 20041-4182. They also have a TDD line of the National Gay and Lesbian Hot Line (800 347-8336) and at the Centers for Disease Control and Prevention's AIDS Hot Line (800 243-7889).

But what's desperately needed is a national group to address the needs of every gay man or lesbian with a disability. Today, write a local or national gay or lesbian publication expressing your concern for such a group or offer to work with others to coordinate its formation.

◆ Even if I'm not physically impaired, I'm emotionally impaired when I ignore the members of the gay and lesbian community who are disabled. Today, let me be more aware of the rights and needs of these members and do what I can to help them be recognized.

Priests are no more necessary to religion than politicians to patriotism.

—JOHN HAYNES HOLMES

Do you feel the need to believe in the same things others believe in or to worship in a recognized "holy place" in order to feel a higher power's love and acceptance? You may look to religious leaders or other gay men or lesbians to learn about who or what they believe in or how they express their spirituality in order to get a sense of how you should be expressing your own spirituality. So you may follow the lead of others who worship goddesses, use the teachings of Native Americans, read the Bible, burn candles or incense as they pray before crude altars, recite the Serenity Prayer, read daily meditation books, attend seminars with motivational speakers, or attend church every Sunday.

But when you're feeling distant from your higher power or disconnected from your spiritual center, you're the only one who can draw near and reconnect. You must take responsibility for the quality of your relationship with a higher power by first acknowledging that your higher power is always with you. You need to open yourself up to "hearing" the messages of faith, trust, love, and acceptance your higher power is always sending to you. Perhaps you can hear these messages better by taking a walk on the beach, holding a crystal in your hands, or seeking insight from a meditation tape. But no matter what method you choose, remember that it's you alone who can interpret the messages your higher power has for you.

◆ Today I'll remember that if I'm feeling distant from my higher power, I'm the one who has moved. So I need to take responsibility for rebuilding this spiritual relationship by making the first move.

As early as kindergarten, such things as appreciating differences and respecting all people can be taught. And as kids get older, teachers should be prepared to respond to the questions they have. Kids don't have any big prejudices to start out with. They learn those things.

—DR. VIRGINIA URIBE

Dr. Virginia Uribe is the founder of Los Angeles school district's Project 10, which uses counseling and support to discourage lesbian and gay teens from dropping out of school. But her program is highly controversial; not only do parents reject the value of such counseling, but most school districts want to avoid the whole topic. When thirty-five Midwestern school districts were mailed a questionnaire about what assistance they provided for gay students in their school districts, only ten responded. And in New York some gay students were so badly harassed that the city supported the formation of a separate mini-school for gay teens who might otherwise drop out.

The amount of violence gay kids face, the harassment, the isolation, and the rejection by their families has led many educators to feel that issues regarding ways of life should not be left outside classroom doors. Robert Birle, San Francisco's Project 21 coordinator for the Midwestern states, agrees: "If schools get beyond looking at gay youth as the problem and look at the homophobic atmosphere instead, we'll get some positive results."

◆ Today, help foster the notion of gay-positive classrooms by providing information or bibliographies to teachers that identify the important contributions gay men and lesbians have made in history, literature, and the sciences.

Whatever strength I brought to this campaign was in my head, not my lymph nodes.

——PAUL TSONGAS

Eight months after Paul Tsongas resigned from the 1992 campaign as a Democratic presidential candidate, his doctors revealed that he had suffered a recurrence of cancer. When the media got hold of the story, it helped to spark a national debate over full medical disclosure for those seeking to occupy the White House. Tsongas's rebuttal expressed his concern that any person with a disease is often seen as the disease itself.

Viewing any gay man or lesbian you know who has cancer, has tested HIV positive, or who has full-blown AIDS primarily as a person with a disease not only belittles that person as a human being, but also shows what little respect or value you have for your relationship with that person. Aren't there strengths your friend, coworker, roommate, family member, or life partner has that are important to you? Doesn't this person enrich your life in some special ways? Isn't he or she attractive to you? Aren't there talents and abilities you admire or envy? Don't you find your life more meaningful with this person in it?

Today, remember that anyone with HIV, AIDS, or cancer is a person first. By looking at who the person is rather than at what disease he or she has, you'll be able to see a much more complete picture.

◆ Let me always see any gay man or lesbian I know as a whole person. Today I'll identify any disease as simply a small part of my friend, lover, roommate, coworker, or family member.

If you feel as if your life is a seesaw, perhaps you are depending on another person for your ups and downs.

—ANONYMOUS

Do you get your "positive strokes" from the gay and lesbian community? Perhaps you get them by being a "mother" to everyone, always mending broken hearts, offering tender hugs, or wiping away tears. Maybe you get them by being a big sister or brother, ready to offer support and advice to anyone on any subject, no matter what time of day or night. Perhaps you get them by being a "rock," never asking for support or always ready to help a still-loved ex move in with a current lover. Or maybe you get them by being a "gay guide," ready to bring some young person out, fix up single friends, or help newcomers feel welcome in the community.

You may do such things as a way to bolster your feelings of self-worth, instead of feeling good about yourself for who you are. By having others value and need you for the things you can do for them, your opinion about yourself may improve. But although you may spend a great deal of time mothering, teaching, guiding, and caretaking, you may rarely get such nice things in return.

Isn't it time you said, "I can't keep doing these things for other people who can't return them—just to make myself feel better about me"? Remember today that your self-worth is of greatest value only when you truly value yourself.

◆ Am I too dependent upon others' reactions to me and the things I do for them to make me feel better about me? Today I'll keep in mind that the price I have to pay by being unable to do this for myself is that I let others rule my life.

But when you more or less surround yourself by a community of queers . . . you create a different universe within that seemingly larger whole, a universe in which you are the norm, in which you are accepted and acceptable. You relax. You laugh, you love, you can suffer loss and openly grieve. Your passions stop embarrassing you so badly!

— JENIFER LEVIN, FROM *THE SEA OF LIGHT*

Can you think of seven people you could call at 2:00 A.M. who would be there for you, no matter what you needed, how you were feeling, or what you had to talk about? These people would make up your support system. Such a support system can keep you from being totally isolated in your way of life, validate your feelings about your sexuality, help you identify with your "love problems" or family matters, comfort you in times of sadness, ease your anxieties and stress, help you cope with the loss of a loved one in a way no straight person could—no matter how close he or she is to you—and make you feel like you belong.

You, like everyone else in the gay and lesbian community, need a support system that's made up of people who reflect who you are so they can share in and identify with your most intimate reality—the fact that you're gay.

Today, create your support group. As you consider people to include, keep in mind the intimate issues you may need to share with them. Exclude people who can't understand or be supportive; include those who can.

◆ Who, in my circle of friends and loved ones, can I always depend upon to be there for me and to understand? Today I'll be selective of those I'll rely upon in my times of need.

*Of course, many lesbians and gay men consider marriage to be
repressive, patriarchal, and disgusting. They see marriage as
based on ownership and production of new workers and consumers.
And they're right! That's certainly the history of marriage, and
for some people, it's the present as well. But that doesn't mean
that same-sex marriages would have to follow that model: we do
almost everything else differently, so why not marriage?*

— WENDY CASTER

Do you want to get married to your lover or life partner? You
may believe that since you're already firmly committed to each
other and want very much to stay together "till death do us part"
that you are married. You may have exchanged rings, had children together, or participated in a commitment ceremony.

But if one of you had a heart attack or were badly injured,
you might not be able to visit the other in the hospital or take
on the responsibility of finding a home health-care provider.
You can't file taxes together. You can't die without some
potential legal problems with your partner's family of origin.

Today, instead of believing that by having an emotional commitment to one another you'll be together forever, focus on
making a more legal and lasting commitment. Make a will so
your life partner will be taken care of after your death; fill out a
living will that names your life partner as one of the decision
makers; and hire a trusted accountant to handle both of your
finances.

♦The list of legal disadvantages to not being married is
long. But today I can do some things that will identify in
writing who my life partner is and how I want him or her
taken care of when my life is over.

[It's all too] easy for gay men who haven't learned how to deal with feelings to become addicted to using sex as a substitute for other emotional needs.

—RIK ISENSEE

For a casual-sex relationship to exist, you need two participants. It's not really possible for one person to escape into sex unless the other person acquiesces. What that means is that even if you feel you're being emotionally open, honest, and vulnerable with a partner, if he or she isn't equally emotionally involved, you haven't achieved emotional intimacy.

Couples who make love in the middle of or after a fight and never process what the conflict was about or how to resolve it learn to use sex as a way of avoiding communication. Couples who find any number of excuses not to cuddle, talk, or express their feelings to one another before, during, and after sex are avoiding opportunities for greater intimacy. Couples who deny sex to one another at times of conflict are using sex to avoid dealing with their feelings.

Instead of jumping into bed at the first sign of conflict or jumping out of bed before any intimacy can be established, strive to become more aware of what it is that you're afraid of feeling. Encourage yourself—and another—to respond to you through words as well as physical embraces.

♦ Today I want my relationships to be healthy. I'll give myself and someone else the space to express thoughts and feelings, to offer support and suggestions, and to be emotionally as well as physically open.

It is possible to be different and still be all right. There can be two—or more—answers to the same question, and all can be right.
—ANNE WILSON SCHAEF

You may have been brought up to believe that there's only one "right" way of doing things: you grow up, go to college, meet a nice member of the opposite sex, get married, raise a family, work hard for your money, you grow old, and then you die.

But getting in touch with your attraction to members of the same sex means you've added another dimension to the way you do things; it may not be right for everyone else, but it's right for you. By challenging the basic concept of "right and wrong," you gain an incredible amount of freedom that enables you to challenge other situations where there may only seem to be a right-or-wrong, yes-or-no, all-or-nothing answer. For instance, rather than view politics in terms of Democrat or Republican, you may be more capable of considering candidates on the Independent or other tickets. Rather than set up your long-term relationship like a "husband and wife" situation, you may be more capable of playing out different roles at different times. Rather than think only of yourself and your needs, you may be much more willing to consider the needs of people of color, those with disabilities, those less educated, those with different religious beliefs, and those of different classes.

Today, be thankful for your ability to see that there are many answers to the questions in life—not just right or wrong.

◆ The binary way of thinking may lead me to disregard many possible solutions to the problems I face in life. Today I'll be true to my reality, which offers me an infinite range of choices.

*Learn to say "no"; it will be of more use to you than to be able
to read Latin.*

—CHARLES HADDON SPURGEON

Why do you find it so hard to say no to people? Why do you
often end up agreeing to do things you don't want to do?
Maybe your parents have asked you not to bring your lover to
a family cookout, and you've gone along with their request.
Perhaps whenever an ex-lover asks for your help, you never
refuse. Or maybe when your life partner asks you not to
spend so much time with your friends, you give in to what he
or she wants.

Sometimes you may go along with what others want because you don't like their disapproval. You may give people
whatever they want in the hope that you'll get something in
return. You may give in because it's the easiest thing to do. Or
you may never say no because to do so invites argument.

If you're tired of allowing your life to be influenced or
controlled by other people's wishes, it's time now to take the
plunge and learn how to say no. The best way to begin is by
saying no in "safe" situations; for example, with a friend who
doesn't have expectations or someone who won't challenge
your refusal to do something. Or, if you're put on the spot by
someone who needs a yes-or-no answer, give yourself time to
make a decision that's right for you by saying, "Let me think
about it and I'll get back to you."

♦ My unwillingness to say no is a result of my eagerness to
please. However, learning to say no is an important way to
develop a strong sense of self-esteem. Today I'll establish
boundaries and priorities for myself by saying say no when
I really mean it.

Death is
The opposite
Of time.

—DENG MING-DAO

Often, when someone dies, you begin to cloak death in meaning, to imagine what happens after death, speculate about reincarnation, or talk about eternal life. But death is opaque to everyone—it remains an unsolved mystery. In its realm, time ceases to have meaning. Hours, days, and even weeks pass by, but often all that can be contemplated is death.

But what really dies? Is anything actually destroyed? Because the stilled body will eventually return to its original components of water and chemicals, it's not really destroyed but merely transformed. What about the person's mind? Does it cease to function or does it make a transition to another existence or a higher plane? No one knows for sure.

When a person dies, the only thing that disappears is the identity—the collection of parts that you once called by a name, someone with a unique personality who had a meaningful role in your life. What dies is the physical matter of that person. There's still someone underneath that identity who doesn't die. Where that person goes or how he or she gets there is, like the passage of time, beyond your capability to control, change, or comprehend.

♦ I'm powerless over anyone's dying. Today I'll focus on my life and its meaning and try to let go of other people's dying. When I do so, the passage of time can flow freely and my life will be much easier to live.

He told me to put it down in writing if it was a matter of sexual preference. I told him I'm not gay, but that I could just as easily lie and put it down. I didn't think it was my place to lie about my friend. Besides, my sexual preference is none of the school's business.

—KARI SWENDSBOE

When Dedham, Massachusetts, High School junior Kari Swendsboe wanted to take a girlfriend to the prom, school officials wouldn't let her—unless she and her friend said they were gay and not just friends. Principal Anthony Zonfrelli told Kari that because under state law the school cannot discriminate against homosexuals, he would allow their going to the dance together as a female-female couple only if she put down in writing that she and her friend were gay. Kari refused and said she could have gotten a date, but "thought she could have more fun going with a friend. Besides," she added, "many of the boy-girl couples who go to the proms are not romantically involved either."

Have any of your friendships with other gay men or lesbians been misinterpreted as romantic relationships? Perhaps your parents assume that every gay man or lesbian you're with is a bedmate. Maybe the fact that you dance with the same person in a bar leads to gossip that he or she is your lover. Or maybe your close friendship with an ex has elicited comments that you haven't ended your relationship.

Today, treat such assumptions made by others with honesty and openness. However, if your explanations aren't accepted, consider any further speculation worth refuting.

◆ Today I'll try to discourage any untrue gossip about my friendships, or if I can't, I'll just accept that some people will believe what they want to believe.

It never occurred to me . . . that I could be a battered woman. After all, I was a strong, articulate, political dyke. I knew . . . that women are not violent, and that lesbians were changing the world to end violence. I know this despite the physical, emotional, and sexual abuse I lived with on a daily basis.

—ARLENE ISTAR

Arlene Istar, a clinical social worker from Schenectady, New York, ended a two-year relationship with a lesbian abuser over a decade ago. The punching, kicking, and hitting she endured challenged her belief in the myth that women—especially lesbians—were never violent.

Because both lesbians and gay men tend to form relationships based on equality, the reality that violence exists in gay and lesbian relationships with almost the same frequency and severity as in heterosexual relationships is surprising. Yet many gay men and lesbians accept violence in their relationships because they've grown up with it. Many battered lesbians and gay men assume abuse is just part of any intimate interaction because that's how their mothers or fathers treated them while they were growing up.

Today you don't have to be victimized in your relationships anymore. Enlist the help of a counselor or friend who has successfully ended an abusive relationship. Then read literature on battering, join a support group, or explore therapeutic recovery. Stopping the cycle of abuse begins with you.

◆ Today I need to recognize if I'm in an unhealthy, abusive relationship. Let me explore my childhood to determine whether or not abuse was in my history with the help of a trusted friend or counselor.

I'm not a gold coin—not everyone is going to love me.

—ANONYMOUS

When another gay man or lesbian shows that he or she doesn't like you, do you react with sadness, self-pity, or confusion? Maybe your phone calls are never returned, or you're told there's no interest in pursuing a friendship or going out on another date. You may ask yourself, "What did I do to deserve this person's rejection or dislike? He/she doesn't even know me! Why can't I be given a second chance?"

Just because you're nice to someone—going out of your way to be friendly and courteous, offering your help, or never having a conflict or exchanging a cross word—doesn't mean that you're going to be liked. You can search your memory for days to discover a time when you might have "blown it" with someone, but you probably won't come up with anything.

The bottom line is that everyone doesn't have to admire you, enjoy your company, or even like you. You don't have to know the reasons why, you just need to accept that such decisions are a matter of personal choice. Today, remind yourself that just as you aren't comfortable with everyone you meet, others aren't always going to be comfortable with you. Your goal shouldn't be to be universally liked, because that's unrealistic. Rather, your goal should be to love yourself enough so that the arbitrary rejections of others don't matter.

◆ When I love myself unconditionally, I don't need to bolster my self-esteem from the number of people who like me. Today I'll recognize that I'm a human being with unique qualities that some people are bound not to like.

No man, for any considerable period, can wear one face to himself, and another to the multitude, without finally getting bewildered as to which may be the true.

—NATHANIEL HAWTHORNE

As Louise Erdrich writes in her novel *Tracks,* "The practice of deception was so constant with her that it got to be a kind of truth." Have you gone so far in your masking of the truth that when you look in the mirror the only reflection you can see is that of the mask—and not your true self?

The truth is, you *are* gay. But will you ever be ready to tell the truth so you can feel more accepting of your sexuality? In William Wyler's *These Three,* a movie based on Lillian Hellman's riveting *The Children's Hour,* Joel McCrea tells one of the girls who has lied his views on lying. "Everybody lies all the time," he begins. "Sometimes they have to, and sometimes they don't. I've lied for a lot of different reasons myself. But there never was a time when, if I'd had a second chance, I wouldn't have taken back the lie and told the truth. You're a lucky girl, Mary, because we're giving you that second chance. Were you telling . . . the exact truth . . . ?"

Have you become such a good liar that you find it hard not to believe the lies? When you strive to internalize something as big as your sexuality—and neglect any desire for fighting for the rights and freedoms you have to be able to live your life as you choose—then you're not simply living a lie. You're trying to be someone you're not.

Today, imagine you have a second chance. Ask, "Can I take back at least one of the lies I've told—and tell the truth?"

◆ Today I'll remember that the truth can set me free. The more honest I am, the more honest my life becomes.

Lesbian sexuality is changing, and women today are smashing the idea that lesbians aren't interested in having sex.

—KITAKA GARA

It used to be that literature written by, for, and about lesbians never detailed what women did when they were in bed together. Instead, phrases like "her bosom swelled with love," "an unknown passion was deeply explored," or "she tasted like the sea" were used to gloss over the reality that the women were, in fact, having sex. The idea that women who were in love with each other could also be in lust has only recently been explored in S/M–based lesbian literature, through lesbian porn-style videos, and at casual sex parties.

On the other side of the coin, deeply intimate relationships between gay men increased shortly after the AIDS epidemic began as men opted for less casual encounters and more long-term, monogamous relationships. Recently the concept of gay men expressing romantic, committed love for one another has been publicized through gay men's support groups and films like *Longtime Companion,* which focused on the concept of men being givers who could provide each other with emotional support.

Just as lesbians can be more physically aggressive with one another, so, too, can gay men be more emotionally assertive with one another. Lesbians, as well as gay men, have much to learn from one another.

◆ Today I won't hold back from interacting with another gay man or lesbian in a different way. There's much I can learn from exploring other ways of expressing how I care for someone.

What is family? Family is when any two people come together and make a home. A nest. That's your family values.
—ANGELA LANSBURY

It's difficult to go through life alone. Eventually you may want to settle down with a life partner in a safe, secure place you can each call home—a home in which you can live the way you want to and freely express your love for one another.

For such a relationship to work, you must share a basic compatibility with a partner who complements your values, outlook, and purpose. You must be able to endure great travails and hardships together, as well as share the heat of passion and love. You must be able to support each other and instill in one another a sense of belonging that comes from working toward shared goals. You must develop a loyalty that can be found in no other type of relationship—you must be each other's lover, friend, confidant, partner, counselor, guide.

Yet you shouldn't define yourselves by your relationship, or force yourselves to stay together in your relationship. If you are lucky enough to spend time together, then you'll find there's much you can experience as one.

Together you can create with one another the family life you always wished you had had. This family can simply be you and your partner. Or you can include children, pets, or close friends in the safe, warm space you call home.

◆ An enduring relationship can become like tempered steel —two people who are joined together like the forged links on a steel chain. Today I'll forge a link with someone I know I'll love for a long, long time.

> *Reputation is what you have when you come to a new community; character is what you have when you go away.*
> —WILLIAM HERSEY DAVIS

Every gay man or lesbian has a reputation. Part of it is provided by society, which builds your reputation as a gay man or lesbian on stereotypical beliefs, negative newspaper accounts, and erroneous information. Another part is supplied from your childhood, which donates your family history as well as the achievement and labels you earned while you were in school. Still another part is furnished by those who knew you in the past, which contributes to the portrait of the person you used to be before you changed negative behaviors—drinking, using drugs, sleeping around, being angry and unforgiving, and so on—into positive ones. A final part is contributed by ex-lovers, who believe they know how you think, what you feel, why you do what you do, and what kind of person you really are.

Sometimes your reputation can get in the way of letting others see you for who you really are: someone who has struggled long and hard to become the positive, healed, person you are today. That's why it's important to show others the things that make up your character.

When you're with others, do you hide behind your reputation or show them your true character? Today, let people see you without characterizations provided by others. Let them see you as *you*.

♦ Today I'll remind myself that while reputation can make someone look at me once, character can make someone look at me twice—and really notice me.

You don't have to be a lesbian to like purple. You just have to understand that color is Nature's way of saying, "I'm here and I want to be loved."

—ODETTE DE CRECY

The color purple has had a long history before its shades evolved into a symbol of lesbian love. Helen of Troy, whose beauty moved men to war, was purportedly born from a purple egg. Cleopatra tried to conquer the city of Tyre, where the secret of purple dye was supposedly kept. Alice Walker, author of *The Color Purple,* wrote: "God gets pissed if you walk by a purple field and don't notice."

To lesbians, lavender is the epitome of difference; for gay men, it's pink. For the gay and lesbian community as whole, the rainbow colors—which include purple—are symbolic of the unity and pride felt by those who dare to be different.

Imagine today that for one hour, you and every gay man and lesbian in the world are the color purple. Think of what the crowded subway trains, the bustling city streets, the jammed shopping malls, the Congress of the United States, and busy airport terminals would look like! You would be able to see firsthand the dazzling energy of the color purple as it beams through the hustle and bustle of daily living, where you and your brothers and sisters usually blend in rather than stick out.

Today, *be* the color purple. Visualize your difference as you stand near others in a crowded elevator or walk along a city street. Be happy in your difference—be happy in your purpleness!

◆ Today I'll be proud to be purple!

> . . . *I was amazed to discover that many people die each year in anti-gay attacks and thousands more are left scarred, emotionally and physically. Bigotry has no place in this great nation and violence has no place in this world. But it happens. Prejudice hurts . . . kills. Please don't be part of it.*
>
> —BOB HOPE

Gay bashing is an increasing problem in the gay and lesbian community. Gay bashing isn't just an inner-city problem; gay men and lesbians have been bashed in small, rural locations as well as in foreign countries.

At the request of the Gay and Lesbian Alliance Against Defamation (GLAAD), actor/comedian Bob Hope has filmed a public-service announcement condemning antigay violence. The tape has been carried as a news item on *Entertainment Tonight* and in *People* magazine. But raising public awareness won't stop the violence; fear of AIDS, combined with homophobia and increased visibility, have made gay men and lesbians more vulnerable to attack.

Take steps to protect yourself from violence. Tonight, if you decide to bring someone home with you, introduce this person to a friend. That way someone will know who you're spending time with in case anything happens to you.

◆ Today I'll take a positive step to protect myself and my rights as a gay man or lesbian. I'll sign up for a self-defense course so I can defend who I am.

Laugh and the world laughs with you, snore and you sleep alone.

—MRS. PATRICK CAMPBELL,
IN A LETTER TO GEORGE BERNARD SHAW

Laughter can turn any disadvantage into an advantage, any negative into a positive. Gay men and lesbians who know this not only look for some positive aspect in the things that upset them, but also go one step farther. After identifying a difficulty, they strive to do something humorous to relieve the tension and lighten their outlook.

Your life may be filled with a variety of difficulties: a longtime lover breaks your heart or a new love interest breaks a date; a longed-for vacation is canceled or a business flight to seal a deal is delayed; an injury keeps you from your daily exercise program; you have a hard time in your recovery from an addiction; your blood test comes back HIV positive. Being able to find some humor in each scenario may be hard, but if you can look at how each incident can enrich your life, you may be able to take a more lighthearted view.

A Zen poem states this idea in another way: "Since my house burned down, I now have a better view of the rising moon." Or, as Art Linkletter once said: "Things turn out best for people who make the best of the way things turn out."

♦ If I can focus on what I can gain from a circumstance rather than on what I've lost, I may be able to find advantage in my disadvantage. Today I'll seek out my gains by employing a more humorous outlook.

*All of my sexual experiences when I was young were with girls.
I mean, we didn't have those sleep-over parties for nothing.*
——MADONNA

One of the questions that faces every gay man or lesbian at some point in their lives is, "What do I do about my parents?" Some gay men and lesbians never come out to their parents, even though a parent may express curiosity about a close relationship with a family friend, drop hints that would encourage discussion, or even point-blank ask, "Are you gay?"

Whether or not you decide to come out to your parents is highly personal. It should never be based on whether a close friend has told his or her parents or because a lover wants you to. Don't feel pressured to do so if you're not sure you'll be better afterward, if you're not comfortable with your sexuality, if you don't have a close friend who can be there in the event your parents' overreact, if you're doing so as a gut response to "getting caught" with another man or woman, or if the emotional climate at home would make your coming out just another problem at an already difficult or sensitive time.

If you get along well with your parents and were raised in a healthy, stable environment, chances are pretty good your parents will be able to deal with your sexuality. But be sure of your motives if/when you decide to come out to them. Always come out from a desire for openness and connection——never for a need to take revenge or inflict hurt.

◆My parents may need some time to think about my coming out to them. Today I'll keep in mind that if/when I come out to them, I need to allow them as much time as possible to accept my sexuality.

OCTOBER 4

*What a person does with his personal life is on his conscience
. . . and he is not responsible to anyone for what he does away
from the job.*

—DALE EVANS

What happens when you're out with your friends on a Saturday night at a gay bar and you spot your boss or a coworker on the dance floor? Or you run into a business client at a meeting of a gay or lesbian professional organization? Or you discover that someone you work with used to be sexually involved with your life partner?

Finding out that someone you work with or associate with on a professional basis is gay—or having that person discover you're gay—can be unsettling, particularly when such knowledge is revealed through membership in a gay or lesbian business, civic, or political organization, by a chance meeting at a gay or lesbian social event, or through mutual acquaintances. You may want control of when and to whom your sexuality is revealed, but these are times when your coming out is totally out of your control.

You might decide to approach an out-of-work "sighting" with an "I won't tell if you don't tell" bargain; you both might be just as scared to have your "secret" known to others on the job. You might play "the invisible person routine," acting as if you don't see the person and hoping he or she doesn't see you. Or you might find that recognizing each other in a gay social setting confirms what both of you suspected about one another—and you gain a workplace ally!

◆ Today I'll remember that my personal life is just that—
mine. How, where, and with whom I choose to spend my
time is a gift I give to others.

I especially like being a gay entrepreneur. I don't have to put up with the pressures of the non-gay, often anti-gay, corporate world. I'm my own boss. And my personal success is directly proportional to the good that I do in creating life-affirming gay culture.

—TOBY JOHNSON

What is gay culture? Most gay men and lesbians consider that their culture has been and is still being formed from the works of authors, artists, playwrights, fashion designers, singers, composers, poets, actors, filmmakers, and others who are also gay.

But gay culture is also made up of the heritage gay men and lesbians have created—the materials that make up their past history as well as the materials in the present that will add to their history in the future. These are the biographies and autobiographies, activists, court cases and legal decisions, and political and social reforms that give evidence of contemporary gay life.

Anything that reflects your life today as a gay man or lesbian can be considered gay culture; gay culture is what makes your life significant, validates your experience, and affirms your way of life.

Today, support the efforts to preserve your heritage as a gay man or a lesbian. If you or an organization you belong to produces materials that reflect your way of life, send copies of it to the National Museum of Lesbian and Gay History, 208 W. 13th Street, New York, NY 10011.

♦ I'll donate items from my personal collection of gay or lesbian literature, film, audiocassettes, or photographs to a library that will care for such treasures. Preserving my culture for future gay men and lesbians means taking care of materials today.

I have never been able to conceive of how any rational being could propose happiness to himself from the exercise of power over others.

—THOMAS JEFFERSON

There may be those in your life who try to force you to conform to their way of living rather than let you live your life in the way that makes you happiest. Your parents, for example, might try to run your relationships by fixing you up with members of the opposite sex or by refusing to include your lover at family events. Your straight friends might invite you to do things with them, but on the condition that you don't wear a certain T-shirt with "that slogan" on it or act in a certain way. Conservative Republicans may push for legislation that makes it more difficult to pursue your way of life with equal protection. Landlords, bosses, or other people in positions of control might discriminate against you or make day-to-day living difficult. Homophobic strangers might harass you, threaten you, or beat you as a way to suppress who you are.

When others try to manage or control you through actual power or power they assume they have, they show a lack of respect for your rights as an individual. Today, refuse to let someone exercise any illegal, unnecessary, or forceful power over you. Contact an attorney, register a complaint with the proper authorities, or reject attempts to draw you into a situation that threatens your personal rights.

♦ When others try to exercise control over me, I'll remain in control. Today I won't let anyone manage me but the only person who has a right to do so—me.

The greatest crime is not to grow, not to be willing to move on to the next stage of life. It is a terrible fate to be stuck forever in one place, wedded to a triumph or a sorrow.

—REEVE LINDBERGH BROWN

The life of every gay man or lesbian is filled with losses. There's the initial loss of acceptance in a society that rejects homosexuality as a legitimate way of life. There may the loss of family security or parental love and affection. There may be the loss of friends. There may be the loss of a job. There are losses in relationships through separation or the death of a life partner. You may even feel like you've lost your ability to be heard, some of your self-esteem, your ability to trust others, or your dignity.

Dwelling on such losses is one way people deal with the sorrows, rejections, and tragedies in your life. While this option certainly puts you in constant touch with the feelings of pain, hurt, sadness, disappointment, anger, and frustration, it does nothing to help you let go and move on from such feelings. Like a car stuck in mud, you constantly spin your wheels and wind up getting nowhere.

It's time to divorce yourself from the losses to which you may have become wedded. Rather than spend years of your life under a rain cloud, get in motion: emerge from under the cloud and look for the sunshine. Today, opt for a course of action by signing up for an adult education course, inviting a friend to dinner, or asking someone out on a date.

♦ Today I'm ready to make a change. I'll stop letting raindrops fall on my head and lift my face up to feel the warmth of healing sunshine.

Woe to him that is alone when he falleth, for he hath not another to help him up.

—ECCLESIASTES

When was the last time you reached out to a gay brother or a lesbian sister and offered your assistance? Perhaps you helped a friend move. Maybe you offered a hug and words of comfort to someone who had been dumped. Perhaps you volunteered to work a few hours at a gay hotline. Maybe you chipped in some money to help an ailing friend pay for badly needed medication. Perhaps you treated someone out of work to dinner and a movie. Or maybe you said yes when a newcomer to a twelve-step program asked you to be a sponsor.

While every gay man and lesbian needs to offer love, support, guidance, and comfort to other gay men and lesbians, there may be those who can't, don't, or won't reach out when they need the help. Those who walk through life indifferent to the help those around them can provide or disconnected from others in the community do so by conscious choice.

Yet you need to try to change their minds. Each person is here on earth to learn lessons from and play teacher to one another. When you see others who have stepped away from the circle of people who can help, always reach out to them with a willing hand. Don't let them shut themselves out of opportunities for growth and connection. Let them learn, by the power of your example, how to reconnect. Let them know that just as they need you, so, too, do you need them.

◆ I know gay men and lesbians need one another. Being helped by someone who knows what it's like to be gay is the only way to get through the tough times. Today I'll freely give of myself to another who may need me.

I hired him, and I thought probably he was gay, but I didn't care. But I later realized that I should have cared, in an affirmative way.

—JACK ROSENTHAL

Jack Rosenthal, editorial-page editor of the *New York Times,* had always thought he was open-minded and accepting of gay men and lesbians. After all, he had hired Larry Josephs, an openly gay staffer. But when Larry died of AIDS in 1991, Jack realized that accepting a gay man or a lesbian was not enough. He had to move beyond his awareness of homosexuality and his acceptance of the individuals he knew, and learn to feel for them in the same way he felt for those in the heterosexual community.

There's a story that illustrates this well. When a father who was also a surgeon was asked by his son the night before the child's upcoming operation what it was going to be like, the father explained, in medical terms, what would go on in the operating room and the recovery process. But after the surgery the son awoke, looked at his father, and said, "You didn't tell me it was going to hurt."

Today it's important not only to let others know that you're gay, but also to allow them to feel what it's like to be a gay man or a lesbian. Casual acceptance of your sexuality is never as meaningful as a commitment to understanding what it feels like to live your way of life every day.

◆ If the straight people in my life can earn my respect, attention, caring, time, and interest, I should earn theirs. Today I'll make those relationships less one-sided by sharing what I feel as a gay man or a lesbian.

In most native cultures, gay men and lesbians held positions as healers, visionaries, and teachers. They were the doctors and lawyers of native societies before the Europeans came. Tolerance used to be indigenous to our culture. We try to reclaim, against opposition from our own people, that we were the holy people, the special people.

—SUSAN BEAVER

In 1492, when Christopher Columbus sailed the ocean blue, he embarked on a journey that ultimately invaded the lands of Native American Indians and eventually led to the destruction of their way of life by white settlers.

Today not only do Native Americans have to endure the repeated celebration of the "discovery" that led to the desecration of their lands, but they must endure as well the discrimination against gay men and lesbians within their tribal communities. Susan Beaver is a Mohawk lesbian who is executive director of Two Spirited People ("two-spirits" is a term used for gays, meaning people with male and female spirits) of the First Nations, a Toronto support and education group. She testified before the Royal Commission on Aboriginal Peoples, a Canadian government council, saying, "With the influence of the church and Europeans, two spirit is a tradition pushed so far away. . . . Your sexuality is not tolerated. . . . If you are strong enough to be who you are, you are ridiculed, harassed, and only sometimes understood as again being 'different.'"

Today, celebrate Columbus Day in a way that honors the gay and lesbian Native Americans who have had to fight for over five hundred years for their rights and freedoms.

♦ Probably the most difficult place for Native Americans to be openly gay is on their own reservations. Today I'll honor Native Americans past and present through my prayers.

What is the source of our first suffering? It is in the fact that we hesitated to speak. It was born in the moments when we accumulated silent things within us.

—GASTON BACHELARD

October 11—National Coming Out Day—has become one of the major gay and lesbian celebrations in the United States and Canada. The holiday was first designated by a group of gay and lesbian community leaders to commemorate the 1987 March on Washington, a highly successful political and unifying event.

The goal of National Coming Out Day is simple: to increase the visibility of gay men and lesbians through a decision to be open about their sexuality with one, two, or a few chosen people—or even to go public with their identity.

How can you go about being "out"? You can do so in a variety of ways. You can use certain opportunities to bring up the subject of homosexuality; for example, you can watch a documentary on gay issues with family members and then discuss the show with them. You can conceal nothing about your sexuality when the subject of homosexuality comes up in your interactions with others. Or you can bring up homosexuality or your sexuality at every opportunity.

Today, think about how public you want to be with your identity. Who do you want to tell and how do you want to tell them? You can come out subtly—by placing your lover's photo on your desk at work—or openly—by taking your lover home to meet your parents.

◆ Today I'll show another that I'm part of the gay and lesbian community by actively and constructively discussing my way of life with someone in my life.

It may sound patronizing, but you're contributing to the health and well-being of the whole church. You've got to hang in.
—REVEREND EDMOND L. BROWNING

In 1992, the presiding bishop of the Episcopal Church, Reverend Edmond L. Browning, spoke to a national meeting of Integrity, a 2,500-member group of gay and lesbian Episcopalians. His message was clear: to build a spiritual community, gay men and lesbians have to stick together and explore their connections, no matter what homophobic religious leaders might tell them.

Religion was once seen as one of the most degrading and shame-inflicting forces against the development of a positive gay image. Now, many gay men and lesbians are finding spiritual comfort and community in traditional denominations.

Is your local church or a church in the denomination of your choice open to *all* persons? If not, you might want to meet with the church's pastor to raise his or her awareness about such exclusion and discuss your specific spiritual needs as a gay man or a lesbian. Or you might want to write to the national headquarters of your chosen denomination to find out if there are places of worship that not only affirm the church's gospel, but also accept and welcome all worshipers.

You shouldn't have to face experiences and challenges in your life without a basis of spiritual support. Today seek out a church that publicly and enthusiastically welcomes gay and lesbian members.

◆ I wish to belong to a congregation that affirms that gay men and lesbians share with all others the worth that comes from being unique individuals created by God. Today I'll seek out such a welcoming, affirming house of worship.

After he [Francis Menuge] died, I thought about how as a child I'd dreamed about becoming a designer. I met someone with whom I fell in love, and we pursued my dream together. When he died, I thought to myself, "Why should I go on?" I really almost walked away from everything.

—JEAN PAUL GAULTIER

French fashion designer Jean Paul Gaultier has built an incredible empire. In 1992 he grossed $80 million—after starting his company just ten years before, with friends who worked with him for nothing. Today, he expects to more than double his volume by launching a fragrance and a jeans line. "Gaultier influences those who influence pop culture," says Hal Rubenstein, men's style editor at the *New York Times*. "He's one of the very few at the top of fashion's pyramid of influence."

But Gaultier would never have started his company without the love, stability, goals, and dreams he shared with his life partner of fifteen years, Francis Menuge, who died of AIDS-related complications in 1990. "We created this thing together," Gaultier says. "Without him there would have been no Jean Paul Gaultier company. Our relationship worked because I can love somebody who is working with me in some way."

Today think of the person you're in love with or the type of person with whom you'd like to fall in love. Does this person share your dreams? Do you work together toward mutual goals? In what ways do your lives connect?

♦ It's not enough to love someone because he or she is attractive, makes a lot of money, lives in a nice home, or is nice to me. Today I'll remember that the love that lasts is based upon two visions we can both see together.

Everyone is more or less bisexual. People just don't want to admit it. I haven't been involved with a woman for years, but one of the nicest experiences—whatever you want to call it, was with a woman.

—JOAN BAEZ

Have you ever asked yourself: "Am I really a gay man or a lesbian?" You may question whether you're a "real" gay man or a lesbian if you have sex with members of the opposite sex or are attracted to them. You may question whether you're gay when you date members of the opposite sex as well as people of the same sex. You may question your inclusion in the gay and lesbian community and wonder if PRIDE parades, National Coming Out Day, gay-rights activism, discrimination, homophobia, gay bashing, and so on truly affect you because of your inability to commit to one sexual preference.

It's one thing to be attracted to men as well as women and to act on those attractions—and then to honestly label yourself as bisexual. It's another thing to be in a "wavering mode," where you constantly question your sexuality or refrain from making a clear-cut decision because of fear, lack of acceptance, or because you believe one way of life will be easier to live than another.

Today, take an honest look at the reasons behind the label of "bisexual" you may have given yourself. Is that label true to what you feel in your heart or simply reassuring in the safety it provides to you?

◆ It may be fear that leads me to say, "I'm in love with a woman/man, but I'm not a lesbian/gay man." Today I'll look at what sex I'm primarily attracted to and decide if bisexual is an accurate, honest label.

A long-term relationship hasn't been tested until it's been exposed to screwing around.

—CHRISTOPHER ISHERWOOD

Having a sexual activity outside a gay or lesbian relationship, whether agreed upon in advance or not, usually shakes up the relationship to some degree. It can trigger insecurities, jealousy, anger, and fears as partners wonder what the other man or woman is like, if he or she is more attractive or a better lover, or ultimately, whether the other man or woman will pose a risk to an established couple's future.

People "fool around" for all kinds of reasons; some may be clear at the time, some may only be clear later on, and some may never really be clear. The more common motivators, however, are to end a relationship, to provide a distraction or an ego boost, or to feel separate.

Good communication and clear agreements, as well as ongoing dialogue, are helpful in providing or restoring trust between partners in a couple and bringing a sense of security to the relationship. When your partner screws around, ask yourself first whether you want to continue in your relationship. If you do, determine whether you can both agree to restructure your relationship to include outside involvements or if you both need to make a commitment to monogamy in order to feel happy, secure, and to grow together.

◆ A crucial variable in my relationship is communication. Another is my willingness to redesign and refine what makes me happy in a relationship. Today I'll make decisions about how I want my relationship and communicate these decisions to my partner.

It is very important that children learn early on that there are different family structures out there than the traditional one.

—JOSEPH FERNANDEZ

After a 1989 federal study showed that one-third of adolescents who kill themselves are young people struggling with their sexual orientation, school officials in Virginia's Fairfax County decided to expand their wide-ranging family-life education program. "We had a moral obligation to combat a devastating trend," says Gerald Newberry, coordinator of the county's family-life education programs. "We needed to communicate to our kids that people are different and that we don't choose our sexual feelings—they choose us."

To help foster respect for gay men and lesbians and different family structures, think about forming a group of creative people in the gay and lesbian community who can work together on a "Foster Family Awareness" program. Contribute your writing, design, artwork, fund-raising, and networking skills to help put together a progay, pronontraditional family advertisement to be seen in local newspapers, on city subways, and posted on government bulletin boards. A few states, including California and Massachusetts, are thinking about ways to discuss homosexuality in the classroom. Let the awareness piece you create suggest some positive, life-enhancing ways in your state.

◆Today I'll channel my creative energies into curbing bigotry by working with other gay men and lesbians to try to teach kids and adults the meaning of the word "homophobia."

If I had to wear high heels and a dress, I would be a mental case.

—K. D. LANG

In what ways do your clothes define who you are as a gay man or a lesbian? Although your career may pressure you into conforming to heterosexual fashion ideals during working hours, the last thing in the world you may want to do is dress like you're a straight woman or man in your off-hours. So when you're away from work, you may be a sweatsuited lesbian, a drag queen, a leather lover, or a T-shirt-and-ripped-jeans dresser.

Clothes may be as important to you as your way of life. You may spend an incredible amount of money on T-shirts—even though you may already own several—handkerchiefs of various colors, western clothing, leather goods, vintage clothing, or sports outfits. You may do this not only because such things are more comfortable to wear, but also because they're more comforting. Wearing such gay- or lesbian-identified ensembles may be your way of showing others who you are. And the more your parents, friends, family members, or employers may object to your wearing such attire, the stronger may be your desire to continue to do so.

Today, be conscious of the clothing you wear and how it makes you feel. Pay particular attention to the things you like to wear and in what ways such things make you feel more comfortable with yourself and your sexuality.

◆ Dressing up for myself—not dressing up to conform to others—is what dictates my fashion sense as a gay man or lesbian. Today I'll balance a fashion purchase made for the benefit of others with a fashion purchase made just for me.

Country radio gets so many songs that they're looking for a reason not to play a song rather than to play one. It's a mistake to say that people in country radio are bigots or that country audiences are narrow-minded homophobes. But . . . it's impossible to discount the fact that this song was more daring than what you usually hear on the radio.

—JAY ORR

When Garth Brooks's album *The Chase* shot to number one on both country and pop charts, a minor controversy erupted over its first single. "We Shall Be Free" was risky and startling, for no mainstream country musician had ever addressed homophobia in a song. One week after he was named *Newsweek's* Entertainer of the Year, Brooks told the magazine: "If your parents are black and white, if your parents are the same sex, that's still traditional values to me."

Other country musicians have begun to recognize their ever-increasing gay and lesbian audience by supporting gay and lesbian issues. Kathy Mattea, Country Music Association Female Vocalist of the Year in 1989 and 1990, wore three red ribbons in honor of three friends with AIDS at a recent CMA awards ceremony and later performed at Nashville's first grass-roots AIDS fund-raising and awareness event.

Today support those musicians who are sensitive to the needs of the community and listen to radio stations that aren't afraid to play their music or air public-service announcements about gay discrimination.

♦ I'll feel empowered by musicians who aren't afraid to take risks. Today I'll listen to songs with meaning—not songs that are demeaning.

OCTOBER 19

When I first came out to him [my brother] he told me, "Don't tell Dad. It will kill him." This gave me visions of myself as the neutron lesbian. "Hey, Mr. Reagan!" I used to say onstage, "I'm a lesbian." Kaboom!

— KATE CLINTON

How did your parents (or will they) react to your coming out to them? How accepting are they (or do you think they'll be) of your lover? If you had to do it over again, would you change how you came out to your parents—or offer words of advice to someone in the process of making that decision?

For most gay men and lesbians, their biological/adoptive family represents a protection against an oppressive and hostile mainstream society. So coming out to family means risking the loss of this support and sense of identity and community.

Yet according to a 1990 survey done by *Out/Look* magazine on the subject of coming out to parents, 74 percent of the respondents were already out to all of their siblings, 76 percent to their mother, and 59 percent to their father. The number of readers who "straightened up"—or "de-gayed"— their households prior to the visits of others usually did so for neighbors, coworkers, or other relatives. But when parents visited, 42 percent never changed or hid items.

So today, leave your copy of the *Joy of Lesbian/Gay Sex* out on the coffee table when your parents visit, wear a gay symbol or button when you go home, and stop lying to your parents about your "friend."

◆ Some gay men and lesbians have been rejected by their biological/adoptive families, but at least they've been honest and received an honest response. I'll never know if my parents will accept me unless I let them know who I really am.

Hatred is the coward's revenge for being intimidated.
—GEORGE BERNARD SHAW

How is it that some people can actually feel hatred for you or for other gay men or lesbians when they don't even know you? How is it that such hatred can lead to vicious attacks that leave victims physically and emotionally scarred—or even dead?

Rather than be subjective about homophobia when an attack occurs or an ignorant statement is made, you need to examine objectively such actions or words. When you do, you'll see that the things others hate the most are often the things they most fear. "We fear something before we hate it" is the only way to explain such senseless and insensitive acts.

Because hatred is often fear's disguise, the best way to alleviate the fear is to make the experiences that precipitate it more familiar. Most gay bashers freely admit that they don't know anyone who's gay. Some are homophobic, closeted gays who are afraid to come to terms with their own sexuality. And some claim that they believe someone who's gay will force them to have sex.

To ease such fears, work with other gay men and lesbians to find ways to ease or remove the fears. Raise funds for gay organizations whose goals are public education and awareness about gay and lesbian issues. Or write letters to those in Congress, urging passage of bills that will include, rather than exclude, gays in all professions.

♦ The media can play a big part in how gay men and lesbians are perceived by others. Today I'll write letters to the editor, articles for mainstream publications, and discuss gay and lesbian issues on call-in talk shows.

We're Here, We're Queer, and We Do Quality Printing.
——AD FOR A NEW YORK PRINTING FIRM RUN BY LESBIANS

How times change! In the gay and lesbian community, gay entrepreneurs are advertising their services not only to gay men and lesbians, but also to the straight business world. In the conservative business world, there's beginning to be quiet recognition that some employees are gay—and that doesn't have to be a big deal. Companies ranging from IBM to USWest have been recognized as having strong antidiscriminatory policies; some, like Chevron, General Mills, and Equitable Company, have donated hundreds of thousands of dollars to AIDS groups and gay and lesbian organizations. *Fortune* magazine even reported on gay employee organizations formed at companies from AT&T to Xerox, a gay corporate network in Chicago with over six hundred members (called "Fruits in Suits"), the openly gay president of a well-known ad agency, a gay Wall Street lunch club, and a group called the National Organization of Gay and Lesbian Scientists and Technical Professionals. American business seems to be saying, "If the best person for a particular job happens to be black, Jewish, or gay, why waste that talent?"

Today use your buying power to support companies that support their gay employees. Urge the company you work for to commit itself to nondiscrimination based on sexual orientation and HIV status. And hold the management of *any* company responsible for behavior that abuses the dignity of any gay man or lesbian in its employ.

◆ Today I'll find out which corporations are gay sensitive, identify which products they produce, purchase their merchandise, and encourage my gay brothers and sisters to do the same.

Is she my "girlfriend" or my "significant other"? My "longtime companion" or my "lover"? Surely, a little ingenuity will solve this problem. So tell me, America, how do I introduce Joyce?

—DEB PRICE

When Deb Price, a lesbian columnist for the *Detroit News,* posed these questions in a 1992 column about her lover, Joyce Murdoch, she was asking the same questions that have stymied gay men and lesbians for decades. For every label that one gay couple uses to identify themselves as more than friends, that same label may be considered degrading, pseudo-heterosexual, or politically incorrect by another gay couple. Within the gay and lesbian community, there seems to be no clear consensus as to how to identify the person with whom you're involved on an intimate basis.

There may also be other labels with which you have difficulty. You may prefer to be called a lesbian rather than a dyke, choose to spell women "wimmin," or take real issue with being labeled homosexual. As a gay man, you may call yourself a fag but resent it when straight people do; you may prefer to think of yourself as queer rather than homosexual.

But how much do such labels really matter to you? If you find that you absolutely *need* a label with which to identify yourself or the person with whom you share your life, then come up with a term that's acceptable to you. But then concentrate your time and energy on being you—with or without a label.

◆ When I introduce the most important person in my life to other people, I'll use a term that we find most comfortable— not a term that's going to be acceptable, "correct," or comforting to others.

Humor is an affirmation of dignity, a declaration of man's superiority to all that befalls him.

—ROMAIN GARY

Sometimes you may not see the importance of humor in your dark times because you're so blinded by your tears. Remaining open to levity even in the most solemn situations can help survivors as well as those who are ill or dying stay both mentally and physically healthy. One medical study done in the United States showed that the immune systems of those who were grieving the loss of a longtime companion had lower activity levels of T cells, one of the body's defenses against illness.

So humor and laughter can help keep your immune system in balance, help you psychologically, enable you to communicate at a time when communication is at a standstill, and restore your sense of pride, so you feel that nothing is so great that it can destroy you or your dignity.

Today, try to take the processes at the end of your life or the life of someone you care for less seriously. Humor during such trying moments as the death of a longtime companion, grieving the loss of a loved one, and dealing with your own illness is of benefit both to the person going through the difficulty and to those around them—the family, friends, loved ones, and care givers.

Today keep in mind a Chinese proverb that states: "You cannot prevent the birds of sorrow flying over your head, but you can prevent them from building nests in your hair."

♦ Today, instead of asking, "Why did this happen to me?" I'll ask instead, "Now that this has happened, what shall I do about it? How can I find the silver lining in the cloud?"

> *Our aim is to recognize each other and for each to learn to see
> and honor in the other what he is—the counterpart and comple-
> ment of the other.*
>
> —HERMANN HESSE

You may wonder, "What's a healthy intimate relationship? How do I find one? How do I know if I have one?" Gay men as well as lesbians often joke about how they begin their relationships: lesbians identify the second date as the one when the U-Haul appears while gay men simply respond, "What's a second date?"

You'll know that you're in a healthy intimate relationship when you've created a space in which both you and your partner can honestly say, "I can be me, you can be you, and we can also be us. In addition, I can grow, you can grow, and then we can also grow together."

How do you create this space? To have such separateness as well as togetherness, you must allow your partner to be him or herself. You must respect and value your partner as he or she is right now. Your acceptance can't be conditional on your partner being the person you want him or her to be or doing what you want him or her to do. This simply means you don't have to like everything about your partner, but you need to acknowledge his or her likes and dislikes, hobbies and interests, feelings and attitudes, and ways of doing things without judging or putting your partner down. By accepting your partner for who he or she is, you give understanding, freedom, and support, all of which help intimacy develop and grow.

◆ I need to resist trying to make my partner be the way I want him or her to be. Today I'll encourage my partner to grow and change, but in ways he or she chooses rather than in ways that I might want.

Some of our students are going to lead a gay or lesbian life. We would want them to have some role models in the faculty, as well.
——DONALD W. MCNEMAR

While most high-school gay and lesbian teachers remain in the closet, fearful of the personal and professional consequences of coming out, elite boarding and day schools are encouraging their gay and lesbian teachers to be open about their sexuality so they can be positive role models for their gay and lesbian students. In 1991 the Gay and Lesbian Independent School Teacher Network (GLISTEN) was created as a vehicle for raising awareness about gay and lesbian teachers and the issue of homosexuality in the prep-school world.

One closeted teacher at a Massachusetts suburban school described her school's attitudes about homosexuality: "We counsel gay students not to come out. They'd get killed . . . male students get harassed just for being in drama or chorus." But at some private schools, gay/straight alliances have been formed, and there are openly gay teachers; courses on gay and lesbian history are offered, while discussion of the gay movement is part of a civil rights course.

Phillips Academy headmaster Donald W. McNemar feels the role-model issue, combined with the alarming rate of suicide among gay teenagers, is a compelling impetus for many gay and lesbian teachers to make their sexuality known. So if you're a teacher, think about coming out at your school. And if you know others who teach, encourage them to be positive gay role models at their schools.

◆ Today I'll view any openly gay teacher as having taken a courageous step for him or herself as well as for his or her students.

Supposedly there is an advertising problem. But I don't see the ratings of "Roseanne" plummeting from having a gay character. . . . And if advertisers do withdraw from homosexuality, TV's weekly format allows all to be forgiven by the next episode.

—JEHAN AGRAMA

While gay and lesbian cinematic representation continues to be negative or nonexistent, television has surged ahead in its positive portrayal of gay and lesbian characters. There have been recurring homosexual or bisexual characters on shows such as *L.A. Law, Hill Street Blues, thirtysomething, Melrose Place,* and *Roseanne.* Popular series such as *Murphy Brown, Northern Exposure, The Simpsons,* and *Quantum Leap* have built episodes around homosexual themes and characters. Made-for-television movies such as *Doing Time on Maple Drive, Consenting Adult, My Two Loves,* and *An Early Frost* have confronted gay and lesbian issues head-on. And talk shows consistently focus on the issue of homosexuality. While some advertisers may be shaky about buying time during homosexual-themed shows, the hesitancy has not stopped the television powers that be from continuing to show gay male, lesbian, and bisexual characters in positive ways.

Today, boycott Hollywood movies that perpetuate stereotypical gay images or negative, violent gay characters. Stay home and watch TV!

♦ There are people who work in the television industry who have achieved power and are willing to treat homosexuality in positive, real-life ways. Today I'll watch their shows or write letters expressing my continued support for their recognition of the gay and lesbian community.

I don't know anyone who feels his or her parents made them gay or lesbian. What parents do, though, is pull closet doors shut by pretending homosexuality doesn't exist. Families are given the keys to the closet doors.

—PAUL MONETTE

You've got a rare set of parents if they aren't racist, sexist, or homophobic in some small way. So one of the greatest challenges you face as a gay man or a lesbian when you want your parents to know about you, your sexuality, and your partner is to come out in a way that challenges them to look at their prejudices and to think of ways to get rid of them. This is already made difficult by the fact that you're different from your parents; your different-ness challenges the connections that bind you as a biological/adoptive family and may cause your parents confusion, anger, or disappointment as they seek to maintain connections.

But the differences caused by your homosexuality may pale beside the revelation of an involvement with someone of a different race, religion, or class background. If your parents don't accept your relationship, you may wonder if your partner is being rejected or excluded because he or she is black, white, working class, Asian, Jewish—or simply because he or she is a gay man or a lesbian.

Anger against such prejudice is justified. When your parents refuse to accept you, your sexuality, or your lover, it's okay to be angry. While they have the key to unlock the closet door, you always have the choice to overcome and confront the closet.

♦ Today I'll become more aware of the privileges afforded me because of my skin color, background, or class, and those denied to my partner, and communicate those differences to my parents.

Children awaken your own sense of self when you see them hurting, struggling, testing; when you watch their eyes and listen to their hearts. Children are gifts, if we accept them.
—KATHLEEN TIERNEY GRILLY

When you watch your child or a friend's child grow and begin to examine the world around him or her, you may feel a longing to protect the child from any pain, sorrow, rejection, humiliation, or disillusionment that might be encountered because of your sexuality. You may even start to worry about the child's eventual exploration of his or her sexuality and hope that if he or she is gay, the coming out will be an easy, positive process.

But shielding the child from pain or trying to fight the child's battles now or in the future could only do the child a disservice. For those are the experiences that help to shape the child's character and teach the child life's greatest lessons. Being a parent or a close friend means you must "mother" the child—not "smother" him or her.

Such a "hands off" approach to parenting can also be applied in your own life. Whenever you run from conflict or difficulty, force yourself to go back and face it. Your heart may pound and you may feel frightened and weak. But just like the child who must face all the hard tests in his or her life, so, too, must you. For it's only when you face your fears and test your limits that you can gain confidence and grow.

♦ When I try to shield myself or anyone else from painful learning experiences, I hinder the normal growth process. Today let me extend a hand when it's needed and let go when it's required.

Prayer is neither black magic nor is it a form of demand note. Prayer is a relationship.

—John Heuss

You know that communication is the key to a healthy relationship. Communication requires two elements: talking and listening. When only you are talking, that's a monologue. When someone else is talking, all you should be doing is listening. Good communication involves a balance between the time you're talking, or giving to another, and the time you're listening, or receiving from another.

Do you use healthy communication in your prayers? If you examine the way you pray, you may find that your prayers are really monologues. You may pray for answers or guidance about your sexuality, pray to be released from the pain or suffering of an illness or injury, pray to be given the strength to get through another day in a homophobic society, or pray for a family that has rejected you. While it's wonderful to converse with a higher power, unless you also allow time to listen, you're not really communicating.

Today, change your way of praying. Limit your requests so you're not listing a series of wishes or demands. Ask instead for the patience to listen and then let quiet reign. You'll find the answers will come to you and guidance will be given when you're truly ready to receive it. An equal balance of talking and listening will help you strengthen your relationship with your higher power.

◆ I know I don't need great faith to pray. All I need is to be willing to ask for help and then receive the help when my higher power is ready to give it to me. Today I'll be ready and willing to communicate with my higher power.

Homohatred exists throughout the world—just be prepared for it but don't let it detract from your pride in who or what you are.

—DANIEL L. OTERO

Exploring your country or the world can be one of the greatest adventures in life. You may enjoy traveling, but dislike constantly being placed in heterosexual social situations or having to hide your sexuality. You may love going to the beach, to the mountains, or on ocean cruises, but wish such trips also offered opportunities to meet other gay men or lesbians. Or you may be hesitant to journey to unfamiliar lands, across the country, or even within your state with a partner or group of gay men or lesbians because you fear homophobia, violence, or hate crimes.

Today opportunities abound for you to travel within the United States as well as abroad with groups of gay men and lesbians or to stay in guest houses or hotels that cater to a gay and lesbian clientele. It's not uncommon to go to any number of metropolitan areas in the United States or overseas and find a gay-owned bed and breakfast, gay and lesbian bookstores, and restaurants and businesses owned and operated by gay men and lesbians. There are any number of travel agencies that cater to a gay clientele or orchestrate all-gay men, lesbian, or mixed cruises or outdoor adventure expeditions.

Today, go to a nearby gay or lesbian bookstore, peruse the travel guides available for the current year, then start planning your fantasy vacation!

◆ Today I'll stop dreaming about an exotic adventure, a backpacking trip, or an island-hopping ocean cruise. I'll sign up for a vacation with other gay men and lesbians.

The art of drag is as old as society itself.

—STEVEN ARNOLD

From ancient civilizations to contemporary times, gay men and lesbians have explored and enjoyed gender transformation by dressing in drag. Some lesbians in the past dressed in men's clothing solely for comfort, in order to perform tasks in a normally masculine profession, or to pass as men; some gay men dressed in women's clothing in order to play roles in theatrical productions or to boldly confirm their sexuality to others. But most gay men and lesbians cross-dress just to be daring, bold, chic, trendsetting—and to have fun!

Cross-gender costuming has given gay men and lesbians the opportunity to break visual definitions of masculinity and femininity. It's a way to proclaim to themselves and the world that gender isn't as important as personal identity. Drag shows give gay men the freedom to be their favorite starlets or harlots; formal events give lesbians the freedom to dress in tuxedos. In those situations, in the guise of entertainment, social intercourse, or a political statement, gay men and lesbians use drag as a form of creative expression.

Today's modern drag queen and butch lesbian exemplify the wit, style, glamour, bravery, freedom, pride, and boldness that symbolize what it's like to live a way of life that's always breaking from the norm.

◆ Today I won't judge another gay man or lesbian because of how he or she chooses to dress. Drag is just another way to say, "I'm gay and I'm proud!"

If two men not related by blood stand naked under one sheet without any necessity, both of them will be subject to Ta'azir [flogging] of up to 99 lashes. . . . If two women commit a similar offense, according to the law, they may be punished with up to 74 lashes. Such is the sentence for the first three transgressions. The fourth time brings the death penalty.

—IRAN'S ISLAMIC PENAL CODE

The provisions on homosexuality of the Islamic penal code have recently come to the attention of gay and lesbian communities in the Western world, primarily through the efforts of Homan, a group formed by gay refugees from Iran. The group's name comes from a male character who has a platonic love relationship with another man in a folktale by Ferdosi, an ancient Persian writer.

Homan's one hundred members, all of whom served time in Iranian prisons before emigrating, now live in various countries throughout the world. But even though they've escaped the Islamic regime, many are frightened for themselves and for their family and friends in Iran. "Now this terror is part of our body and psyche," says Arman, the spokesperson for Homan.

Today, join together with others in the gay and lesbian community to urge your representatives in Congress to grant asylum to people like Arman. Because interpretations for asylum vary widely, emphasize in your letter that asylum be granted based on a fear of persecution due to an individual's sexuality.

♦ Today I'll let this country's decision makers know that asylum should be granted to gay men and lesbians who would be tortured or killed if they were forced to return to their homelands.

"As president, what's the first thing you'd change?"

"Redecorate the White House and institute health care. Health care comes first. We're going to do that by doing away with the defense budget. We don't need it, because I'm going to have dykes on bikes lining the country."

—JOAN JETT BLAKK

In the "perfect" gay and lesbian world, you would work with your brothers and sisters to create a country in which you always felt safe, your needs were always met, and your way of life was no big deal. Gay men and lesbians who were bodybuilding champs would protect drag queens and "lipstick" lesbians from harassing homophobes as well as enforce the law. Members of gay and lesbian mountain clubs would be in charge of environmental issues. Lesbian entertainers would provide the music while gay men would serve drinks and dish up nutritious meals. And, of course, free health care would be provided to everyone regardless of HIV status. In effect, we would take care of our own the same way those in government take care of their own!

You can achieve some of your vision of a "perfect" gay and lesbian world. The month of November always signals time for a change. Whether on the federal, state, or local level, you have the opportunity to listen to candidates, look at their records, contact gay and lesbian organizations to learn how they're voting, and make conscious choices. Today, campaign for an openly gay candidate or support someone who's for progay legislation.

♦ My rights and freedoms as a gay man or lesbian won't be protected unless I get involved. Today I'll spread the word to others about candidates I'm supporting who I know will work hard to protect my rights and freedoms.

I had a meeting with [U.S. Senator] Sam Nunn's [D-GA] staff, I had a meeting with [U.S. Senator] Joe Biden's [D-DE] staff last week, and tomorrow I'm meeting with a staffer for Senator Edward Kennedy [D-MA]. Why am I having these meetings? Because I want to know what is going on in terms of public hearings for the queer civil rights bill.

—MICHAEL PETRELIS

How political is the life you live? Do you regularly read gay publications to keep abreast of legislation that affects you? Have you ever volunteered to work for a candidate for political office or canvassed communities regarding political issues that affect them? Do you engage in political discussions with your friends? Do you exercise your right to vote?

Michael Petrelis, an ACT-UP member in Washington, D.C., has no problem demanding hearings at the beginning of legislative sessions. "And the way I do that is to put on a tie, shave and go and have a civilized meeting as an inside lobbyist in Washington." He's not afraid to speak his mind to presidential candidates, presidents, cabinet members, or members of Congress. He has been known to urge gay-rights lobbying groups such as the Human Rights Campaign Fund to "flex a little more activist muscle" on behalf of all gay men and lesbians, urging them to demand "open lesbians in the president's cabinet."

Today, get politically active and get out to vote. Remember that your vote can help make the gay and lesbian community more politically powerful.

◆ Voting is such a basic freedom that sometimes I take it for granted. But imagine what life would be like for gay men and lesbians if we couldn't vote! I'll choose to exercise my freedom and let my voting voice be heard.

*[Ronald and Nancy Reagan] think it's abnormal. I certainly
don't think they feel that whatever someone's sexual preference is,
is OK. They think God made men and women to make love, and
any variation on that theme is in some way blasphemous.*

——PATTI DAVIS

When your parents raised you, they may have made you
follow their basic "rules of life"—rules like look both ways
before you cross the street, pick up your toys, eat your
vegetables, don't talk to strangers, be home by curfew, be
courteous to your elders, mind your manners, do your home-
work, and so on.

But not once did your parents ever tell you, "Don't love."
They also probably never said, "Don't fight for what you
believe in." They probably never advised, "Let others walk all
over you." They probably never urged you to be dishonest.
And they probably never said, "Let others tell you you're an
abnormal, horrible, disgusting, sick person."

Parents who instill values in their children that are quickly
"clarified" or "revised" when their son or daughter comes out
to them are giving mixed messages. It's not okay for your
parents to say, on the one hand, "Be honest," but then tell you
never to bring up the subject of your sexuality again. It's not
okay for them to say, "We love you," and then reject you.

Today, create a set of rules that are right for you. Be
honest. Fight for what you believe in. Know that you're a
wonderful person. And, most of all, *love*.

◆ The most painful mixed message my parents have given
me is: "We love you, but not if you're gay." Today I'll reject
this condition on their love and tell them that the *only* love
that exists for me is unconditional love.

> *Last night at twelve I felt immense,*
> *But now I feel like thirty cents.*
>
> —GEORGE ADE

Do you remember times in the distant past—or even more recently—when you may have begun a date or a night out with a clear head, an upbeat mood, and a lightness in your step? You may have felt like you were on top of the world, filled with high hopes and great expectations.

But then, the morning after, you may have crawled out of a bed you shared with someone you barely knew, drowned yourself in a vat of coffee to sober up, looked in the mirror at a horrifying reflection you barely recognized, then tried to remember your behavior during the previous hours. You may have felt like you'd rather crawl under a rock than try to make it through the day.

Such morning afters can be scary or humbling—it's all in how you look at them. If you view them as scary, then chances are you won't deal with the events of a previous evening. While that may feel good over the short term, there's a strong possibility that a similar situation might occur. But if you can view the morning after as humbling, you'll probably be able to deal with what happened so the situation isn't repeated.

There is dignity in being humble. You can apologize to someone you may have offended, confide in a trusted friend about your behavior, and then tell yourself that it will never happen again.

◆ I can limit the damage I may have created last night by taking a walk to clear my head and then talking it over with someone who will listen. I'll promise myself that tonight I won't do anything that'll make me feel like thirty cents tomorrow.

You pray in your distress and in your need; would that you might pray also in the fullness of your joy and in your days of abundance.
—KAHLIL GIBRAN

Have you ever contacted your higher power through prayer and not asked for anything? Instead, have you listed all the people, places, and things in your life for which you're grateful? Have you thanked your higher power for nature's beauty—the brilliant foliage, the crisp morning air, a breathtaking sunset, or the gentle moonglow? Have you expressed your gratitude for the senses you have or for your mobility? Have you bowed your head in thanks before enjoying a delicious meal? Have you conveyed your happiness about sharing your life with a beloved partner, with a loving circle of friends, with a warm extended family, or with an accepting family of origin?

Too often you may pray in times of need—when you're filled with sorrow over the loss of a partner, in poor health, depressed, or weak in spirit. You may tend to pray more fervently and regularly when you feel most threatened and helpless. But after things calm down and you feel better about yourself or your life, the lines of communication with your higher power may grow quiet.

While your higher power is always there to listen to all of your prayers, today make a resolution to pray often and consistently. Remember, you don't have to need to pray in order to pray; you can simply pray as a way of staying in touch with your higher power.

◆ Just as I would call a close friend on a regular basis to share the good and the bad in my life, so, too, can I call on my higher power. My prayers can be wishes for help for what I need as well as messages of gratitude for what I've been given.

NOVEMBER 7

The fire rose like two branched flames like the golden antlers of some enchanted stag.

—KATHARINE MANSFIELD

It's a simple fact that burning wood produces fire. Yet do you know that when fire feeds on fire, it can create a rare condition that yields the greatest illumination? Chinese philosophy teaches that when two flames come together, they yield light more magnificent than either could have given forth alone.

This philosophy illustrates what can happen when you join with other gay men and lesbians to achieve a common purpose or goal. When one person cooperates with others, the accomplishments can often be greater than what the individuals could achieve on their own. Sometimes the combination of energies can come down to just two people, a few, or a small group. As long as the individuals who are drawn together don't sacrifice their individual power but, instead, lend this power to their communal endeavors, they can often create a positive situation that benefits others and encourages individual growth.

In the case of activities and interests in the gay and lesbian community, situations that bring others together in harmony can spark ideas, create inspiration, and generate the necessary momentum for growth and action. If the group interacts with one another by contributing individual energy and power, the results can be like fire upon fire. Such results can illuminate the world!

◆ Today I'll be careful not to lose my energy in my involvement in any gay or lesbian group—fire feeding on fire can also mean the swift exhaustion of energies. I'll keep in mind that group integration, not individual disintegration, is the key.

Experience is a hard teacher. She gives the test first and the lessons afterward.

—ANONYMOUS

You probably wouldn't argue with the statement that the best way to learn anything is through personal experience. But think back to some of the ways you may have handled the more difficult situations in your life—coming out to your friends or family, your first gay relationship, being harassed at school, ending a relationship, asking someone out on a date, dealing with a coworker's gossip about your sexuality. Did you try to handle such things on your own? When a close friend advised you not to adopt a certain tactic, did you ignore the advice? Did you feel that you had all the answers or were the only one who knew the right thing to do?

Today you may be more accepting of the idea that you can learn much from others. By becoming more open-minded and trusting of the wisdom and advice of other gay men and lesbians, you may be more willing to learn from them. When you do, you'll probably no longer have to do everything "the hard way." Learning from others means that you don't have to repeat their mistakes.

Today, reach out to others in the gay and lesbian community who can be your teachers. Listen to the lessons they give you, prepare yourself for the tests of life, then apply what you've learned.

♦ In the past I wasn't always the best student—no matter who was giving the lesson. Today I'm tired of doing everything the hard way. I'll let others teach me so I can benefit from their experiences.

I had come in time to learn that it was a mistake to smile a friendly smile when somebody made a fool of me.

—MARCEL PROUST

When you're harassed by one or more people whose expressed purpose is to cause emotional rather than physical hurt, how do you respond? Even though you may feel angry, hurt, or humiliated, do you suppress such feelings and instead show forgiveness, compassion—even friendliness? You may do so because the person insulting you is a parent or family member, and fear that defending yourself may cause the confrontation to escalate. You may do so because you're outnumbered by a gang of strangers on a deserted street. Or you may do so in order to hold on to a job, keep an apartment, or maintain a relationship with a person whose services you may need.

Yet smiling a friendly smile to individuals who are treating you badly may only end up doubling the emotional damage they inflict. To paraphrase Buddha, holding on to anger or any other negative feeling is like grasping a hot coal—you're the one who gets burned.

Today, don't let others walk all over you with their words. When a family member insults you, say that you don't need to hear their unkind words and walk away. When you're verbally abused by those with whom you have a work, rental, or professional relationship, inform them that their words constitute harassment and that you're not afraid to report them.

♦ Today I'll let my body language, my facial expression, and my words defend me from malicious attacks because of my sexuality. I won't smile a friendly smile at another unless he or she deserves it.

Change occurs when one becomes what she is, not when she tries to become what she is not.

—RUTH P. FREEDMAN

Do you feel like you're always trying to hide your sexuality from others in order to make them happy or more comfortable? Perhaps you accept that your parents don't want your lover to accompany you home during the upcoming holidays. Maybe you remove your earrings or political buttons when you're around your straight friends. Perhaps you laugh at antigay jokes your coworkers make or even tell them yourself. Or maybe you dress, walk, talk, or behave in ways that make you appear to be straight instead of gay.

Yet think of how much time and energy it takes to be who you aren't instead of who you are. Consider all the stress and tension you must go through to make sure you're giving others what they want, when you're giving very little to yourself. Realize that when you're bending over backward to increase the comfort level of others, you're doing very little to make yourself more comfortable with yourself.

You don't have to disguise or minimize your sexuality any longer. You don't have to think first of others and then yourself. Who you are and what's right for you needs to be of primary importance. Today, take the time to be who you are. Put your energy into you. Make yourself comfortable with you. Bend over backward for yourself so you can grow as a gay man or a lesbian.

◆ Today I won't change my outward appearance for others, hide the things that are important to me, or behave in ways I don't want to behave. I'll be happy being gay and not compromise this happiness for the benefit of others.

But he did that job, which few men wanted, until a wet spring day in 1951, when I knelt and looked at the small, round hole dead center in his wet, greenish-gray forehead below the line of his red hair. I noticed some of the men in his squad turning away from me so I wouldn't see them crying softly as they put him on a litter so we could carry him with us. He was one of us, a soldier.

—LUCIAN K. TRUSCOTT III

Lucian K. Truscott III, a retired army infantry officer, once commanded an infantry rifle company in the first year of the Korean War. Among the 150 or so men under his command in the bitter cold Korean mountains was at least one gay soldier. The other men in Truscott's unit knew the soldier was gay because he was very effeminate; they often ridiculed him to his face. The soldier's job in the unit was BAR (Browning Automatic Rifle) man. It was a job few men wanted; the weapon was big, weighing more than twenty pounds. The soldier's slight build — about five feet seven inches and 140 pounds — probably made his job even harder. But the worst part of the job was that the weapon was so reliable and deadly that the Chinese invariably went for the BAR man first.

The fact that the soldier was gay had no bearing on the bullet that killed him or on how well he performed his job. He, like many soldiers killed in battle before and after him, was a good, brave — and gay — soldier.

This Veterans Day, remember those brothers and sisters who have laid down their lives for everyone: those who loved them, those who were like them, even those who disliked them.

◆ Today I'll honor the memory of gay men and lesbians in all branches of the military who have lost their lives in the line of duty.

Even if both partners are out to their parents and relatives, all problems do not magically disappear.
—D. MERILEE CLUNIS AND G. DORSEY GREEN

Life partners Pat and Lee always dread the holiday season. They hate the fact that they always spend the holidays apart, yet for years they've gone to their respective childhood homes to spend holidays. Both Pat and Lee feel torn between their loyalty to their parents and their love for one another. They can't see the point in coming out to their parents, who are in their seventies, because it would upset them. Yet when they discuss upcoming holidays, both feel that the other is applying pressure to come out so they can spend their holidays together—and with their families.

Perhaps you and your partner vehemently disagree about how out you should act toward your biological/adoptive families. You may blame each other for causing the separation during the holidays or feel that the other is not taking the relationship seriously by refusing to come out to parents.

But even if you both came out to your respective parents and got to spend the holidays together, don't assume that you'd have a Norman Rockwell time together. In fact, the holiday stresses you might face could even be worse.

Today, accept that coming out is an individual process and a personal decision. If you and your partner can't be together over the holidays, set aside time before or after to celebrate your own holiday together as a couple.

◆ Traditional family holidays are always very hard for nontraditional couples. Today I'll talk with my partner about the special plans we can make and share together this year that will help us to enjoy the holidays.

Imagine what it would be like if you never threw out any of your trash. It wouldn't take long to accumulate more plastic packaging than furniture, and you'd find yourself virtually unable to move. We need to clear the debris out of our minds.

—MARGO ADAIR

A mandala is traditionally a diagram or painting that one uses during meditation. The painting is usually brightly colored and extremely complicated. To see this as a soothing picture on which to meditate, the meditator begins focusing on the outer edges of the picture and gradually works inward. By the time the meditator has reached the center of the picture, the chaos of the outer edges should have been dissolved so the mind can be opened.

But a mandala doesn't have to be a brightly colored, complicated drawing. A mandala can be repeating a chant, reciting a favorite psalm, staring at a burning candle, holding a gay symbol in your hands, progressively relaxing your muscles, visualizing the good cells in your body destroying the bad cells, going for a long run, or taking life in an uncomplicated, slow, relaxed way.

How can you make your daily activities into a mandala? You don't have to achieve greatness or feel terrific in order to be calm and relaxed. Today, simply enjoy all the little things you do. Think of these things as mandalas that can help you feel alive, centered, and happy in the moment.

♦ I know that meditation isn't the cure for AIDS, and it won't eliminate homophobia from the world. Today I'll live my life simply and efficiently, taking pleasure from life's little treasures.

I can say to my gay friends "Men are shits," and they agree. It's a kind of sisterhood in a way.

— SARAH JESSICA PARKER

Do you think that every man and woman of color loves all people of color? Or that every Jew loves all Jews? Or that each Native American loves all Native Americans?

In every group of people, there are always those who aren't liked by others, who don't fit in, who aren't moral or ethical people, or who have beliefs that run contrary to those of the group. But often people who are part of a minority feel pressure to accept everyone in their community, lest the power of the entire group be damaged. So members of minority groups will often urge unity and plead acceptance of all members rather than turn their backs on those who split off into subgroups, those who speak out against the group's needs, and those who won't contribute to the efforts of the group as a whole.

The same is true in the gay and lesbian community. You're bound to have difficulties with some gay men or lesbians. There may be those within your community who disagree with issues that are important to the majority of gay men and lesbians. There may be those who feel that what they want and how quickly they can get it is more important. And there may be those who simply aren't very nice people.

Today, strive to find unity in disunity. When the actions or behaviors of a few threaten the community, channel your energy into keeping the majority together so the individual efforts of others won't damage the community as a whole.

◆ Today I'll accept that we're all individuals, with separate needs and issues, but that we are all united with the same common thread of our sexuality.

I'm looking out a large window now and I see about forty dogwood and maple and oak and locust trees and the light is on some of the leaves and it's so beautiful. Sometimes I'm overcome with gratitude at such sights and feel that each of us has a responsibility for being alive: one responsibility to creation, of which we are a part, another to the creator—a debt we repay by trying to extend our areas of comprehension.

—MAYA ANGELOU

Writer and actress Maya Angelou, author of *I Know Why the Caged Bird Sings,* wrote the above passage when she was asked, "What's the meaning of life?" In trying to arrive at a definitive answer, she realized that her view changed from week to week. "When I know the answer, I know it absolutely," she said. "As soon as I know that I know it, I know that I know nothing."

If you've tested HIV positive, are a person living with AIDS, or are battling cancer or another illness, it may be difficult for you to find some meaning in life. Every day, every hour, every minute, every second might be so precious to you that it may be hard to step back and look at life as a whole.

Today, do like Maya Angelou did and look out of a window where you live. What do you see? Whether you look out over a serene country scene or a busy city street, you can come up with answers to the meaning to life. Seek to find some meaning, if only for a moment.

◆I know that there's a purpose and a meaning to my life. Today I'll accept that there's a reason for my creation. I'm part of some grand design that requires my presence on earth for a certain amount of time.

Do they miss me at home—do they miss me? 'Twould be an assurance most dear, to know that this moment some loved one were saying, "I wish he were here."

—CAROLINE ATHERTON BRIGGS MASON

Estrangement from family members because of your way of life can be particularly painful as the calendar year draws near the times of traditional family celebrations: Thanksgiving, Hanukkah, Christmas, and New Year's Eve. Right now it may be hard not to think about holiday times you've shared with your family in the past. You may find yourself pulling out old photo albums, having dreams about family members, staring at an item displayed in a shop window that you know a family member might like, wondering whether or not you should send a card to your parents, or hoping that every time the telephone rings it will be someone in your family.

Yet the only way to repair the broken bridges that keep you from connecting with family members is for you to take the first step. What that means is that you can't concern yourself with how the bridge broke, exactly when it broke, or who caused it to break. Instead, you need to concentrate on drawing the opposite sides of the bridge closer together so they can be reconnected.

To do so, begin with your end. Pick up the telephone. Write a letter. Or send a card. You don't have to say much. Your message can simply be, "I miss you a lot."

♦ Today I'll forget harsh words spoken in the past or the reasons why I'm not connected with my family. Instead, I'll show my parents, my siblings, or other family members just how hard it is not to have them in my life.

*I want to love somebody and be loved, but being in love—
that's so out of control, irresponsible, and obsessive. I'm too old for
that shit.*

—ALIX DOBKIN

Growing older in the gay and lesbian community can bring
with it new challenges and problems. Retirement, mild or
serious health problems, changing sexual needs, problems
with aging parents and adult children, changes in financial
status, and needs for housing and personal care can be much
easier to face with a long-term partner. But what happens
when a long-term partner has died before you or you've
grown older without settling down? The social opportunities
you may have to meet a potential partner can decrease with
age; so, too, can your desire to explore a new relationship.

Yet growing old can also bring new joys and freedoms. In
embarking on a new relationship when you're older, you're
able to reap the benefits of maturity, of knowing pretty much
what you want out of life, and of being able to choose exactly
the type of person you'd like to be with. In terms of sexual
activity, you can bring to an intimate relationship not only a
familiarity with your own body but also a willingness to
explore more sensual activities such as cuddling, caressing,
massaging, and other forms of nongenital contact.

Today, recognize that love isn't necessarily reserved for
the young. Love is for anyone, no matter what their age. Love
is truly for those who are young at heart!

◆I can view my age as a barrier to pursuing an intimate
relationship or a benefit. Today, let my years as a gay man
or a lesbian contribute to helping me form a mature and
meaningful relationship.

It is a stupefying grief. It comes over me sharply, at unexpected moments, in the middle of me cooking something he would have liked, or hearing music he enjoyed. . . . I stop, I cry; I let the feeling feel me. And then I do the hardest thing: I put aside the guilt I feel about surviving and being well, and continue with my life.

—DOUG FEDERHART

How many times have you found yourself filled with sadness several months or even several years after the loss of a loved one? How many times have you told others you were happy only to discover you were crying as you said the words?

Such things happen because grief is a feeling that can't be suppressed. It has a life of its own. It makes itself known according to its own schedule. It comes and goes when it wants to—sometimes nudging us with little pangs of pain or punching us hard in the heart. You may find that you can shut yourself off from feeling grief at certain times in the day or even deny that it exists, yet that won't make grief go away. It will wait until a certain song comes on the radio, a familiar scent at a fragrance counter fills your senses, a photo falls out of your wallet, or you notice that the date on your calendar has particular meaning. At such times grief simply can't be held back. Like a dam that bursts, grief can become more intense the harder you try to contain it.

Today, experience your grief. When you give grief the time and space to be freely expressed, you may find it easier to get on with the rest of your life.

♦ Today I won't cut myself off from feeling grief. I'll let each wave in my ocean of grief crash down over me until the tide eventually takes the waters away from the shore of my heart.

It's important that institutions begin to recognize the real family relationships out there in the world.

—SUE HYDE

When Cambridge, Massachusetts, passed the domestic partnership ordinance, it became one of eighteen municipalities in the country to allow couples to register as "domestic partners"; other cities include Seattle; San Francisco; Madison, Wisconsin; Ithaca, New York; West Hollywood and Berkeley, California. By paying a small fee, same-sex domestic partners receive two wallet-sized cards certifying their status and entitling them to receive benefits usually reserved for married couples. Under the ordinance, passed late in 1992, the city of Cambridge allows domestic partners visitation rights in the city hospital and jail and access to the school records of their partners' children. The city also extends health benefits to the partners of municipal employees.

Gay and lesbian couples who registered in Cambridge when the law went into effect said the law didn't afford them special privileges; rather, it corrected discrimination that already existed and remedied an unjust situation. Although the city of Boston defeated a similar ordinance, Children's Hospital in Boston extended benefits to the domestic partners of its employees.

Today, work with other gay men and lesbians in the city where you live to urge the city council to pass a similar ordinance.

♦ Today I'll support a domestic partnership ordinance as more than just a symbolic recognition of my relationship. It can benefit my partner as well through the extension of health-care benefits.

I still shiver with a kind of astonished delight when a gay brother or sister tells of that narrow escape from the coffin world of the closet. Yes, yes, yes, goes a voice in my head, it was just like that for me. When we laugh together then and dance in the giddy circle of freedom, we are children for real at last, because we have finally grown up.

—PAUL MONETTE

When you're isolated from a sense of community, when you have the feeling that you're alone in the way that you feel, or when you suspect that no one else is the way you are, it doesn't matter what age you are. When you experience such things, it's easy to feel like a lost, lonely child. You may feel as if you're growing up all alone in the world without a role model who lives your way of life and without supportive friends who understand your attractions to people of the same sex.

Ideally you should be able to meet other gay men or lesbians with whom you can play and work and then grow from such interactions. But until you come out of the closet, the extra pressures your unwillingness puts on you can detract from your ability to nurture yourself in positive, healthy ways.

A gay and lesbian community is not automatically going to build itself around you. You need to do it for yourself. Today, tell three people that you're gay.

♦ Today I'll remember that closets are for kids' toys—not for living my life. I won't be able to understand and explore the joys in being a gay man or a lesbian until I first acknowledge my sexuality.

As much as I shy away from public attention, I felt it was something I had to do for Howard and for all the gay spouses and widowers who are ignored by society.

—BILL LAUCH

One of the complications of gay and lesbian relationships is that the couple usually doesn't have the support that a heterosexual couple takes for granted during the course of a relationship and in the event of a partner's death. Unless you're out to people at work, you won't get condolences from coworkers, understanding from your boss about unexplained absences or your inability to focus on a project, or paid funeral leave. Without a will that specifies desired funeral arrangements and property disposal, the biological/adoptive family can exclude you from postmortem decisions, prohibit you from attending the funeral, ignore the wishes your partner communicated to you, and take ownership of possessions belonging to you and your partner.

But aside from the legal and social aspects involved in the loss of a loved one, there are also emotional issues to face. Adjusting to an environment where your lover is now missing can be extremely hard. Unless you have a network of supportive friends to rely on, even the simplest of tasks can seem monumental.

Today, no matter your or your partner's age, accept the reality of each other's death. Accidents can happen, so it's best to be prepared now. Arrange to meet with a lawyer to discuss desired funeral arrangements and division of personal and financial property.

◆ Today I won't avoid the "what ifs" concerning my death or the death of my partner. Our advance planning can prevent adding unnecessary legal, financial, and other hassles to the already difficult mourning process.

If you think that this time, for the first time, you're going to get everything right, that Mom and Dad aren't going to fight, that nobody's going to drink too much, that everybody's going to be happy, then you're bound to be disappointed.

—DENISE LANG

In her book *How to Stop Your Relatives from Driving You Crazy*, Denise Lang gives two strong words of advice to all those people who get stressed out over the holidays, including those who grew up in dysfunctional homes, gay men and lesbians who may or may not be out to their families and who may or may not be going home with their partners, those who have never been able to get along with their parents, and those who feel like they're never in control when they're in family situations.

Her two words of advice are: Grow up! When you return to your childhood home and all of its memories, its not uncommon for you to regress—become a child all over again. You enter into a world where, as in the past, your needs aren't met, your parents are fighting, there's too much drinking, unhealthy behaviors abound, your way of life is attacked, your lover is ignored, and no one is happy.

This Thanksgiving, be an adult. Decide when, where, and for how long you want to spend time with your family. Keep your expectations low. Let the past go. And when your limits have been reached, leave.

♦ When I'm around family members this holiday, I'll try to imagine they're relatives in someone else's family. Distancing myself in this way can help me see them more as humorous characters in my life than as real-life relatives.

Inside her breasts there are volcanoes smouldering. Do you think we can reach her before she explodes?

—RUTH GENDLER

Often lesbians are given the label "sensual" while gay men are labeled "sexual." The basic sweat-pouring-off-you sex, accompanied by ecstatic cries of pleasure, has long been thought to be part of the activity that goes on in the back room of a gay men's bar rather than in the bedroom of a lesbian.

So when *On Our Backs,* a magazine that proclaimed it was for "the adventurous lesbian," debuted in 1984, few thought it would last. But a decade later, *On Our Backs* has survived, lesbian parties and sex clubs have been formed, lesbian porn videos are being made and marketed, lesbian publishers are calling for S/M and sex-based manuscripts, and lesbian authors are writing sex scenes in which whipping, bondage, fisting, and sex toys are the reality rather than a character's titillating fantasy.

The notion that "A lesbian's G-spot is a romantic hug" is disappearing as fast as the cliché that all gay men want is sex. Gay men are now pursuing romance while lesbians are actively pursuing their sexual expression. Even the most radically feminist lesbians are accepting sex toys and sex acts that were once labeled "politically incorrect."

Today, don't accept any tired clichés about your sexual nature. As a gay man, you aren't necessarily aggressive, promiscuous, objectifying, and genitally focused. As a lesbian, you aren't always monogamous, nurturing, and searching for romantic love rather than sexual pleasure.

◆ What I do to my body, who I do it with, and where I do it is part of my private life. Today I'll welcome the freedom to make sexual or romantic discoveries in my own way.

Enthusiasm is one of the most powerful engines of success. When you do a thing, do it with all your might. Put your whole soul into it. Stamp it with your personality. Be active, be energetic, be enthusiastic and faithful, and you will accomplish your objective.

—RALPH WALDO EMERSON

What's the biggest challenge you face in your life right now as a gay man or a lesbian? Maybe you want to be more out to friends, family, or coworkers. Perhaps you and your life partner are struggling through a difficult period together. Maybe you're confronting a life threatening disease. Perhaps you're tackling a chemical addiction or a compulsive behavior. Or maybe you're trying to break unhealthy relationship patterns so you can look forward to a more healthy relationship in the future.

Whatever challenge you want to tackle, face it head-on. If you let another day go by without doing something about it, you won't get any closer to making it happen. So go for it! Set a goal that will prompt you to take action. A goal could be coming out to the person closest to you at work, scheduling a time when you and your partner can discuss your relationship, finding an AIDS buddy, going to a twelve-step meeting, or dating a few people before settling down with one person.

♦ Procrastination won't move me any closer to meeting the challenge I've set for myself. So today I'll live by the motto "Act now."

Some people would rather die than burst the myth that families are unimaginably nice places where nothing bad ever happens.
—DONNA MINKOWITZ

When you grow up in a dysfunctional family, you learn a different kind of "normal" from the rest of the population. You learn, for example, to trust mixed messages, half-truths, and lies. You learn that you're a problem, you're in the way, you're stupid, or that you'll never amount to anything. You learn not to ask for what you want, and not to look forward to anything. You learn that sometimes parents behave in ways that are hurtful or embarrassing.

But even though these may be some of the things you learned when you were growing up, you might choose now to believe that you're "wrong" because of your way of life rather than accept the fact that your parents were "wrong" to treat you the way they did when you were a child. Finding fault with yourself may be much easier than finding fault with those who were supposed to nurture you, support you in all your endeavors, protect you from harm, teach you trust, and surround you with love.

Today it's okay to let go of the myth that you grew up in a perfect family, raised by a perfect set of parents. While it may be too hard to look back and remember the reality of your childhood, look at what's true in the present: you're a worthwhile, wonderful gay person who is "right."

♦ Today I'll think about my parents and remember that even though we may have shared a difficult past, the present reality is that I'm an adult. I no longer have to feel like a child who has no power and no choices when I'm around them.

I've spent my whole life exploring the truth and reporting the truth. I just went in and told them I had AIDS.

— JEFF SCHAMLZ

There's an often heard phrase in twelve-step programs that says, "You're only as sick as the secrets you keep." What that means is that as long as you hold things inside or keep them to yourself, you'll never get well. It's only when you can begin to let go of some of the things you're hiding or holding on to that healing can begin. For once you vocalize your fears, talk about your mistrust, confess your past behaviors, or discuss your memories, you bring your feelings out of darkness and into light. Darkness hides, but light heals.

Part of the process of healing when you have a positive HIV status or AIDS is telling people about it. How do you do that? Jeff Schamlz, *New York Times* assistant national editor, simply told others the truth. You, too, can do the same. Once you let the truth be known to those who ought to know, exploring healing options and enlisting the support of others can be easier.

Today, tell someone you have AIDS or have tested HIV positive. Then explore a healing program that includes eating right, exercising, meditating, and spending quality time with caring, nurturing people. Healing with AIDS means dealing with AIDS.

◆ Today I'll resolve that the only secrets I'll keep will be the plans for a surprise party or the purchase of a special gift for a loved one. Those are healthy secrets that won't make me sick!

I think Harvey Milk is a good example of this. He lived with absolutists, with people who committed suicide, with people who couldn't get on with their lives. I think he was troubled by this absolutism that he saw around him in the gay community.

—OLIVER STONE

Are you an absolutist? This means you see things only in terms of black and white. You might immediately say no, I'm a flexible, spontaneous, easygoing person. But in an intimate relationship, are you willing to see that there are more choices than making a long-term commitment or having no commitment at all? Are you willing to accept that not everyone is going to be okay with your sexuality? Can you accept your parents' refusal to let you bring your lover home for the holidays this year—"but maybe next year"—or do you set ultimatums with them? Are you someone who objects to sharing space at a festival or in a bar with gay members of the opposite sex?

Probably the most nonabsolutist role model you've had in the gay and lesbian community was Harvey Milk. Milk was elected to and served on the San Francisco Board of Supervisors, but was murdered because he worked hard to find the "gray areas" that would bring together gay politics and inner-city politics.

Today, honor the memory of "the Mayor of Castro Street" on the day of his assassination. Before you make any either-or decision, try to find at least two more options. Then make a decision from four choices.

♦ On November 27, 1978, the gay and lesbian community lost a positive, powerful role model. Today I'll say a prayer for Harvey Milk and express my gratitude for the open way he lived as a gay man, worked as a gay business owner, and served as a gay politician.

Worry is a form of fear, and all forms of fear produce fatigue.
A man who has learned not to feel fear will find the fatigue of
daily life enormously diminished.

—BERTRAND RUSSELL

Do you worry about how your parents will react when you tell them you're gay? Do you worry about your safety when you leave a bar located in a high-crime area of the city? Do you worry about losing your job if your boss or company finds out you're gay? Do you worry about AIDS or breast cancer? Do you worry about growing old and being alone? Do you worry what will happen to your partner after you die or what will happen to you after your partner dies?

Such worries, while valid, are really based on your fear of the unknown. When you worry, each of your questions can be followed by further questions. While it's okay to worry about things that matter, like your well-being or the well-being of others, unless you can do something to ease your worries, you're only wasting your time—and letting fear control you.

Today, make a list of all the things you're worried about. Then, after each entry on your list, write suggestions detailing things you could do to ease the worry. For example, if you're worried about what will happen to your partner when you die, you can write a will. But if you can't find a way to ease a worry that's out of your control—for example, how your parents may react to hearing you're gay—then let the worry go.

◆ I'm only using my energy foolishly by regretting what happened yesterday, what might happen tomorrow, or what other people think, say, or do. Today I won't worry about things over which I have no control.

I don't think homosexuality is a choice. Society forces you to think it's a choice, but in fact, it's in one's nature. The choice is whether one expresses one's nature truthfully or spends the rest of one's life lying about it.

——MARLO THOMAS

In 1993 the Archives of General Psychiatry revealed research into a study of lesbianism in twins that confirmed what was previously discovered in a 1992 study of male homosexual twins: sexual orientation in women as well as men is largely inborn rather than a matter of upbringing or choice. Professor Michael Bailey and his coauthor of the study, Dr. Richard Pillard, analyzed 108 pairs of female twins and forty-five adoptive sisters. The analysis concluded that the twin sisters of the lesbian identical twins, who shared identical genes with their sisters, had the greatest percentage of lesbians among all the sibling groups.

How does this study affect you? Dr. Nanette Gartrell, a psychiatrist and associate clinical professor at the School of Medicine at the University of California, San Francisco, comments: "So many of the laws that prohibit same-gender sexual behavior . . . are based on the assumption that a gay life-style is a choice, rather than something that is inherent. Studies like this make us think a lot more about how inappropriate these laws are." But David Halperin, a professor at the Massachusetts Institute of Technology counters: "The argument that lesbian and gay people have a claim not to be discriminated against should be made on ethical or moral grounds; it can't be finessed by science."

◆ Today I'll discuss with other gay men and lesbians my feelings on the subject of discrimination based on the true expression of my sexuality.

> . . . *what was completely forbidden for me to do would be to kill myself. . . . If I were to commit suicide, I would be throwing God's gift back in his face.*
>
> —DR. RAYMOND A. MOODY

You may have had suicidal thoughts at one time or another in the past. When you were initially coming to terms with your sexuality as a youth, when your first gay relationship ended, when your parents overreacted or rejected you because of your way of life, when you struggled to be happy in a heterosexual relationship or marriage, when you had to deal with the death of a partner or close friend, or when you first learned you were HIV positive—all these difficult situations may have led you to contemplate or even try suicide.

Then, for years, you may have been able to let go of all thoughts of suicide and lead a relatively happy, stable life. But today, for whatever reason, you may once again be feeling unhappy, hopeless, depressed, and suicidal. That's when you know you need to call someone. Talk it out with a friend, bring it up at the next meeting of a support group you belong to, or make an appointment with a counselor or a spiritual adviser. When you open up, you'll find friends and peers who can be understanding and caring.

You are not alone. Everyone feels like giving up from time to time. But today, don't give in to the feeling. Open yourself up to the caring and love you can receive from another human being.

◆ If a friend of mine felt down on life, wouldn't I want to help? Today I'll think about who I can open up to when I feel like giving up. There *are* people who care about me.

A lot of people feel that sex is going to liberate them. Sex is an animal function. That's like saying, "I'm going to eat apple pie tonight, and that's going to liberate me." Sex never liberated anybody.

—RITA MAE BROWN

The most common term used to refer to a same-sex partner is "lover." That word implies, assumes, and requires sexual contact. But if you and your partner aren't being sexual, are you still lovers? While a heterosexual couple might continue to see themselves as married if they went through a period of reduced sexual contact, a gay or lesbian partner may interpret the same situation as signaling the end of the relationship.

Gay and lesbian couples frequently attach powerful meanings to sexual contact. After all, you're defined as a person who is sexually attracted to and/or has sexual relations with a member of the same sex. So acting on this definition is one way to express yourself freely as a gay man or a lesbian.

Yet reduced sexual activity when the "romance stage" of a relationship has passed—the first six months or so—is normal. When couples are in conflict or a partner is stressed, sex may be suspended. And when couples have been together for a long time, sometimes one or both partners lose interest in being sexual.

Today, develop ways to handle conflicts in your relationship more openly and constructively. Couples who can talk about their issues can often work on their sexual wants and needs as well.

◆ Today I won't feel threatened or frightened by my lack of sexual interest or my partner's. Not having sex doesn't mean we can't be in love with each other.

I cannot give you the formula for success, but I can give you the formula for failure—try to please everybody.

—HERBERT BAYARD SWOPE

Principles are rules or codes of conduct that you set for yourself on how you want to live your life—like being honest, striving to be on time for your appointments, and taking responsibility for paying bills and budgeting your money. You may also set certain principles for how you want to live your life as a gay man or lesbian, like not changing the pronoun when you talk about your lover with other people, including your "gay family" at traditional or religious holiday celebrations, and boycotting companies or organizations that discriminate.

But when you compromise any of your "general life" or "gay life" principles for someone else's benefit, you jeopardize the strength of that principle and its importance to you. If you want to be honest but lie to cover up another's actions, you compromise that principle. If you boycott a discriminatory company that manufactures a particular food and then eat this food in order to avoid conflict at a family dinner, then you've compromised yourself and let someone else's desire dominate.

Today, abide by the principles you've set for yourself, even if doing so won't please others in your life. To let your principles triumph over the demands or desires of another is a victory for your inner peace.

◆ Is anyone making demands on my principles? Today I'll be true to myself and my principles and not make any compromises I'll later regret.

DECEMBER 3

*Weep with me when I weep. Laugh with me when I laugh.
Don't be afraid to share this with me.*

—St. Anthony's Hospital

There's wonderful advice for care givers contained in a St. Anthony's Hospital (Alton, Illinois) brochure titled, "Twenty-five Tips to Help Those Facing a Serious Illness." The brochure emphasizes that whether you're an AIDS buddy, volunteer in a hospital, provide home health care for gay men and lesbians, or are the partner or close friend of someone who's seriously ill, the main function you can provide is to be there emotionally for the person who's sick. Tell the person he or she looks good, don't be afraid to touch or have physical contact, be positive, show that you care, and try to understand and share in all the person's feelings.

The brochure suggests that someone who's seriously ill may say, "Maybe I need to talk about my illness. Find out by asking me: 'Do you feel like talking about it?'" Even though you might be afraid to bring up the subject with your buddy, friend, or partner, the next time you're together ask the question. You may find that he or she has a lot of sad emotions that need to be expressed. While your logical mind may think that expressing sadness could be detrimental, you're wrong; it's actually a very cleansing, healing, and beneficial activity. As Shakti Gawain says, "Sadness is related to the opening of your heart. If you allow yourself to feel sad, especially if you can cry, you will find that your heart opens more and you can feel more love."

◆ Today I'll allow someone who's sick or dying to be sad. I'll give him or her the space in which to cry and express sadness. I'll also give myself the opportunity to embrace this sadness as part of my feelings as well.

Most of us who grew up in small places leave there, not just because there was nothing to do but because it was very uncomfortable for us. Younger people and even older people coming out in rural areas feel very isolated. It's important that we remember our roots.

—JULIE BARON

In an attempt to reach out to gay men and lesbians in rural areas, the National Gay and Lesbian Awareness Project, a Los Angeles–based group dedicated to promoting lesbian and gay visibility, ran ads in both *Time* and *People* magazines. The ads featured a diverse cross section of gay men and lesbians, along with the slogan "We're Your Family, Neighbors, and Friends . . . and We're Gay."

Most gay and lesbian advocates agree that the strongest support in isolated areas comes from positive gay and lesbian role models outside or within those communities. "It comes down to getting adults who are gay or lesbian to speak out," says Scott Thiemann, a gay youth educator at a Spokane (Washington)-based organization called Outreach to Rural Youth.

Most gay men and lesbians who came out in small towns and then left recall that for information on homosexuality they went to guidance counselors, schoolteachers, and local gay men and lesbians. So today, remember your roots. Provide positive gay materials for the school you once attended or offer to speak to an assembly of students.

♦ I can't count on my homophobic hometown to help young gay men and lesbians who are struggling in isolation with their sexuality. Today I need to reach out to these young people in some way so they don't feel isolated and alone.

We need to see ourselves in a larger context. I think it would be good for us to get more involved in the world.

——NEIL MILLER

To research and write his book *Out in the World: Gay and Lesbian Life from Buenos Aires to Bangkok,* Neil Miller traveled to twelve nations. He spoke with South African miners, Australian AIDS activists, a lesbian couple legally married in Denmark, and Japanese men who told him that to be "gay in private . . . is acceptable" as long as they maintain a heterosexual facade. What Miller discovered was that many gay men and lesbians in America are very impatient and angry that things haven't changed quickly enough for them. Going to other countries helped him to see that gay Americans don't realize or appreciate how far they've already come. "I was in Czechoslovakia right after communism fell," he explains. "There was the first gay newspaper, the first lesbian group, and people were really excited, young, and idealistic."

Before you can judge how far you've come in America as a gay man or a lesbian, it's important to see yourself not in terms of your own issues and needs but as just one gay man or a lesbian within an entire world of gay men and lesbians. To get an idea of this larger context, read books that detail gay and lesbian life in foreign countries or travel to countries that aren't as enlightened as America. Doing so may help you to appreciate the rights, freedoms, and opportunities that already exist for you at home.

◆ In countries such as Egypt, two women can't rent an apartment or go to a movie together. In Argentina, gay bars are still routinely raided by police. Today I'll find out more about the lives of my brothers and sisters around the world, and appreciate the freedoms I enjoy here.

I felt really bad. . . . I felt really dirty about it. I felt there must be something wrong with it that they kept it a secret.
—DINA BILLMAN

Do children of gay and lesbian parents have difficulties with gender and social development when they know their parents are gay? In the early eighties Dr. Martha Kirkpatrick and two colleagues completed a ground-breaking study of children of lesbian mothers and concluded there was no evidence to support the belief that children have such difficulties. Other researchers in later studies arrived at the same conclusion.

While children of gay and lesbian parents sometimes have trouble at first accepting their parents' sexual orientation, most become quite supportive and mature in handling the issue. When twelve-year-old Cameron Calderon-Melendez of Brooklyn was asked why he didn't tell any of his friends about his father, he replied, "They're still immature. They don't know about that stuff." When sixteen-year-old Dina Billman was home sick from school and found books about gay parenting and how to be a gay father in her parents' closet, at first she was in shock. But when her father was diagnosed HIV positive, she began attending a support group. Since his death Dina says, "I tell everybody that he was gay. Really, I'm proud of it. I'm proud of who my father was."

Today, show your children you're proud of who you are. Doing so will let your kids know it's okay to be proud of you for who you are and of themselves for who they are.

◆ Today I'll show my children that they can be proud of me and proud of themselves, no matter who we are or what we do.

DECEMBER 7

We all live under the same sky, but we don't have the same horizon.

—KONRAD ADENAUER

Often people remember December 7, 1941, not as a day of global tragedy but as a day for hating Japanese people. They may also see it as a time to treat Japanese Americans with contempt and suspicion; because of the attack, many loyal American-born Japanese citizens were treated cruelly, viewed not as citizens of America but as a threat.

Within the gay and lesbian community, there's a need for acceptance of all special-interest groups, whatever racial, ethnic, or other commonality draws them together. Even though what unites you with every gay man and lesbian is the way of life you share, there are times when different groups of gay men and lesbians need to be together. Gay men and lesbians of color need to work on racial politics that affect them in a profoundly unique way. Gay and lesbian people of Asian descent and their friends, gay Native Americans and Native Canadians, the hearing impaired and disabled, and Jewish groups have special needs to gather together and speak in their own words in an environment that affords them understanding and harmony.

Today, work cooperatively with the special-interest groups within your gay and lesbian community. Or if you're a member of a special interest group yourself, work to promote unity among and between other members of your group.

♦ I accept that a diverse group of gay men and lesbians can never effectively deal with each individual's particular needs. Today I'll support the efforts of every gay man and lesbian to find comfort and common grounds within the community.

What must I do is all that concerns me—not what people think. It is easy in the world to live after the world's opinion; it is easy in solitude to live after our own—but the great man is he who in the midst of the crowd keeps with perfect sweetness the independence of solitude.

—RALPH WALDO EMERSON

Are you fast approaching the time of year when you need to hide your sexuality from parents, family members, siblings, and hometown friends? Will you and your partner separate for the holidays, acting as if you're college roommates going home for school break instead of staying together like the married couple you are every other month of the year?

You might be like a chameleon this time of year, changing your sexual "color" to please others, hiding your true self and your way of life to protect your sexual identity or avoid hurting someone else. While chameleons survive in the wild because they're adept at hiding from predators, your choice to hide isn't based on survival but on being dependent on what others think about you. In doing so, you're making someone else's needs more important than yours.

This holiday season, don't be a chameleon. There are no predators out there—only people. Their thoughts and feelings may be different from yours, but that's okay. You have your own brilliant colors to show them.

◆ Do I "change colors" for the approaching holidays to please others or make life easier for me? I'm not living well if I'm spending some of my life hiding my true self. Today I'll tell myself that it's okay for me to be different, too.

> *Christmas was a miserable time for a Jewish child. . . . De-*
> *cades later, I still feel left out at Christmas, but sing the carols*
> *anyway. You might recognize me if you ever heard me. I'm the one*
> *who sings, "La-la, the la-la is born."*

> —FAYE MOSKOWITZ

Not only do Jewish gay men and lesbians often face a complete lack of understanding—even hostility—when they
come out to their parents, but they also face problems because of their Jewishness within the gay and lesbian community. This schism can become particularly evident when you
want to share holidays important to your culture with a
non-Jewish partner or non-Jewish friends in the community.
Times of cultural importance to Jewish gay men and lesbians
are often ignored by the gay and lesbian community as a
whole. Rosh Hashana, Yom Kippur, and Hanukkah are rarely
recognized or celebrated by non-Jewish members of the gay
and lesbian community. Rather, Jewish gay men and lesbians
are often urged to "get into the Christmas spirit" and participate in all the tree trimming, stocking stuffing, and caroling
festivities.

Today, you don't have to get into the Christmas spirit or
even deal with the Christian spirit. Welcome the Hanukkah
season with Jewish friends and family who understand its
meaning in your life, or share its meaning with a non-Jewish
partner or friend who respects your religious beliefs.

♦ Today I'll share with my non-Jewish friends in the gay and
lesbian community the Jewish celebration of Hanukkah. I
can be proud of my Jewish traditions as well as my gay
culture.

Two may talk together under the same roof for many years, yet never really meet.

—MARY CATHERWOOD

How do you and your partner communicate your wants and needs? Are you able to say, clearly and effectively, what you want and need? Or do you want your partner to figure out what you want or need so you don't have to put energy into getting clear yourself and asking for what you want?

Trying to maintain an intimate relationship without expressing your wants and needs is like trying to drive a car without a steering wheel. Even though you may be able to move ahead, you won't be able to change directions, avoid difficult spots in the road, or stop in one spot for a while. You can't make forward progress in this type of relationship because it doesn't allow you to connect as a couple through open, clear communication.

There's a difference, for instance, in *announcing* your wants and needs and *expressing* them. Saying "I'm cold" is an announcement that leaves out any specific request of a need. But saying, "I'm cold. Would you move closer to me so we can share your comforter?" expresses what you want clearly and effectively in a way that helps your partner to understand what he or she can give you.

Today, even though you may be hesitant to communicate a clear and straightforward message to your partner because you're afraid of being criticized or not getting what you want, take the risk. Chances are good that you might get what you want!

◆ My partner deserves clear messages; so do I. Today I'll ask that we express what we each need in a way that helps us better understand each other.

Feeling is a breath orgasm.

—JOSEPH KRAMER

Feelings are intimately connected to your breathing. When your moods change, your breathing changes. When you're nervous about coming out to someone, your breathing may be quick and shallow. When you're calm and peaceful lying next to your lover, your breathing may be slow and regular. When you're frightened in a situation of potential harassment or violence, your breathing may be fast and irregular. When you're emotionally shut down, you may even forget to breathe.

While most of the time you may be able to get in touch with how you're feeling from the way you're breathing, sometimes when you're emotionally shut down you may not know how you feel. To get in touch with such feelings involves becoming more familiar with how your body's responding, almost in the same way you'd become more conscious of your physical responses to a lover's touch.

Pay attention right now to your breathing. Then ask yourself the following questions: "Is my jaw tense? Is my stomach in knots? Is it hard for me to talk? Is it hard to keep quiet? Are my teeth clenched? Are my eyes stinging? Are my palms sweaty?" After you've assessed your physical responses, ask yourself, "What am I thinking?" Once you know what you're thinking and how your body's responding to these thoughts, you can clarify and then express your feelings.

♦ Since feelings are a normal part of living, releasing them is like the letting go I experience during orgasm. Today I'll pay attention to my breathing, my body, and my thoughts so I can let out how I feel.

Love says, mine. Love says, I could eat you up. Love says, stay as you are, be my own private thing, don't you dare have ideas I don't share. Love has just got to gobble the other, bones and all, crunch.
— MARGE PIERCY, FROM *BRAIDED LIVES*

Long- or even short-term intimate relationships can be confusing for gay men and lesbians. It can be easy to lose the sense of your individual boundaries and your partner's until you seem to become one person. Then your needs become "our needs," your goals become "our goals," your likes and dislikes become "ours."

Then, when your relationship changes—your partner asks for space, leaves for a short time, makes changes in himself or herself, or begins to behave differently—you may feel threatened, wounded, and desperately lost, unsure of who you are, what you need to do, and where you're now going.

Such blurring of boundaries in a relationship rarely indicates a healthy relationship. At first such blurring may seem to be a normal part of the process of connecting intimately with someone. As time goes by it may become a familiar way of operating together, so comfortable that you can't imagine being with your partner in any other way. But you need to maintain individuality or you won't be able to stand on your own two feet—with or without your partner.

Today, adjust your focus in your relationship so there are no blurred areas. For you to love well and to be involved in a healthy way, you need to always know where both you and your partner stand.

◆ If I feel confused and lost whenever my relationship changes, it may mean that I have become too enmeshed with my partner. Today I'll keep all the pieces of myself together so I can stand alone as well as with my partner.

*A synagogue or church that admitted only saints would be like
a hospital that admitted only healthy people. It would be a lot
easier to run, and a more pleasant place to be, but I'm not sure it
would be doing the job it is here to do.*

—HAROLD KUSHNER

Before you completely accept yourself as a gay man or a lesbian
so you can live your life as a happy, healthy, whole gay person,
one of the biggest areas of concern may be your spirituality. You
may struggle long and hard to reconcile a way of life to a
childhood religion that rejects it. You may explore options for
spiritual comfort through meditation, spiritual retreats, fasting,
chakra alignment, and other New Age offerings. But if you
haven't yet found your "spiritual center," you may be tempted to
give up and call Dial A Gay Atheist, a twenty-four-hour recorded
telephone commentary/information line that's been in operation for years through the American Gay Atheists, Inc.

Yet before you turn your back on organized religion,
consider the Metropolitan Community Church (MCC). It
was founded by Reverend Troy Perry as an alternative denomination that welcomes all gay and lesbian people into its
fold. MCC has evolved into a denomination, with international missions, a seminary, an extensive AIDS and prison
ministry, and a department of people of color. This welcoming church and congregation may be just what you need for
your spiritual awakening!

♦ There are hundreds of MCC congregations, missions,
and clergy in North America. Today I'll contact the MCC
International Offices at 5300 Santa Monica Boulevard,
Suite 304, Los Angeles, CA 90029, (213) 464-5100 to
find a church near me.

DECEMBER 14

The ballet world is more uptight about the issue of sexual preference. It's that codpiece out there; it's supposed to be just for the women in the audience.

— PETER DiMURO

Although it's a well-known fact that many men in dance are gay, the American dance establishment has spent decades aggressively promoting a heterosexual image. They've done this by emphasizing dance's athleticism and by giving extra publicity to male dancers who are married. Even though more and more dancers are willing to proclaim their homosexuality, ballet-company spokespeople continue to publicize their dancers who are husbands and fathers and contend that the majority of the men in their companies are straight.

Why? Boston choreographer Peter DiMuro explains that many corporate and individual funders don't want to be associated with an organization that has a gay identity. New York choreographer Bill T. Jones agrees. He feels that he has been denied funding because of his sexual preference and his decision to be open about it.

But should dance companies—or any other company, group, or organization, for that matter—hide the truth about their gay and lesbian members for the sake of funding or because of their audience's attitude? Today give your financial support to those dance schools and amateur and professional companies that accept *all* their dancers for who they are.

◆ I believe that dance companies should be proud to reflect the multicultural and multiracial values of their dancers as well as to accept their sexuality. Today I'll convey this belief to the management of a local dance company.

It is not enough merely to exist. . . . Every man has to seek in his own way to realize his true worth. You must give some time to your fellow man. Even if it's a little thing, do something for those who need help, something for which you get no pay but the privilege of doing it. For remember, you don't live in a world all your own. Your brothers are here too.

—ALBERT SCHWEITZER

When was the last time you made extra food purchases at the grocery store for your gay men and lesbian friends who were out of work? Have you recently made a clothing donation to a worthy charity? Even though you may not have kids, have you picked up some games and toys to donate to collections for needy children this holiday? Will you be writing out a check at the end of the year to give to a worthy gay or lesbian organization? Are you planning to prepare a special meal for your AIDS buddy or volunteer to help deliver food to people with AIDS? Will you be including your gay and lesbian friends who have no place to go this holiday in your plans?

Doing something for others, with no concern for what you'll get in return, is what giving is all about. When you give of yourself, what you get in return is often invisible. You may not see the excitement in the eyes of a child who has a new toy or hear more than a softly spoken "thank you" for what you did for a brother or sister in need. But trust that your actions have touched a place deep inside, where it really matters.

♦ Giving without getting is an act that comes totally from the heart. Today I'll volunteer my time or donate material goods to show someone else that I truly care.

DECEMBER 16

Once you have lived with another it is a great torture to have to live alone.
—CARSON MCCULLERS, FROM *THE BALLAD OF THE SAD CAFÉ*

You may view the gay and lesbian community as the perfect portrait of serial monogamy, where everyone drifts in and out of relationships with such frequency and ease that it seems as if everyone's involved, just coming out of being involved, or just about to get involved. Because of this, the pressure on you to connect with someone else can be great. "It's not right to be alone" is the message you may receive from other gay men and lesbians. You can't just be connected to yourself.

Being gay and single can be very unsettling, particularly at this time of year. Most of your friends may be in couples. Everywhere you go you may see couples shopping for each other, dancing together, hosting parties, and decorating their homes. You may feel lonely and empty.

How can you feel better about being single? Rather than scramble to be with the next person who's available, think about how wonderful it would be if you knew a lot of people who were single. Take out a personal ad in a gay or lesbian newspaper to announce the formation of a singles' group in your area. Arrange potlucks together, discuss topics of interest, and focus on making friends rather than lovers.

♦ Today I'll reach out to others who are single. I'll form a supportive network of single people who are happy being with themselves—the same way I'm happy being with myself.

The preservation of health is duty. Few seem conscious that there is such a thing as physical morality.

—HERBERT SPENCER

How often do you allow yourself to become hungry, angry, lonely, or tired during a day? Maybe you find that you're too busy to eat, too rushed to be gracious, too busy to meet new people or make plans with old friends, or too restless to take a time-out to recharge your run-down batteries. When you're feeling any of those feelings, you're not taking good care of yourself. And when you're not feeling good physically, your emotional health is going to suffer.

Starting today, you need to pay attention to your physical well-being. Did you exercise yet today? Decide now when you'll go for your run or walk or set aside time to work out at the health club. When and what will you eat today? Forgo eating fast-food meals or snacking on empty calories and begin the day with a good breakfast. Pack a healthy lunch and plan to serve fresh fruits and vegetables with tonight's meal. Have you been feeling lonely lately? Call a friend today or scan the calendar pages in the gay and lesbian newspaper for fun activities for the weekend. Are you getting enough sleep? Tonight, don't take any work home. Instead, get to bed early after taking a warm, relaxing bath.

You can change your hungry, angry, lonely, and tired feelings by calling a halt to them. Doing so can help you feel refreshed and renewed.

◆ Today I'll make healthy choices for my body that can help to nurture my emotional well-being. Taking care of my body can be good for my soul!

I can understand people simply fleeing the mountainous effort
Christmas has become. . . . But there are always a few saving
graces and finally they make up for all the bother and distress.
——MAY SARTON

At the end of every holiday season you may vow to do things
differently next year. Maybe you tell yourself you're going to
buy your presents earlier, budget your money more wisely,
spend more time at home with your partner and less time
with your parents, participate in more gay and lesbian than
straight celebrations, or plan that special holiday party you've
always talked about with your gay and lesbian friends.

But now you may feel as if you're never going to have
enough time to do all the things you want to do. The daily list
of things to accomplish may barely get touched. Your eve-
nings may be spent aimlessly drifting from store to store
without finding the "perfect" gift for your partner. And you
may resent all the office parties, client luncheons, business
trips, and family obligations that take you away, once again,
from your partner and the gay and lesbian community.

Today, seek to balance your time between those things you
have to do and those things you *want* to do. Like dividing up an
even number of candies, you can give one to "them"—those
who require your presence at certain events—and then one
to "you," so you can do something you'd really like to do.

◆ Today I'll set aside time to do something that I *want* to do
with my partner or with the gay and lesbian community.
There's nothing I *have* to do unless I want to.

Remember that pain has this most excellent quality: if pro-
longed it cannot be severe, and if severe it cannot be prolonged.
— SENECA

Do you believe that because of illness, relocation, or a forced
separation, this may be the last holiday season you'll share
with your life partner, your family, or your friends? Whether
you or someone else will be going away, the pain you may feel
about the upcoming separation or anticipated loss can seem
insurmountable. You may spend every minute of every day
fearfully focusing on the time when that special person or
people will be far away from you or no longer in your life. You
may long to freeze time or wish your pain would go away.

But your sorrows will pass, just as your happiness sometimes does. Your pain will ease up, just as your pleasure
sometimes does. Nothing ever really stays the same. Nothing
ever stands still. Nothing remains unchanged. Life is all about
change—about tides coming in and out and about people,
places, and things moving in and out of your life.

What you need to do right now—which is all you can
really do—is take a deep breath and endure the present
moment. Keep in mind the words "And this, too, shall pass
away." This present hour will not endure, nor will the time in
the future endure. Time passes, and so will the pain.

◆ I need to have strength, patience, faith, and a strong
belief that I can get through each moment of today. Time
passes quickly; perhaps I can find some pleasure in it to
sweeten and soothe my pain.

A man who trims himself to suit everybody will soon whittle himself away.

—CHARLES SCHWAB

Prior to your going home for the holidays, have your parents laid down the "laws" that will govern your interactions with other family members? You might be told not to mention the "L" word or the "G" word. You might learn that relatives have been informed ahead of time that you're bringing home your room-mate—"and that's how you must refer to him." You may be warned not to "spoil" all your mother's hard work or ruin the holiday dinner by talking about your personal life. Or you may be requested to come home dressed "like a lady" or "like a gentleman" and not like "one of *those* kind of people." "We won't have any of *that* in our house" may be the final words you're given on the subject of you, your sexuality, and the holidays.

But here's a major truth in life: No matter what the circumstance that brings people together or who those people are, *someone* is bound to be mad or displeased with you. So trying to appease everyone will only whittle you down to a wooden image of who you really are.

The solution to this is to live your life to please yourself, not anyone else. Inform your parents that changing your style of dress, the subjects you discuss, or the ways you behave won't change who you are or your way of life. Suggest to them that you're willing to compromise about certain things when you come home, but only if they're willing to compromise, too.

♦ I need to be my own person this holiday season. I don't want to lie, hide, cover up, or disguise the truth in order to make myself into someone I'm not. Today I'll respect who I am and ask that others do the same.

Words are the freezing of reality.

—TIMOTHY LEARY

Have you ever started an argument with your partner by saying, "Do you know what your problem is?" and then launched into a litany of all your partner's shortcomings or character defects? Have you ever called your partner by an ugly name or used adjectives to describe his or her behaviors? In the heat of an argument, have you used words to stab, slap, or inflict pain?

There's an old Paul Bunyan tale about a winter that was so cold that the words anyone spoke immediately froze in the frigid air. When the spring thaw arrived, everyone walked around with their hands over their ears because the sounds made by all the words thawing at one time were deafening.

The things you say are like such words. They can "freeze" in the mind of the listener and never be forgotten. Even when you've reconnected after a conflict, the words may be revived—they may echo in the listener's mind or be returned to you in kind during a future conflict.

Think of how you feel inside when a stranger yells at you from across the street, "Hey, dyke!" or "Die faggot!" Such words can startle, hurt, frighten, and humiliate you. Today, think first about the things you want to say in a conflict with a loved one. Though the words may come from your anger and not from your heart, that doesn't make them any less painful or lasting.

♦ "Let's talk about it" are four words I'd much rather use when I'm in conflict with my partner. Today I won't be insensitive, unkind, or cruel in the remarks I make. I'll let my words lead the way toward resolution.

It usually happened . . . particularly at the beginning of a holiday. Then, when I was hoping for nothing but sleep and peace, the chattering echoes of recent concerns would race through my head, and the more I sought rest the more I could not find it.

—JOANNA FIELD

Stress, anxiety, fear, and worry are especially strong before holidays. The upcoming travel to your childhood home, the dreaded separation from your partner, the worry over not being around other gay men and lesbians, having to attend an unfamiliar twelve-step meeting, or reaching the decision that you need to come out to your parents can take precedence over anything or anyone else. Yet there are ways to find peace and serenity amid all the nervous energy you may have.

Instead of focusing on the things you don't like about the upcoming holiday events, you can focus on the things you would like to do. Such things may be as simple as looking forward to seeing a sibling, enjoying the sight of snow on pine trees, or anticipating the excitement of your niece or nephew when you give them a special present.

You can also have a special gift exchange with your partner or gay and lesbian friends. You can listen to a meditation tape, go for a run, or take your dog on a walk through the woods. Or you can sleep an extra hour in the morning or curl up with a favorite book and a hot chocolate tonight. Today, put the stress of the upcoming holidays to rest by remembering to think of yourself first.

◆ I'll have a nice time this holiday season by putting my energy into the things I enjoy. Today I'll stay calm and serene by focusing on things I can look forward to.

The courts are not prepared to acknowledge, let alone honor, nontraditional family structures. Therefore, difficult as it may sound, it is particularly important for . . . [gay] couples to discuss custody and visitation arrangements in the event that the relationship dissolves.

—D. MERILEE CLUNIS AND G. DORSEY GREEN

Generally, gay couples with children are divided into three family groups: "nuclear," where the children are born to or adopted by the couple; "blended," where the children come from a parent's prior relationship; and "extra-blended," where the children come from the prior relationships of both partners. While your family group may start out happy and whole, over time you and your partner may decide to separate. How you handle your breakup and future interactions with your children becomes critical.

If your breakup is difficult and you're a nonbiological/nonadoptive parent, your partner may decide to restrict or deny access to the child. It's helpful to have thought out all the possible breakup scenarios beforehand, rather than wait until you're in the midst of a breakup to hash things out.

In meeting with a therapist or mediator to negotiate visitation/custody arrangements, your primary concern should be to make the end of the relationship less traumatic for the child. You might want, as a general guideline, to allow each parent's continued involvement with the child. This way the child isn't forced to deal with a potentially hostile court arena.

◆ As much as I hate to admit it, nothing lasts forever. Today I'll encourage my partner to think about how we would best handle a separation to preserve our relationships with our children and ensure the least amount of disruption to their lives.

*Look at your own life: Who really is there when you're up?
Who's going, "Congratulations! I'm really happy for you"?*
—Tom Cruise

The word "community" can mean different things to different gay men and lesbians. In small towns, all the gay men or lesbians may know each other. In midsized cities, the gay men and lesbians may at least have "heard the name" or recognize others by sight. But in larger cities, there may be any number of disparate communities. Most of these may actually be friendship circles, or groups of gay men or lesbians who know each other, socialize together, and support one another.

Creating a strong support network for yourself and/or your relationship is what community is really all about. When your way of life differs from the majority of the population, your community can offer a space in which you're never viewed as a stranger or someone who's different. When you have to work, travel, or interact in an uncaring, unaccepting, or even hostile environment, your community can offer you love and acceptance as well as protection. When you have to deal with illness or the pain of loss, your community can be there to understand and help get you through.

Today, strengthen your community by reaching out to each person, listening to what's going on in his or her life, and sharing what's going on in yours.

♦ When I'm isolated from my community, I don't have role models for my choices, friends to balance my relationships, or support for who I am. Today I'll strive to build a community of gay men and lesbians who can support and nurture each other's individual growth.

There is nothing sadder in this world than to awake Christmas morning and not be a child. . . . Time, self-pity, apathy, bitterness, and exhaustion can take the Christmas out of the child, but you cannot take the child out of Christmas.

—ERMA BOMBECK

You, like many gay men and lesbians, may have longed as a child to be given presents at Christmas that reflected what you really wanted. Instead, you may have been given what you were told you should like because you were a little boy or a little girl. "Boys don't play with dolls, they play with guns," or "Girls don't play with race-car sets, they play with toy ovens," your parents may have informed you after they read your Christmas list.

But today there may be a little child inside you who still wishes to go to the Christmas tree and find that present he or she always wanted. As a little girl, you may have longed for a Lionel train set, an air rifle, a package of plastic army men, or a dump truck. As a little boy, you may have wished for a Barbie doll—complete with accessories—or a toy kitchen appliance, ballet shoes, or an art set.

Today, make a resolution to give yourself that gift you've always wanted. Decide to buy that present in the new year so it'll be waiting for you under the tree next Christmas morning, or make an early New Year's resolution to give yourself that gift before the end of the year.

♦ When I was growing up, there were many Christmas mornings I woke up as an excited child, only to be disappointed later on. Today I'll make sure that child never gets disappointed at Christmas again.

It is tragic how few people ever "possess their souls" before they die. . . . Most people are other people. Their thoughts are someone else's opinions, their lives a mimicry, their passions a quotation.

—OSCAR WILDE

"If only I could be more like so-and-so," are the first words spoken each day by an ailing person who wakes up to to fight a terminal illness. "But I'm too weak, too self-focused, too unhappy with myself. I'll never be as lighthearted or as courageous as my friend."

It often takes a major crisis to bring us to the edge—that place where you're asked to face yourself and a particular challenge in your life. When you're at the edge, you need to be willing to close your eyes and jump. Sometimes you may turn away before you get anywhere near the edge. Other times you might get right up to the edge, but then hesitate and look around for someone to tell you what to do. Still other times you may toe the edge and imagine that it's not you there anymore but someone else—someone braver, more self-assured, and more confident.

Yet when you can trust that it doesn't matter who you are, you can give up being someone else and take that leap yourself. When you choose to trust, you may discover that when you push off from the edge, you can fly. That's always the message of the soul: No matter how bad things get, *you can always fly.*

♦ Sometimes I think I'll fall if I try to live out the rest of my life just being me. But maybe I'm mistaken. Maybe when I'm able to surrender everything—including my wish to be or act like someone else—then I won't ever fall.

I pounded on my car and screamed, "They misspelled it! They misspelled it!" For some reason, that offended me more than anything else.

—ELAINE NOBLE

When openly gay Massachusetts representative Elaine Noble walked out to her vehicle one night in 1984, she noticed it had been vandalized. Written on her car, in large letters, was the word "LESBEAN." It may seem humorous that Noble was more outraged that whoever damaged her car misspelled the word "lesbian" than the fact that her car had been damaged. But her anger was an expression of her frustration at the ignorance of the homophobic individuals who misrepresented a symbol of pride in her sexuality and her way of life.

Should you feel ashamed, humiliated, or shaken when you hear or see graffiti labels like "fag," "dyke," "lezzie," "homo," "queer," "bulldyke"? Or should you feel outraged that others dare abuse a designation of your gay pride?

You can be proud to know or say that you're a lesbian or a gay man, proud of your homosexuality, proud to be someone who loves others of the same sex. But you don't have to be proud of labels that are homosexist in nature. *They* are offensive, not who you are.

Perhaps the next time someone calls you by a name they feel will degrade you in some way, you can retaliate. You can think to yourself, "That's *Mister* Homo/*Ms.* Bulldyke to you, buddy. And I'm proud of it."

◆ Today I'll let gay pride manifest itself in my life. I'll live by the motto "The few, the proud, the gay" as part of a community of other proud gay men and lesbians.

The iron chain and silken cord are both equally bonds.
—FRIEDRICH VON SCHILLER

In foreign countries where elephants are used as working animals, a baby elephant is often trained early on for future work by being taught that it can't escape. To accomplish this, one of its legs is fastened by a heavy manacle and chain to a metal stake driven deep into the ground. Whenever the elephant tries to walk farther than the chain, it's held back. Over time, the elephant learns that the farthest distance it may go is the length of the chain. This training is so effective that if a silken cord were tied to its leg and connected to a thin wooden stake, it wouldn't try to escape.

In some ways you may live your life like that baby elephant. You may be afraid to explore your freedoms as a gay man or a lesbian. Such freedoms may be as basic as expressing how you feel through letters written to congresspeople and newspapers or calls to radio and television talk shows. They can be as personal as using your creative gifts to portray the gay way of life through language and the arts or by dressing in ways that help you feel freer as a gay man or a lesbian. They can be as visible as marching in a PRIDE parade or wearing a button with the pink triangle on it. Or they can be as radical as becoming a gay-rights activist and organizing protests and rallies to promote and protect the freedoms of gay men and lesbians everywhere.

♦ It's never too late to challenge my freedom. Today I won't remain fettered like a baby elephant, passive and convinced there's no way to feel free. I'll use the personal power and strength I've been given to break loose and explore the freedoms I have.

DECEMBER 29

A strong life is like that of a ship of war which has its own place
in the fleet and can share in its strength and discipline, but can
also go forth alone to the solitude of the infinite sea.

—P. G. HAMERTON

Are you able to achieve a balance in your life between socializing and solitude? You may be someone who's very active in
the gay and lesbian community—your weeknights may be
spent attending group meetings or volunteering, while your
weekends may be occupied at bars or with friends. Or you
may be someone who fights tooth and nail to avoid going out
at all; you may crave solitude in order to pursue hobbies,
read, meditate, or take care of your animals.

If you're around others day in and day out, you're never
going to learn what it feels like to be by yourself. Likewise, if
you're isolated a lot, you'll never learn what it's like to
interact with others. Your health and happiness depend on
creating a sound balance between the two.

Look back over yesterday. Take note of the time you spent
with others or in solitude. Then decide how to balance
today's activities. If you're going to be around people all day
long, maybe you can spend some time alone tonight. If you're
going to be alone for a good deal of the time, then maybe you
need to experience being part of those around you. Ask
yourself: "Should I spend my time tonight in the company of
others or in the company of myself?"

♦ Today I'll decide whether it might be good to travel in
solitude on an infinite sea tonight or to seek my own
balance within the fleet of gay men and lesbians around
me.

. . . we ourselves are only fragments of existence, and our lived life does not fill the whole of our capacity to feel and to conceive.

—PAUL VALÉRY

Your feelings as a gay man or lesbian can sometimes be bigger than you are, particularly when an act of discrimination, abuse, hatred, or violence has been perpetrated against a member of your community. It's important that you band together with other gay men and lesbians in order to share your feelings and to release them. To experience such strong emotions with a crowd of like-minded people can be beneficial, for it takes you away from the sometimes frightening strength of individual feeling and sweeps you up in a collective current of emotion.

But while it's necessary for the gay and lesbian community to band together during times of difficulty, tragedy, or sorrow, it's also important that you give yourself time to acknowledge your own feelings, too. The difference between one individual and a group is that the former can choose what he or she wants to do with their emotions.

Today, you can feel rage and let it out. You can feel sorrow and survive it. You can feel love and express it. You can react to your feelings as they come to you as well as express the feelings of the rest of the community. Today, let your feelings flow free—with and without others.

♦ Today I'll be unified with myself as well as with members of the gay and lesbian community. I can feel my feelings as well as "our" feelings.

And lastly, a resolution that gay men should be as supportive of lesbian health concerns as lesbians have been about gay men's health concerns.

—MICHAEL SMITH

When Boston gay radio-talk-show host Michael Smith was asked about his New Year's resolutions, he quickly supplied a list. But then he paused, gave the above resolution, and added in a somber voice, "That's a resolution I don't think people will keep."

Too often you may end a year and begin a new one with the noblest of agendas in your heart. This agenda may include one or more resolutions based upon selfless giving to gay friends of the opposite sex. As a gay man, you may wish to give your time and energy to a lesbian friend who's undergoing breast-cancer treatments or surgery, having a difficult pregnancy, or dealing with a drinking or drug problem. As a lesbian, you may wish to give your time and energy to a gay male friend who has tested HIV positive or is struggling with full-blown AIDS.

Before you become too wrapped up in your own day-to-day hassles or those of other gay men or lesbians in the New Year, ask a gay friend of the opposite sex how you could best help him or her stay healthy this coming year. Give your friend advice on how he or she could do the same for you. Then make a resolution in each other's presence to contribute in these ways to each other's health and well-being for the next 365 days.

♦ This is the time of year to dream up resolutions you hope you can keep, you despair of keeping, or you wish others would make. Today, think of three resolutions. Make one for yourself, one you'll give to someone else, and one that you put out into the universe.

INDEX